LACAN'S SEMINAR
ON "ANXIETY"

THE LACANIAN CLINICAL FIELD

A series of books edited by
Judith Feher Gurewich, Ph.D.
in collaboration with Susan Fairfield

Introduction to the Reading of Lacan:
The Unconscious Structured Like a Language
Joël Dor

Lacan and the New Wave in American Psychoanalysis:
The Subject and the Self
Judith Feher Gurewich and Michel Tort, eds.

The Clinical Lacan
Joël Dor

Hysteria from Freud to Lacan: The Splendid Child of Psychoanalysis
Juan-David Nasio

Lacanian Psychotherapy with Children: The Broken Piano
Catherine Mathelin

Separation and Creativity: Refinding the Lost Language of Childhood
Maud Mannoni

What Does a Woman Want?
Serge André

Lacan in America
Jean-Michel Rabaté, ed.

Lacan
Alain Vanier

Lacan's Seminar on "Anxiety": An Introduction
Roberto Harari, translated by Jane C. Lamb-Ruiz

Structure and Perversions
Joël Dor

LACAN'S SEMINAR
ON "ANXIETY"
An Introduction

ROBERTO HARARI

TRANSLATED BY JANE C. LAMB-RUIZ
REVISED AND EDITED BY RICO FRANSES

OTHER

Other Press
New York

Production Editor: Robert D. Hack

This book was set in 11 pt. Berkeley by Alpha Graphics of Pittsfield, New Hampshire.

10 9 8 7 6 5 4 3 2 1

Library of Congress Cataloging-in-Publication Data

Harari, Roberto.
    Lacan's seminar on anxiety : an introduction / by Roberto Harari.
        p.   cm.—(The Lacanian clinical field)
    Includes index.
    ISBN 1-892746-36-0
    1. Anxiety.   2. Psychoanalysis.   3. Lacan, Jacques, 1901–   I. Title.
    II. Series.
RC531 .H288 2001
616.85'223—dc21

                                                00-066911

Don't ask how
what you hope for
will be,
don't let
anyone
name it
for you.

—H. A. Murena, *El demonio de la armonia*
(The Demon of Harmony)

Halfway between Desire and the Idea appears, nevertheless, the platonic concept of a productive Eros, this impelling that is quieted not with visions but with works, not with contemplation but with actions. True entelechy of the process is not the pure vision of the Idea but productive action."

—E. Trías, *The Artist and the City*

No. Fatigue, why?
It's an abstract sensation
of concrete life
—something like a scream
to be screamed,
something like anxiety
to be suffered.
To be suffered completely
Or to be suffered as . . .
Yes, to be suffered as . . .
That's it: as . . .
As what?
If I knew I wouldn't have this false fatigue within me.

—F. Pessoa (Alvaro de Campos),
"No, It's Not Fatigue"

Contents

Foreword

CHARLES SHEPHERDSON

The problem of anxiety is a nodal point at which the most various and important questions converge, a riddle whose solution would be bound to throw a flood of light on our whole mental existence.

Introductory Lectures on Psychoanalysis[1]

Anxiety is precisely the point of rendez-vous where all of my previous discourse awaits you, including a certain number of terms which up to now may have seemed to you insufficiently related. You will see how anxiety is the terrain on which these terms are knotted together, and thereby assume their places more clearly.

L'Angoisse, 11.14.62[2]

---

1. Sigmund Freud, *The Standard Edition of the Complete Psychological Works of Sigmund Freud*, 24 volumes, trans. and ed. James Strachey et al. (London: Hogarth Press, 1953). References will be given by volume and page number (in this case, *SE* 20:393).

2. Lacan's *Seminar X: L'Angoisse* has not been published, but transcripts are available and are conventionally referred to by the date of each session (since in some cases more than one transcript version exists). This is also Harari's practice in the present volume.

X   FOREWORD

I

It is always a good idea to read Freud. And no one obliges us to recognize this fact more than Lacan. The reading of Freud that one finds in Lacan is so protracted, so elaborate, difficult, and mystifying—but ultimately so rewarding—that it tends to destroy much of what we think we know about psychoanalysis.

Reading Lacan thus has a tendency to produce anxiety. It deprives us of the safety and distance afforded by a secure knowledge of Freudian theory, forcing us to encounter Freud's text in all its disorienting proximity. But if Lacan is right to call anxiety the knife-edge that separates desire from *jouissance*,[3] then the experience of returning to Freud—even if it entails anxiety, and even if it requires that we relinquish a degree of knowledge—may thereby rekindle our desire in relation to psychoanalysis.

II

Such is the aim of Other Press, and this book is a fitting example of that endeavor. It derives from a course taught by the Argentinian analyst Roberto Harari in Buenos Aires in 1987, which focused on *L'Angoisse*, Lacan's unpublished seminar on the con-

---

3. See Jacques Lacan, "The Names-of-the-Father Seminar," trans. Jeffrey Mehlman in *Television: A Challenge to the Psychoanalytic Establishment*, ed. Joan Copjec (New York: Norton, 1990), p. 94, where anxiety is materialized in the knife held by Abraham, and poised to strike at Isaac's throat. When the angel descends to stay Abraham's hand, this is God's messenger, announcing the law that separates desire and *jouissance*, and thereby transforming Abraham's relation to God, saying in effect: "What God desires is that you should not use sacrifice as an attempt to satisfy His *jouissance*." Anxiety is thus the threshold that must be crossed on the path that distinguishes two different modes of relating to the Other.

cept of anxiety. *Seminar X: L'Angoisse*, took place in 1962–1963, and is the last seminar that Lacan gave at the Sainte-Anne Hospital in Paris. At the start of the following academic year, Lacan was excluded from the approved list of training analysts in his own society, and in the wake of this second major upheaval in the French analytic community, he moved to the École Normale Supérieure, where he gave the well-known course that has since been published in English as *The Four Fundamental Concepts of Psychoanalysis.*[4]

The internal affairs of psychoanalysis thus provide a dramatic context for this seminar, but its external conditions are perhaps even more important. For during the decade following the war, French philosophy had undertaken the massive project of inheriting and reworking the German philosophical tradition. Although the French appropriation of German thought had begun much earlier (Sartre's *Being and Nothingness* appeared in 1943, and Kojève's famous lectures took place in the 1930s), the end of the war brought with it a new and profound engagement with German philosophy, under the native influence of existentialism. France saw the publication of many important works in 1962.[5] Heidegger's two-volume work on Nietzsche appeared in a French translation, as did Gadamer's *Truth and Method*, Georg Lukacs's *Existentialism or Marxism*, Binswanger's *Mélancholie et manie, études phénoménologiques*, and a number of important

---

4. See the "Minute" of the International Psychoanalytic Association concerning the Study Group of the Société Française de Psychanalyse in *Television*, p. 79–80. See also Jacques-Alain Miller's remarks on *Seminar XI* in "Context and Concepts," *Reading Seminar XI: Lacan's Four Fundamental Concepts of Psychoanalysis*, ed. Richard Feldstein, Bruce Fink, and Maire Jaanus (New York: SUNY Press, 1995), pp. 3–15.

5. *Bibliography of Philosophy*, vol. IX (1962), published by the International Institute of Philosophy (Paris: Librarie Philosophique J. Vrin).

works by Jaspers, Marcel, Karl Barth, and others. Levinas's great work, *Totality and Infinity* was published that year, Foucault's *Mental Illness and Psychology* appeared, and the first two volumes of Ernest Jones's life of Freud were translated into French as *La Vie et l'Oeuvre de Sigmund Freud*, together with Freud's *Three Essays on the Theory of Sexuality* and the *Introduction to Psychoanalysis*.[6] It was a period of remarkable philosophical renewal. Major texts by Hegel and Schopenhauer were published in French that year, Heidegger's *Being and Time* appeared in its first English translation, and France saw the first three volumes of Kierkegaard's *Oeuvres*, including *Fear and Trembling*, *Repetition*, and *The Concept of Anxiety*. As Harari notes, Lacan is fully aware of these developments, and explicitly refers to a number of these texts in the course of the seminar itself (especially Heidegger, Kierkegaard, Sartre, and Hegel). It is clear, therefore, that Lacan intends his engagement with anxiety to be more than a narrow psychoanalytic account. As technical as the seminar may be in places, Lacan clearly regards the topic of anxiety as an opportunity: it offers a chance to demonstrate the true philosophical depth and importance of Freudian theory, and to reveal that it can stand as a genuine contribution to questions that are being posed in the culture at large—even if, as Harari points out, the psychoanalytic approach does not coincide with that of existentialism or phenomenology.

The cultural and philosophical horizon of Lacan's *L'Angoisse* is thus formidable, but the arguments that we find in the seminar itself, with respect to Lacan's own theoretical development, are equally stunning. There is a radical reworking of the famous

---

6. Michel Foucault, *Maladie Mentale et Psychologie* (Paris: Presses Universitaires de France, 1962). *Mental Illness and Psychology*, trans. Alan Sheridan (New York: Harper and Row, 1976).

thesis on the "imaginary body" that will challenge and disrupt most of the secondary literature on Lacan in the English-speaking world. (Lacan argues that the imaginary cannot be understood as a *Gestalt*, but is organized around a hole which makes the body-image cohere, giving the concept of bodily unity an entirely different character than the usual accounts of the "mirror-stage" would suggest, and at the same time illuminating many practical issues such as tattooing, body-piercing, eating disorders, and even drug injection.[7]) There is an extended and difficult revision of Lacan's account of the Hegelian dialectic of recogition, in which the "relation to the other" is fundamentally reconfigured. There is an elaborate treatment of the "object a," together with a close exegetical account of Freud's important text, *Inhibitions, Symptoms, and Anxiety*—an account which Harari follows and explores in great detail. And there is a profound and detailed encounter with the concepts of "emotion" and "affect," which many English readers have been told does not exist in Lacan's work. Anxiety, Lacan insists, is not an emotion but an affect—a fact which should induce us to account for the difference between emotion and affect in a manner that is more precise. In the course of his discussion of this issue, Lacan also uses the concept of anxiety to develop a very clear and useful distinction between "acting out" and the "*passage à l'acte*" (in suicide, for example), which can be regarded as two possible transformations of anxiety, two destinies for the subject in anxiety. Harari explores this distinction at some length, pointing out how anxiety can thereby help to clarify the distinction between desire and *jouissance*. In a way, Lacan's discussion of anxiety here

---

7. For an account of this development of the imaginary, see Phillip Julien, *Jacques Lacan's Return to Freud: The Real, the Symbolic, and the Imaginary*, trans. Devra Beck Simiu (New York: New York University Press, 1994).

can be viewed as a creative return to Freud's earliest theory, in which anxiety is the result of an excess of libidinal tension: anxiety amounts to being filled with phallic *jouissance*, and if this leads to acting out, it is precisely as an attempt to evacuate the body of *jouissance*, in order that desire might emerge. In this sense, Harari says, acting out is a message addressed to the analyst, a symbolic act that calls for interpretation, unlike anxiety itself, which is not a symbolic phenomenon, and which—if it does not find a symbolic foothold in this way—may culminate in a *passage a l'acte* that puts an end to any possible desire. One can perhaps already begin to see why Lacan speaks in this seminar of anxiety as the knife that separates desire and *jouissance*, if only it is held in the right hands.

Given the vast scope of the seminar, and the enormous complexity of its philosophical background, we will not pretend (nor is it necessary) to rehearse Harari's claims in advance. Instead, let us simply consider one of the opening arguments in his analysis, in order to get a sense of how he works with the problem of anxiety. Taking his point of departure from Freud's *Inhibitions, Symptoms and Anxiety*, Harari observes that if we take Freud at his word, there must be a difference between an "inhibition" and a "symptom." An "inhibition" often appears as a loss of some function, which is due not to organic damage or disease, but to something that concerns the subject. In Freud, we often find examples of inhibitions, particularly in relation to *movement* and *locomotion*. In *Studies in Hysteria*, for example, we find the famous case of Elizabeth von R., who is sometimes unable to walk or even stand up. Inhibitions, however, can have a somewhat broader range, and Freud also speaks of anorexia nervosa and impotence as inhibitions, which likewise impede a basic bodily function. But these disorders are also thought of as "symptoms." What then is the difference between an *inhibition* and a *symptom*?

One answer, Harari says, might be that whereas an inhibition seems to impede or disable a bodily function (such as eating, sexual activity, or locomotion), a symptom includes an element of creativity, replacing the inhibited function with something else (delusional perceptions, compulsive exercise, risky athletic stunts like bungee-jumping, or some other activity). The symptom would thus be the "compromise-formation" that substitutes for what is lost through the inhibition. This is a tempting explanation, but Harari claims that it cannot be correct. Anorexia is the inhibition of a function, but surely we also regard it as a symptom. The same can be said of impotence, which is not merely an inhibition but also a symptom. For Harari, this does not mean that the distinction between inhibition and symptom is blurred, but only that we cannot approach it accurately by descriptive means. In other words, we cannot approach Freud's concepts by appealing to the kinds of diagnostic gestures that one finds in the *DSM*, wherein a list of features or phenomenal attributes can be accumulated in order to arrive at a diagnosis (shortness of breath, loss of appetite, increased heart rate, and so forth). Such a list will not enable us to distinguish an inhibition from a symptom.

From this simple terminological starting point, then, we are already confronted with a fundamental procedural difference between psychoanalysis as such and the diagnostic classifications of psychiatry, which are based on "symptoms" understood as phenomenal manifestations (in the manner of medical diagnosis—reduction in body weight over a certain percentage, amenorrhea, and so forth). If Freud insisted on the distinction between "inhibition" and "symptom" in spite of the apparent identity of these terms at the level of the manifest phenomena, this does not mean that the terms are identical, but only that they cannot be grasped by the procedures of psychiatric classification. "Such classifications are useless when unconnected to structure and limited to a phenomenological description." Harari thus begins with a classic and far-reaching principle of Lacanian theory, according to which symptoms should be understood in terms of *structure*, rather than in terms of their *phenomenal manifestation*. This would be one difference between the Freudian approach and psychiatry, from a Lacanian point of view.

One can restate Harari's point in somewhat different language by recalling Lacan's distinction between the imaginary and the symbolic: if Lacan refuses to understand the symptom at the imaginary level, insisting on a difference between "phenomenon" and "structure," it is because this distinction encourages us to recognize that the presence of a particular symptom is not in itself sufficient to make a diagnosis. At the level of "behavior" or "appearance," the same symptom (impotence, for example) may in fact be manifested by a hysteric, an obsessional, or even a psychotic, and the real question is therefore to understand how this symptom is related to the position of the subject, and what it reveals about the relation between the subject and the Other. That "structural" question is the basis for grasping the status of the symptom in psychoanalysis, as distinct from any inhibition that may be present.[8] This may help to explain why homosexuality never functioned for Lacan in the way that it did for psychoanalysis in the United States. Like sexual abstinence or dietary practices, a homosexual act may be the act of a normal subject, or that of a hysteric or obsessional. It is not enough, in itself, to serve as the basis for any diagnosis whatsoever. Only a decision at the structural level will allow us to determine how the phenomenon should be understood in relation to the life of the subject. Thus, if Freud

---

8. For more discussion of this "structural" perspective on diagnosis, see Joël Dor, *The Clinical Lacan* (New York: Other Press, 1999).

insisted upon the difference between an "inhibition" and a "symptom," we may say that the *inhibition* concerns the disruption of a vital function (movement, eating, and so forth), whereas the *symptom* is a theoretical entity, a construction that must be distinguished from its phenomenal manifestation. This also explains why Lacan claimed that the symptom is something that only comes to be formulated during the course of the analysis itself.

Harari's book is full of observations of this kind, and the reader who is not daunted by a few diagrams and some technical details along the way will be richly rewarded by his exposition. It is not possible to do justice to such a wealth of material in a few words, but it may be useful simply to introduce the English-speaking reader to this text—to "introduce" in the sense of "leading to." Let us therefore recall some of the elementary issues that set the stage for Harari's analysis, for readers who are not immediately at home in the atmosphere of Lacanian theory. Beginning with Freud's own work, let us follow the development of his account of anxiety, sketching out along the way how this work has largely been interpreted. This will allow us to see more clearly how Lacan's own reading amounts to a genuine and important alternative to the canonical interpretation of Freud. This brief trajectory may help to orient readers who are less familiar with the Lacanian framework, and bring us to the threshold of Harari's text. It may also allow us to see, in a basic and orienting way, how anxiety came to play such a fundamental role in relation to so many other basic concepts of psychoanalysis.

III

The "Extracts from the Fliess Papers" (1892–1899) provide us with Freud's first efforts to define "anxiety neurosis." Freud's emphasis falls on "neurosis," which he is only beginning to conceptualize, but the problem of anxiety already draws his particular attention: it is not merely an object to be categorized, or placed alongside other elements in a diagnostic table, but an enigma to be pursued, a perpetual question that runs through the entire analysis, and eventually takes on the status of a guiding thread as Freud sets out on the more ambitious project of distinguishing different types of neuroses, and sorting out their possible causes. Anxiety thus acquires from the very outset of Freud's work an especially important status, and plays an organizing role in the emerging structure of psychoanalytic theory as a whole.

This is a point that Freud himself would make many years later, in his *Introductory Lectures on Psychoanalysis*: "The problem of anxiety is a nodal point at which the most various and important questions converge, a riddle whose solution would be bound to throw a flood of light on our whole mental existence" (*SE* 16:393). For Lacan, too, the problem of anxiety has a special status, and emerges as a particularly urgent issue in his work precisely at the moment when a number of apparently well-established Lacanian dicta need to be brought together more clearly: "Anxiety is precisely the point of rendez-vous where all of my previous discourse awaits you, including a certain number of terms which up to now may have seemed to you insufficiently related. You will see how anxiety is the terrain on which these terms are knotted together, and thereby assume their places more clearly" (11.14.62).

We should stress this fact at the outset, for it will encourage us to view anxiety in its connection with the entire architecture of Freudian thought. This perspective, in which anxiety serves as a "nodal point" or "point of rendez-vous" where a variety of fundamental issues converge, may help us to avoid a certain number of easy solutions, as we follow the thread of anxiety through the labyrinth of psychoanalysis. For when we consult the numerous dictionaries and handbooks of psycho-analytic theory that are proliferating today, things arrange themselves a bit too quickly.

We are told that Freud's thinking about anxiety undergoes a change during the course of his work, and that he presents us with two distinct theories. Initially, we are told, he regards anxiety as the result of a failed or inadequate discharge of sexual energy. Somatic sexual excitation that is blocked or inappropriately discharged is transformed, Freud says, into anxiety.⁹ This would be the thesis found in the "Fliess Papers," when Freud writes: "it is a question of a physical accumulation of excitation—that is, *an accumulation of physical sexual tension.* The accumulation is the consequence of discharge being prevented" (*SE* 1:191).

This is the "pipe and valve" theory of sexuality, so dear to the detractors of Freud, for whom the entire doctrine can be reduced to a conflict between the force of "libido" (construed as a biological urge) and the counterforce of culture with its moral constraints. And yet, as we shall see, the first theory is far more complicated than this. For the moment, however, let us stay with the canonical story in order to take our bearings more clearly.

Initially, then, anxiety would arise from the repression of sexual libido. When physical tension accumulates without an adequate release, anxiety is produced as a result: "What finds

9. "Inappropriate" discharge. The claim here is already more complex than one might expect, for it means that anxiety will result not only from abstinence or insufficient discharge—which seems, at first glance, to be Freud's point—but also from forms of sexual satisfaction that in some way inhibit or alter that discharge, including (Freud says) masturbation, coitus interruptus, and even the use of condoms, the last of these posing a problem, according to Freud, because of the *psychic* barrier it erects. This already indicates that Freud's "first theory" is more complex than one might be led to believe from the theory of "physical discharge" that dominates the handbooks and dictionaries.

discharge in the generating of anxiety," Freud writes, "is precisely the surplus of unutilized libido" (*SE*: 20:141). We are dealing, it would seem, with a physical theory in which "anxiety arises out of libido" (*SE*: 7:224). Later, we are told, Freud changes his view, and argues that anxiety should be situated at the level of the ego. Henceforth, anxiety—and the question of "affect" in general—will have to be approached, not as a purely physiological phenomenon, but as matter that bears on the ego. As Freud says in *Inhibitions, Symptoms and Anxiety*: "This new view of things calls for examination of another assertion of mine —namely, that the ego is the actual seat of anxiety . . . Anxiety is an affective state and as such can, of course, only be felt by the ego. The Id cannot have anxiety" (*SE* 20:140).

Libidinal surplus is no longer enough to explain anxiety, understood as an "affective state." Instead, anxiety is said to arise as a response when the ego is threatened with some danger. According to this canonical story, then, we have moved from a theory of physical tension and discharge to a theory of the ego and its defenses.

In thinking about phobias, for example, which he regards as the externalized manifestation of an unconscious thought that the subject cannot bear to confront directly, Freud now claims that anxiety must be connected with this psychic operation by which the ego attempts to defend itself, avoiding some sort of traumatic encounter by constructing a phobic object in which anxiety can be expelled and partially contained. Accordingly, in his account of the phobia of Little Hans, Freud writes that "it was anxiety which produced repression, and not, as I formerly believed, repression which produced anxiety." He now concludes that "anxiety never arises from repressed libido" (*SE* 20:108–109).

In effect, with the second theory, the psychic dimension of anxiety is brought to the foreground. As Moore and Fine observe in *Psychoanalytic Terms and Concepts*, a handbook produced by the American Psychoanalytic Association: "In his *first theory of anxiety*, [Freud] theorized that libido which had not been adequately discharged was transformed into anxiety . . . Freud's *second theory of anxiety* (1926) approached it from the standpoint of the ego."[10]

Thus, in the second theory, anxiety is no longer the result of a somatic process (sexual tension that has not been released), but signals a disturbance in the position of the subject. Thus far, the matter seems simple enough, but we can already begin to see in these formulations the beginning of a theoretical divergence: between the "defensive response of the ego" and the "disturbance in the position of the subject," the labyrinth of psychoanalysis will offer two very different paths to the theoretical conquistador. And anxiety will play the part of Ariadne's thread, guiding us on our way through these alternatives.

Before tracing these different paths, however—in order not to lose our way—let us follow our initial map a little further, which tells us that Freud has passed from a physical to a psychic account. This transformation is conspicuously marked in the *Introductory Lectures on Psychoanalysis* (1917), where Freud addresses his medical students, acknowledging that they may expect him to explain anxiety as a purely physiological phenomenon. Is not anxiety, even today, understood as a neurological disturbance, a disequilibrium in the brain whereby the synapses are overworked or in need of chemical regulation? Are not the famous SSRIs dedicated to fixing these energy-channels by modifying the levels of seratonin that regulate the neural pathways?

---

10. *Psychoanalytic Terms and Concepts*, ed. Burness E. Moore, M. D. and Bernard D. Fine, M. D. (New Haven: The American Psychoanalytic Association and Yale University Press, 1990), p. 25.

Why should we get lost in the detours of philosophical speculation, or do battle with the Minotaur of "the subject," when a direct route to the somatic imbalance is readily available? Read Heidegger and Kierkegaard if you like, but science tells us that the path to anxiety is neurological.

Nevertheless, Freud's way proves rather different from this. Introducing the topic of anxiety, he writes:

> You will certainly expect psychoanalysis to approach this subject too in quite a different way from academic medicine. Interest there seems mainly to be centered on tracing the anatomical paths along which the state of anxiety is brought about. We are told that the medulla oblongata is stimulated, and the patient learns that he is suffering from a neurosis of the vagus nerve. The medulla oblongata is a very serious and lovely object. I remember quite clearly how much time and trouble I devoted to its study many years ago. Today, however, I must remark that I know nothing that could be of less interest to me for the psychological understanding of anxiety than a knowledge of the paths of the nerves along which its excitations pass. [SE 16:393]

This is why, as Moore and Fine also note, it is only with the second theory that Freud arrives at a properly psychoanalytic account: "Freud's second theory of anxiety shifted emphasis from a basically physiological perspective to an unmistakably psychological one," and he thereby "provided a concept that has much wider application and greater explanatory power." On this account, only the second theory allows anxiety to be detached from the physiological sphere and established as a properly psychic phenomenon. This is what we stressed at the outset, in claiming that the thread of anxiety will allow us to follow the very formation of psychoanalysis as a field of research.

This development of the theory has another consequence, moreover, for anxiety, having been detached from its somatic confinement, can now be linked to a whole variety of neurotic phenomena, from hypochondria and phobias to hysterical attacks and obsessive behavior, and including also frigidity, impotence, and eating disorders (all these examples being Freud's own). No longer regarded as a purely physiological effect, but established as a properly psychic phenomenon, anxiety can now be displaced and transformed into other symptomatic formations. Whether it is displaced onto an external object that condenses into a phobia, or warded off by a ritual activity designed to prevent anxiety from arising; whether it appears in the form of a hysterical paralysis, or is indeed transfigured in some other way by the workings of the psychic economy, anxiety now has the status of a genuinely psychoanalytic concept. In all these cases, anxiety must be understood, Freud says, not as the product of a physio-chemical malfunction or accumulated tension, but in terms of a disturbance at the level of the subject: in each case, the symptom arises because the ego seeks to defend itself against anxiety.

This would also explain—since we have mentioned the difference between "inhibition" and "symptom"—the further difference between "symptom" and "anxiety," for if the symptom is an effort to bind anxiety (as in the case of obsessional rituals, which are designed to keep it at bay), the presence of anxiety would indicate that the symptom has not succeeded in its task. This is why Harari says (in contrast with the administers of SSRIs) that analysis should not automatically aim to diminish anxiety, or to restore the equilibrium of the ego. On the contrary: Lacan argues that anxiety should be administered in small doses, and that it can be put to work in the unbinding of the symptom. As he says of anxiety in *Seminar XI*, "in my experience, it is necessary to canalize it and, if I may say so, to take it in small doses, so that one is not overcome by it. This is similar to bringing the subject into contact with the real."[11] Here again, anxiety serves to elucidate the distinction between the desire of the subject and the *jouissance* of the symptom; but this time it also emerges as a force that the analyst is able to enlist: anxiety is not a symptom to be eliminated with pharmacological tools, but a power that the analyst should handle. Anxiety, therefore, is not a symptom for Freud, any more than a symptom is an inhibition.

This view of Freud's development is not limited to the American Psychoanalytic Association. A similar account is given by Dylan Evans in his *An Introductory Dictionary of Lacanian Psychoanalysis*:

> Freud developed two theories of anxiety during the course of his work. From 1884 to 1925 he argued that neurotic anxiety is simply a transformation of sexual libido that has not been adequately discharged. In 1926, however, he abandoned this theory and argued instead that anxiety was a reaction to a "traumatic situation."[12]

Here again, in the development of Freud's thought, we would seem to be faced with a simple shift from a *physical* theory of "libido" to a properly *psychic* explanation in which the ego responds to some danger.

One further point merits attention here, for Evans makes it clear that anxiety is not only a reaction *on the part of the subject,*

---

11. Jacques Lacan, *The Four Fundamental Concepts of Psychoanalysis,* trans. Alan Sheridan (New York: Norton, 1978), p. 41.

12. Dylan Evans, *An Introductory Dictionary of Lacanian Psychoanalysis* (New York: Routledge, 1996), p. 10.

but is characterized by Freud as a response *in the face of some danger*. We must therefore account for what the phenomenologists would call the "subjective" and "objective" correlates of anxiety. As Moore and Fine put it, "Freud's second theory of anxiety (1926) approached it *from the standpoint of the ego*, conceiving of anxiety *as a response to a threat* to the individual." An additional task for the second theory is therefore to understand the nature of this "danger" or "threat." As Richard Boothby notes,

> Freud clearly found it difficult to determine the nature of the danger. In *The Ego and the Id* he remarks that "what it is that the ego fears . . . cannot be specified; we know that the fear is of being overwhelmed or annihilated; but it cannot be grasped analytically." [*SE*, 19:57][13]

In short, as if it were not already problematic enough to negotiate the difference between the "ego" or the "subject" as the second theory of anxiety develops, we are now obliged to confront the "danger" to which anxiety responds. This danger or trauma will entail a complex meditation on the "object" of anxiety, an object that is not reducible to a real, objective threat (an object of "fear"), but which rather brings us up against the void, the negativity, and the absence which have so preoccupied the philosophers in their accounts of the subject, being, and nothingness. And here again, as we shall see, the path of psychoanalysis divides, branching in different directions, becoming for some readers a question of the ego and its mechanisms of defense, and for others a question of the subject and its relation to the Other. These two formulations are in no way equivalent, and we must be careful to account for them precisely. As Harari shows, Lacan's

---

13. Richard Boothby, *Death and Desire: Psychoanalytic Theory in Lacan's Return to Freud* (New York: Routledge, 1991), p. 143.

account is in some respects directly opposed not only to the theory of "defense," but to some of Freud's own formulations.

In spite of the conflict that supposedly separates the continental tradition from the American schools of psychoanalysis, the same story is told in the new French *Dictionnaire de la psychanalyse*, though the dates are somewhat different (Moore and Fine having located the shift in 1926):

> In what has been called his first theory of anxiety (1896–1907), Freud associates the genesis of anxiety with unsatisfactory sexual intercourse . . . In 1908, in his preface to Wilhelm Stekel's *Nervous Anxiety-States and their Treatment* [*Nervöse Angstzustände und ihre Behandlung* (Berlin and Vienna, 1908)], Freud changes his mind and places anxiety in relation to uterine fantasies. The following year, in a note appended to the *Interpretation of Dreams*, he makes birth the prototype of the affect of anxiety. This is an idea Rank takes up in 1924, making birth itself a trauma.[14]

Here again, an initial theory, in which anxiety results from a failed or insufficient discharge of sexual tension, is replaced by an account in which anxiety appears as the ego's response to a traumatic experience, which is to say, an experience that the subject is not prepared for, but which comes as a shock or a surprise.

This formulation on the part of the *Dictionnaire*, and the reference to Rank, point the way to yet another development. For on the basis of this second theory, in which anxiety appears in response to a "threat to the ego," Freud and other theorists of trauma will go on to speak of war experiences, violence, the trauma

---

14. *Dictionnaire de la psychanalyse*, ed. Elizabeth Roudinesco and Michel Plon (Paris: Fayard, 1997), p. 498. All translations are mine.

of sexual abuse at an early age, and other events for which the subject is not prepared: all these are now events which can be characterized as a "threat to the ego," and not merely as an organic injury. The "danger," in other words, is not simply a real threat, but also and perhaps especially consists in the overwhelming or unexpected character of the event—what Lacan will call its "real" dimension, which is to say, not its external empirical reality, but its excessive character in relation to representation, its capacity to escape symbolic and imaginary presentation, and the ego's faculties of codification. For Lacan, anxiety must be understood precisely in connection with this limit of representation, this margin or border of symbolization, which will also explain, as Harari shows, how anxiety should be situated in relation to desire. As for Freud, his account thus redefines the term "trauma," which in medical parlance had previously meant simply a physical injury. As a result, the symptoms or "nervous states" associated with anxiety, however varied they may be (dizziness, fainting, obsessional handwashing, phobia, frigidity, or eating disorders), can now be conceptually grouped together in relation to "trauma," and linked to anxiety as an ordering principle, these symptoms being understood not as a simply physical effect (the accumulation of libidinal energy), but as an attempt to respond, after the fact, to a traumatic experience that took the subject by surprise at the time of its occurrence. Here again, the symptoms of anxiety no longer have a purely physical origin, but are now seen in their connection with memory and the psychic economy, as an attempt to bind the energy of the trauma, which was earlier unbound. It is therefore no surprise, perhaps, that the *DSM-IV* manual classifies "post-traumatic stress disorder" under the heading of "anxiety disorders."

We can now take another step, for these observations allow us to stress the *temporal* factor of anxiety—a matter which is of the greatest significance in the accounts of anxiety that we find in Kierkegaard and Heidegger. In one sense, the "traumatic" element of the theory suggests that anxiety is primarily bound to the past (a real event), and Freud himself points out in *Beyond the Pleasure Principle* that the subject who wakes up in the middle of the night, troubled by a nightmare that brings him back to a traumatic situation (in violation of the principle of pleasure), is providing us with evidence of a "compulsion to repeat," a "repetition compulsion" that binds the subject to a *traumatic past*. And yet, in *Inhibitions, Symptoms, and Anxiety*, when Freud distinguishes between anxiety and fear, he links anxiety to the future, noting that whereas fear has an object (in the present, one might say), anxiety has no object, but is rather a mode of waiting or distressed anticipation, a form of "anxious expectation"—as though the threat were *impending from the future*. A double structure is thus opened by the problem of anxiety: on the one hand a temporal structure, *a matter of memory* (both repetition and anticipation) which may well shape the time of anxiety in a distinctive way (in contrast, for example, to the time of desire); and on the other hand a peculiar form of the *relation to the object*, since anxiety is distinguished from fear in having no object, and being rather a relation to "the nothing."[15] Anxiety is not only a temporal structure, then, but a relation to the void or

---

15. Readers of Heidegger will note that precisely the same difficulties arise in *Being and Time* when Heidegger speaks of anxiety, which, although it is primarily a relation to the future (what Heidegger calls "preparedness for anxiety"), also entails a different relation to the past, since *Dasein*, in being prepared for anxiety rather than fleeing from it, is thereby brought into a different relation to its own finitude, thrownness, and death—its *Gewesenheit*, to use a term Lacan quotes from Heidegger in his famous "Rome Discourse." See Martin Heidegger, *Being and Time*, trans. John Macquarrie and Edward Robinson (New York: Harper and Row, 1962), pp. 184–192 (section 40) et passim. References follow the German pagination given marginally in the English edition.

to absence which the philosophers have likewise addressed, and which Lacan will develop in terms of the "object a," the object of lack, an "object" (if we can still us this term, as Lacan insists we must) that is not captured or presented in the imaginary or symbolic, but is rather the very condition of representation, and of the ego's coherent functioning—the lack that must find its place in order for the subject to emerge. In this respect, Lacan's account takes a step forward in relation to Freud: defiantly claiming that Freud was mistaken in believing that anxiety has no object, Lacan announces that anxiety indeed has an object, and that a proper articulation of the "object a" will allow us to be more precise than the philosophical tradition, which is lost in the abstractions of "being" and "nothingness," and is consequently unable to clarify the clinical aspects of the body's relation to this void.[16] Here too, on both these issues, Harari's analysis casts some interesting light.

The *Dictionnaire de la psychanalyse* is therefore quite accurate in linking "birth" and "uterine fantasies" together as instances of trauma, even though one of these appears to be a real external event while the other is something decidedly psychic. In fact, as the editors go on to observe, Rank's thesis on the "birth trauma" would reactivate the entire polemic over Freud's early "seduction theory." Is trauma, and the "shock" of trauma, to be

---

16. Again, readers of Lacan who may be quick to conclude that the philosophical tradition has somehow failed to touch on discoveries that only psychoanalysis can elucidate may wish to look more closely, for in speaking of anxiety, Heidegger likewise notes that "it still remains obscure how this is connected ontologically with fear," and that "for the most part they [anxiety and fear] have not been distinguished from one another." He also points out that, while anxiety does indeed confront us with a sort of nothingness, or an object that is "nowhere" ("anxiety is characterized by the fact that what threatens is *nowhere*"), this "nowhere" cannot be grasped by a pure negativity or nothingness: "'Nowhere,' however, does not signify nothing" (p. 186).

understood as a real event (as in war and sexual abuse), with empirical grounding in a past occurrence, or does its traumatic status rest on something irretrievably psychic? These debates are still with us today in the furor over "recovered memories" of abuse, and indeed throughout the field of trauma studies.[17] And the question of the proper treatment for such traumas would appear to hang in the balance, depending on how the object (the "trauma" or "threat") is conceived. For Freud, however, the step has been taken, and there is no going back: the "danger" that triggers anxiety has an inescapably subjective dimension, and cannot be reduced to the principles of "empirical reality" governing the organism and its survival. This is a theoretical watershed that will affect the entire conceptual apparatus—not only the logic distinguishing the "instinct of self-preservation" (organic life) from the "ego instincts" (the self-preservation of the ego), but also the conceptual status of the "object" associated with this "danger," which must henceforth be detached from the objective threat to life that Freud associates with animal "fear." Given these consequences following from the "danger" that is present in anxiety, one cannot reduce the problem of the psyche by returning to a "realist" account of the trauma or threat to the ego. The thread of anxiety must be followed through the labyrinth until the Minotaur of the "subject" is confronted.

Let us follow the enigma of this traumatic event a little further. In Freud's account, birth is indeed the prototype of this shock, the first "danger" to which the ego responds with anxiety, and it indeed seems to be a "real danger," to which the child

---

17. See, for example, Ruth Leys, "Traumatic Cures: Shell Shock, Janet, and the Question of Memory," in *Tense Past: Cultural Essays in Trauma and Memory*, ed. Paul Antze and Michael Lambeck (New York: Routledge, 1996), pp. 103–145. Allan Young, *The Harmory of Illusions: Inventing Post-Traumatic Stress Disorder* (Princeton: Princeton University Press, 1995).

responds as if its life were at risk (by crying, appearing panicked or distressed, urinating, and so on); but Freud will soon extend this example to a broader sequence of "threats" or "traumatic events," from loss of the mother (the so-called "separation anxiety"), to loss of love, object-loss, and also castration, which he elaborates in terms of "castration anxiety":

> Anxiety appears as a reaction to the felt loss of the object; and we are at once reminded of the fact that castration anxiety, too, is a fear of being separated from a highly valued object, and that the earliest anxiety of all—the 'primal anxiety' of birth—is brought about on the occasion of a separation from the mother. [SE 20:137]

For Freud, then, anxiety would appear to be the affect that arises with the *threat of separation*. This threat, Freud explains, presents us with a *danger to the ego* that is quite distinct from an actual *threat to life*. We would seem to have passed from the level of the organism and its survival, to the level of the ego and its integrity. And yet, here too, there are several interpretive paths.

As Harari explains, moreover, Lacan's formulation appears to be directly opposed to Freud's on this point (or at least to a certain reading of Freud), for where Freud seems to speak of anxiety as a response to separation or loss, Lacan insists that anxiety is not a response to the loss of an object, but rather arises *when lack fails to appear*. As Samuel Weber observes, "Anxiety, therefore, arises not from the loss of an object, but rather from the loss of this loss, or, as Lacan puts it, 'when the lack comes to be lacking' (*quand le manque vient à manquer*)."[18] On this account, Freud does not present us with a theory in which separation (loss

---

18. Sam Weber, *Return to Freud: Jacques Lacan's Dislocation of Psychoanalysis* (Cambridge: Cambridge University Press, 1991), p. 159.

of the mother, or an object) is itself a cause of anxiety, or the index of a lack that must somehow be overcome or ameliorated; he rather presents us with a lack that is the condition of the subject's emergence, a constitutive lack-in-being that characterizes human existence as such (as the philosophers also say, when they speak of the peculiarly human relation to death and negativity). And it is precisely the failure to register this lack—its "foreclosure" or nonemergence—that gives rise to the experience of anxiety.

This is clearly a different understanding from the apparently more common-sensical account in which the disappearence of the mother, or the loss of a favorite toy, gives rise to anxiety in the child—as if some threat to the ego were at stake. For Lacan, the point is virtually the opposite of this: anxiety is not a response to the loss of the object, but is fundamentally the affect that signals when the Other is too close, and the order of symbolization (substitution and displacement) is at risk of disappearing. Anxiety is thus present in the moment when Abraham is prepared to sacrifice everything to an inscrutable and apparently insatiable Other, whose appetite knows no limit, and demands everything of the subject; and this anxiety is transformed, channeled in the direction of desire, by the pact of symbolic law precisely when God refuses to let this sacrifice occur, putting the ram in place of Isaac, and thereby establishing a new relation to the Other, in which God's desire is no longer confused with this devouring *jouissance* that the subject must somehow appease. We thereby see more clearly how anxiety is situated by Lacan, as the threshold that the subject must cross on the way toward desire and symbolic mediation.

Thus, as Harari shows, it is not enough to speak of the "symbolic law" (as if the mere fact of language were enough to guarantee the subject's position within it), for we must also recognize that lack is the enabling condition of this relation to the Other. This is why Lacan insists, in his account of the fort-da game, that the child is not simply trying to master the trauma of the mother's departure by using the spool of thread as a symbolic substitute. Both points (the fact that it is not simply a matter of the symbolic order, but also a matter of the object a, and the fact that it is not a question of compensating for a loss, but on the contrary of establishing lack), must be stressed in this connection. In the famous fort-da game, it is not a question of restoring the lost object for Lacan, or overcoming the loss of the mother by symbolic means. What is at stake in the game of disappearance and return is not the arrival of symbolic mastery, but the loss of the object a, which is the condition for the emergence of the child's desire. This is a moment of "radical articulation," in which the necessary alienation of the subject is secured. Anxiety thus appears at a very primitive level in the constitution of the subject, in a primordial relation to desire:

> If the young subject can practice this game of *fort-da*, it is precisely because he does not practice it at all, for no subject can grasp this radical articulation. He practices it with the help of a small bobbin, that is to say, with the *objet a*. The function of the exercise with this object refers to an alienation, and not to some supposed mastery. [*SXI* 239]

We are now in a position to see more clearly the difference between two interpretive paths that can be taken through the labyrinth of anxiety, and why we have stressed the distinction between the "ego" and the "subject." For what, in fact, is the nature of the "danger" that threatens the ego in anxiety? Given the diversity of examples in Freud's text (loss of love, castration, birth, and so forth), a number of questions arise. How, then, should we really understand this "threat to the ego"? Is it a real danger, understood as a threat to the organism, and construed in terms of "self-preservation"? Or is it a danger of a different kind, related to the "ego" and its integrity, and thus construed in relation to the "principle of pleasure"? Or is it, still rather, a danger that arises when lack appears to be compromised? The distinction between "fear" and "anxiety" is enlisted to help with these questions, but Freud will also wonder about the difference between an "external" danger (an oncoming storm or an impending threat, such as a battle in war) and an "internal" danger (an unconscious thought, or a libidinal charge that the subject cannot tolerate), and it will not be long before all the ancient debates over the status of the "trauma" in psychoanalysis (whether it is "real" or "imagined") are reactivated with still more complexity as the theory of anxiety unfolds. The shift from the "first" to the "second" theory thus raises a number of questions, and we should not pretend that these accounts of Freud's "two theories" put everything nicely in place, as though it were simply a matter of a shift from a "physical theory" to a theory of "the ego and its danger."

Before turning to our final section, let us follow our thread one additional step. For in the face of these questions, Freud now produces a series of distinctions, separating *Realangst*, *automatische Angst*, and *Angstsignal*. *Realangst* ("realistic anxiety") is anxiety in the face of a real danger, an external situation that threatens the individual's safety. In principle, then, this is a form of anxiety that we can regard as a natural, adaptive mechanism, a response at the level of the "instinct for self-preservation." The other two, by contrast, would be forms of neurotic anxiety, in the sense that they arise, not because a "real danger" is present, but rather because there is a disturbance in the psychic economy —a disturbance in the "ego" or the "subject." *Automatische Angst* is anxiety that is produced automatically in a situation that the subject regards as traumatic, not because of any "real" danger, but because the ego is threatened in some way. Accordingly, Freud speaks of a "threat to the ego," and more precisely of a threat that is due, not to a real external event (in which case it would be a matter of "realistic anxiety"), but rather to the *increase in tension* that the psychic apparatus must seek to discharge or avoid. It therefore concerns an increase in tension that must be managed by the psychic economy, whether this tension arises from an external source (an argument one wishes to avoid, or a situation that causes distress) or internally (as with a nightmare that wakes us up in a state of confusion and apprehension, or a wish that the subject finds intolerable). Freud's third term, *Angstsignal*, is similarly concerned with psychic tension, but it arises not so much in the face of an actual, present experience that "automatically" produces distress, as in *anticipation* of a threat that is impending. The "signal" in signal anxiety is the indication of something *about to occur*, so that signal anxiety and automatic anxiety would both be phenomena that arise, not simply by an encounter with "reality" (a "real danger"), but in relation to the workings of memory and the psychic economy—the one being based on a present that automatically registers as "threatening" (on the basis of past experience), the other being based on anticipation of a danger (which is likewise a projection of previous experience).

These distinctions will prove especially helpful in tracing the paths of Freud's interpreters, for as we shall see, the distinction between "*Realangst*" on the one hand, and *automatische Angst* or *Angstsignal* on the other, is easily lost—depending in large part on how one interprets the term "ego." We will therefore do well to look more closely at this development, to see not only what emerges in Freud's account, but also how Lacan takes up that account, in a way that is itself subject to transformation.

These final clarifications should prepare us to place Harari's reflections in their proper horizon.

IV

We have said that Freud's theory is more complex than the handbooks would suggest, and that the division of his account into two simple moments cannot do justice to the issues that confront us in anxiety. Even the earliest theory is far richer than the dictionaries would have us believe. We would seem to be faced with a physical theory of accumulated tension in which "anxiety arises out of libido" (*SE* 7:224); but in fact, Freud does not say that anxiety can be understood as a purely *physiological* effect—another name for the "accumulated tension." Already in the "Extracts from the Fliess Papers," Freud is more exacting than this. He argues, instead, that anxiety is produced by a *transformation* of physical tension:

> it is a question of a physical accumulation of excitation—that is, *an accumulation of physical sexual tension*. The accumulation is the consequence of discharge being prevented. And since no anxiety at all is contained in what is accumulated [that is, in the physical excitation itself], the position is expressed by saying that *anxiety* has arisen by *transformation* out of the accumulated sexual tension. [*SE* 1:191, Freud's italics]

If indeed "no anxiety at all is contained in what is accumulated," so that the physical tension itself cannot be called anxiety, we are faced with *a distinction between anxiety and physical tension*, such that "anxiety has arisen by transformation." What then does it really mean to speak, as Evans does, of a "transformation of sexual libido"? Can we really maintain that Freud's first theory adheres to a simple version of "physical tension and discharge," as if the question of the ego or the subject has not yet emerged? Is not Freud already more precise than this, claiming as he does that anxiety is not merely a physical phenomenon? What then is really entailed in the "transformation" he points to, and how does this transformation affect our understanding of what Freud calls "libido" ("anxiety arises out of libido"?) [SE 7:224]. Much of the weight of Freud's early analysis will come to rest on these questions. Let us separate "transformation" and "libido," and subject them to closer analysis.

Anxiety, Freud says, is not simply a physiological phenomenon—another name for the accumulated tension, but rather arises from a certain transformation. The transformation of sexual tension into *anxiety* must therefore be distinguished from its transformation, for example, into another somatic symptom such as impotence or frigidity, in which anxiety may not be present to consciousness. Accordingly, in his first formal paper on "anxiety neurosis" ("On the Grounds for Detaching a Particular Syndrome from Neurasthenia under the Description 'Anxiety Neurosis'" [SE 3: 85–115]), after providing a descriptive catalogue of the various manifestations that make up the clinical picture of the syndrome (including general irritability, anxious expectation, foreboding, hypochondria, the inclination to moral anxiety, disturbances of respiration, heart palpitations, vertigo, agoraphobia, and a number of digestive disturbances, including anorexia and bulimia), Freud proceeds to show that each of these entails a different form of transformation, in which "sexual tension" is gathered or dispersed, registered or suppressed, accumulated or displaced, along pathways that belong not only to the physical apparatus, but also to the psychic economy. This is why Freud does not simply speak of "anxiety" as if it were a unitary phenomenon, but rather of various modalities of anxiety: already in the Fliess papers he is able to specify cases of "hysterical anxiety" and "anxious melancholia," (for example *SE* 1:196), and to claim that "there is a kind of *conversion* in anxiety neurosis just as there is in hysteria (another instance of their similarity)" (195), adding later that "The famous *anorexia nervosa* of young females seems to me (on careful observation) to be a melancholia where sexuality is undeveloped," and that "melancholia appears in typical combination with severe anxiety" (200).

In short, since anxiety is manifested in other neurotic phenomena, we cannot pretend that anxiety is simply the automatic result of a physical tension that has not been discharged. Even in the "first theory," anxiety is not reduced to accumulated tension, but is construed in terms of a transformation that can take a number of paths. It is this diversity of paths that opens the labyrinth of the subject. Anxiety is thus clearly understood as a "subjective" phenomenon, even if it entails a physical component. We are therefore already in the domain of an "affect" which cannot be grasped at the level of physiology, but involves a psychic dimension. This is a point Freud will make again in developing the concept of the sexual "instinct" (or "drive" in the French vocabulary): a drive is not a simple physiological urge, but a concept "on the border of the psychic and the somatic." Indeed, Freud says that a drive is never known except through its "representatives," and these too will be capable of various transformations, displacements, and "vicissitudes." In fact, if a drive can be repressed, as Freud argues it can, this is only because the representatives of the drive can be displaced or "transformed," which already means that the drive cannot be grasped in terms of an automatic sequence of cause and effect, or as a strictly physiological mechanism, but belongs to another order of reality. Anxiety thus entails a "transformation" of physical excitation, and brings us to the border between the physical and the psychic, where the question of "affect" should also be situated. Contrary to received opinion, therefore, we should not be too quick to suppose that Lacan's notorious emphasis on the "symbolic order" automatically amounts to a neglect of affect— as if affect had nothing to do with representation, or as if we knew what an "affect" really is. As Freud himself observed in 1926, "Anxiety, then, is in the first place something that is felt. We call it an affective state, although we are also ignorant of what an affect is" (*SE* 20:132).

The problem lies not only in the matter of "transformation," but also in the meaning of "libido." For in fact, the very gesture that makes anxiety the result of a transformation of physical tension in the first theory paradoxically also means (contrary to what many readers of Freud believe today) that "libido" cannot be properly understood as a form of somatic energy. Freud is exacting on this point. Even in the first theory, he does not say that the "libido" has been dammed up, but rather speaks of "*an accumulation of physical sexual tension*" (*SE* 1:191, original italics). "Physical sexual tension" accumulates, then, but as for the "libido" and even the "sexual libido," that is a matter that takes us into the psychic domain. It is this refinement concerning "libido" that allows Freud to account for the apparently paradoxical observation that patients who suffer from "anxiety neurosis," which is due to an *accumulation of somatic sexual tension*, often feel at the same time that *their desire has diminished*. Freud is explicit:

> A further point of departure is furnished by the observation, not so far mentioned, that in whole sets of cases anxiety neurosis is accompanied by a most noticeable decrease of sexual libido or *psychical desire*, so that on being told that their com-

plaint results from 'insufficient satisfaction,' patients regularly
reply that that is impossible, for precisely now all sexual need
has been extinguished in them. [*SE* 3:107]

Freud's first account of "anxiety neurosis" thus confronts us with
a *division between somatic excitation and sexual desire*, and from
this division his first reflections on the "libido" are born.[19] Thus,
what is at stake in anxiety neurosis, which is characterized by
the handbooks as a purely somatic phenomenon, is nevertheless more correctly understood as the result of a process in which
somatic excitation does not find its proper path through the
psyche, into the sphere of consciousness. Tension builds in the
organic sphere, but instead of passing a certain threshold and
entering the subject's awareness (that is, registering as "sexual
desire"), the tension is ignored, displaced or not registered, and
this is why the somatic excitation accumulates without being
discharged. *This* accumulation, due in part to the character of
the psychic economy, is then transformed into the experience
of anxiety. It is therefore not a matter, even in the first theory,
of a purely somatic energy simply failing to find expression in
organic release. One wonders whether the dictionaries are a re-
liable guide through our labyrinth of anxiety, and whether it is
really possible to conclude that, with the "first theory," psychoanalysis has not yet begun, as if we had to wait for the second
theory to find a "properly psychological" account of anxiety. In
any case, it is always a good idea to read Freud.

---

19. As Strachey himself observes that, while the term "libido" is used
in more than one way by Freud, particularly in these early works, it is nevertheless quite clear that "In the present paper [Freud] distinguishes between
'somatic sexual excitation' on the one hand and 'sexual libido, or psychical
desire' on the other" (*SE* 3:88).

Given these observations, how can the handbooks conclude so quickly that the first theory is not yet properly psychoanalytic? If we look at the more general theoretical architecture, the reason is not hard to find. In the passage from the Fliess papers that we have been discussing, Freud defines "anxiety neurosis" as an entity that he wishes to distinguish from "neurasthenia":

> it is a question of a physical accumulation of excitation—that is, *an accumulation of physical sexual tension*. The accumulation is the consequence of discharge being prevented. Thus anxiety neurosis is a neurosis of damming-up, like hysteria; hence their similarity. And since no anxiety at all is contained in what is accumulated, the position is expressed by saying that *anxiety* has arisen by *transformation* out of the accumulated sexual tension. [*SE* 1:191]

Anxiety neurosis is therefore "like hysteria" in being a neurosis of "damming-up," but we must note that they are crucially distinguished: with the former, it is a question of *physical* energy, while in the latter case it is a *psychical* matter (hysteria being notoriously defined in terms of "unconscious thought"). Several points follow from this distinction, simple as it may appear. First of all, it allows Freud to claim that "anxiety neurosis" is completely preventable (if only one changes one's sexual behavior), while at the same time announcing that it is not treatable by psychoanalysis (since it is not really a matter of "unconscious thought"). Hysteria, by contrast, is treatable by analysis, but cannot be prevented by the same physical intervention. Secondly, this observation allows Freud to distinguish still more broadly between "actual neuroses" and "psychoneuroses" or "traumatic neuroses," the former designating neuroses based on the actual, ongoing experience of failed satisfaction (*aktuell* meaning "present," "immediate," or "current"), while the latter group, though typified by hysteria, des-ignates all neuroses based on the inscription of memories from the past—a psychical conflict that has been repressed, or a trauma that has been unconsciously fixed in the unconscious, where its effects are able to operate without the subject's con-scious knowledge (in keeping with the famous formula stat-ing that "hysterics suffer mainly from reminiscences" [SE 2:7]). The larger schematic value of this second distinction can be seen from the fact that, in the "Extracts from the Fliess Papers," Freud proceeds to draw up a table of classification separating (1) neur-asthenia, (2) anxiety neurosis, (3) obsessional neurosis, (4) hysteria, and (5) melancholia (together with mania), adding categories for (6) some "mixed" modes and (7) their ramifica-tions. He then divides these categories in two groups, claiming that the first two are forms of "actual neurosis," while the rest are amenable to analysis, being properly "psychoneuroses."

The peculiarity of this classification is that *it appears to leave anxiety outside the realm of psychoanalysis.* Anxiety neurosis is an "actual neurosis," and as such it does not belong to the do-main of psychoneuroses. Such was Freud's apparent conclusion, and in 1912 he summarized these early views, saying:

> The essence of the theories about the 'actual neuroses' which I have put forward in the past and am defending today lies in my assertion, based on experiment, that their symptoms, unlike psychoneurotic ones, cannot be analysed. That is to say, the constipation, headaches and fatigue of the so-called neurasthenic do not admit of being traced back historically or symbolically to operative experiences and cannot be un-derstood as substitutes for sexual satisfaction or as compro-mises between opposing instinctual impulses, as is the case with psychoneurotic symptoms. [SE 12:249]

Like neurasthenia, anxiety neurosis is an "actual neurosis": it is viewed as having a physical cause, and therefore as not being treatable by analysis. To be sure, this physical cause is considerably more complex than we might hastily conclude, and it clearly entails a subjective dimension in which "libido" and "psychical desire" are involved. Freud's point is therefore not to argue for some kind of physical reductionism, but simply to show that anxiety neurosis can be usefully distinguished from the psychoneuroses, since the first, with its complex intertwining of somatic excitation and a psychic apparatus that fails to register that excitation in a normal way (i.e., resulting in "desire" and thus in the act that would lead to satisfaction), is different from the second, which involves a memory that fails to reach consciousness, and is transformed into a somatic symptom, such as a hysterical paralysis. If the psychoneuroses are susceptible to treatment by psychoanalysis (which follows the chain of unconscious thought) while anxiety neurosis is, according to Freud, not treatable by analytic means, this cannot be taken to mean that the latter neurosis is purely somatic, as if it had no bearing on the psychic domain. It only means that anxiety neurosis should be treated, according to Freud, by what we would call "behavior modification" rather than by analytic means. Such would be Freud's initial account of anxiety neurosis, as the result of sexual excitation or energy that has not been "sufficiently discharged." This formulation—which is clearly a shorthand for a process that is more complex—is what leads the dictionaries to conclude that only the second theory of anxiety really opens the door to a genuinely psychoanalytic account.

And yet, given this broader horizon of the Freudian architecture, we are now in a position to see that "anxiety neurosis" does not encompass anxiety as such, for anxiety also appears in

obsessional neurosis, in phobias, and elsewhere. "Anxiety neurosis" does not designate that neurosis that is characterized by
anxiety, but that neurosis in which anxiety can be traced back
to the accumulation of sexual excitation. Other forms of anxiety are therefore possible, and in the Fliess Papers Freud accordingly speaks of "anxiety hysteria" and "anxious melancholia,"
(for example *SE* 1:196), also noting that obsessional rituals can
be regarded as an effort to prevent anxiety. This means that the
question of anxiety runs across the entire table of analysis, including both "actual" and "psycho-" neuroses. As we stressed
at the outset, anxiety is an enigma whose various resolutions will
structure the entire architecture of analytic theory. Nevertheless, one can see from these remarks how the handbooks, following a narrow path through the theoretical labyrinth, have
come to their conclusion, as if reading by synecdoche: taking
the part for the whole, they have focused only on the form of
anxiety that appears in "anxiety neurosis," and misconstruing
that form in a way that excludes its subjective dimension (and
all the considerations that follow concerning the "libido" and
"psychic desire"), they have then taken this part of anxiety for
the whole, and concluded that anxiety as such is reduced by
Freud to a physiological effect, so that Freud's "first theory" of
anxiety amounts to a (somewhat laughable) theory of physical
discharge. Strachey observes however, commenting on the term
"libido," that while this term is not rigorously fixed in Freud's
usage, and while he indeed speaks of "an accumulation of libido
which is kept away from its normal employment," and which
can be situated "entirely in the sphere of somatic processes," it
is nevertheless also clear that even with the first theory, anxiety
is not a purely somatic phenomenon, but involves a particular
relation to the psychic apparatus, and the conscious emergence
(or nonemergence) of "sexual desire," which appears not only

because of its "quantity" of tension, but also because of the paths of transformation that are available to it—one of which is described as "anxiety neurosis," while other forms of anxiety are also possible.

These remarks therefore clarify what the dictionaries tend to avoid, namely, that we cannot construe the development of Freud's thought as if it were a matter of passing from a "purely somatic" account of anxiety as tension, to a properly analytic account of anxiety as "psychic." For both theories (if one insists on maintaining these "stages" of thought), a complex relation between the body and the mind is clearly in evidence. As Nunberg has pointed out with respect to the two theories, "It is of no great import whether one adheres to the former or the latter conception, for both refer to a disturbance of instinct life, which, indeed is both a psychic and a physical phenomenon."[20] One can see, then, that the narrative, with its neat divisions, tends to obscure precisely those details and complications that constitute the matrix of problems out of which psychoanalytic theory will progress as a theoretical enterprise.

If we now turn to the "second theory," we are told that Freud shifts from a theory of surplus excitation to a threat at the level of the ego. But how should we understand this development? Let us follow our thread a little further, in order to see where it leads. For some interpreters, anxiety is now part of an adaptational response to reality. To speak of a "threat to the ego" is to say that the ego must respond to some danger. But the nature of this danger must be elaborated, and it is precisely in order to clarify this matter that Freud now produces the distinctions we have mentioned, between "realistic," "automatic," and "signal"

---

20. Herman Nunberg, M. D., *Principles of Psychoanalysis*, preface by Sigmund Freud (New York: International Universities Press, 1955), p. 188.

anxiety. In the case of "realistic anxiety," there is an actual danger, and we therefore do not call this anxiety neurotic, but regard it as a healthy adaptive response (the "fight or flight" mechanism). But in other cases, as when the ego responds phobically to an innocent or harmless object that has somehow become libidinally invested, or attached to an unconscious association that the subject cannot tolerate, the ego will respond with anxiety that we may justly call neurotic rather than realistic. This neurotic anxiety manifests itself in two types, Freud says, as "automatic anxiety" and as "signal anxiety." The former designates a response that comes immediately, in the presence of particular situations. "Signal anxiety," by contrast, concerns a more complex phenomenon, in which the ego anticipates a danger, responding to a "signal" that appears to foretell of some impending threat. Automatic anxiety is thus linked to the immediacy of the present situation, while signal anxiety is more concerned with expectation and the future.

Despite the apparent difference between realistic and neurotic anxiety, we should note a certain parallel between this account of the ego and explanations of animal life. We will see that Lacan's view is very different on this point. According to this account, however, "signal anxiety" has a clear connection to an instinctual response, in which self-preservation is manifested. For an animal, an example of signal anxiety would be the response to a sudden sound in the woods that causes the deer to flee. A similar response can be seen in humans, when they anticipate a real danger. But in the case of neurotic anxiety, the signal does not indicate a real danger, but a psychic conflict that cannot be faced. The ego then responds defensively, suddenly refusing to speak, or abruptly leaving the room, or succumbing to an attack of panic or dizziness, for example, and thereby warding off a conflict that appears to be impending. On this view, *anxiety* in general is understood as a *defensive response of the ego*, while *neurotic anxiety* is a *malfunctioning of this defensive response*, a flaw in the adaptive function of the ego. The link between the adaptive function of anxiety and its maladaptive distortion—in cases where the ego is "defensive" and the danger is a "conflict" rather than a real threat—is therefore clear. As Moore and Fine explain, in keeping with our example of the deer in the woods:

> In response to this signal reaction, defensive operations of the ego are then set into motion. In situations of objective danger [Freud's "real anxiety"], the anxiety is part of the adaptive response, while in situations of psychic conflict, the signal may prompt a warding-off from consciousness . . . In its most refined and functionally efficient form, the anxiety signal is limited to a "thoughtlike" awareness and ability to cope with specific danger situations. In contrast, when the intensity of the anxiety experience is very much greater, it may not remain under control, leading to temporary functional disorganization of the affected person. It is then described as a *panic* or *traumatic state.* [p. 25]

According to this account, anxiety is not clearly distinguished from fear. Anxiety at its best ("in its most refined and functionally efficient form") is a natural adaptive mechanism, a "thoughtlike . . . ability to cope," while its malfunction (the "deer caught in the headlights" and paralyzed by immobility) would entail a traumatized reaction that is inappropriate to the situation, and puts the individual at risk. The analytic treatment of anxiety would thus aim at reducing the neurotic form of anxiety (the "temporary functional disorganization"), thereby restoring the

adaptive function of the ego (in which anxiety performs a healthy
and natural role).[21]

---

21. It is this adaptive function that Winnicott has in mind when, in *Playing and Reality* for example, he speaks of a child who makes positive use of a
transitional object, as a stage in a developmental process that allows him to
separate from his mother. "He was fed at the breast for four months and then
weaned without difficulty . . . Soon after weaning at five to six months he
adopted the end of the blanket where the stitching finished. . . This very soon
became his 'Baa'; he invented this word for it himself as soon as he could use
organized sounds . . . This is a typical example of what I am calling a *transitional object*. . . if anyone gave him his 'Baa' he would immediately suck it and
lose anxiety" [D. W. Winnicott, *Playing and Reality* (New York and London:
Tavistock/Routledge, 1989), p. 7.] Anxiety is regarded here as the distressed
reaction of the child to the loss of the mother, and the healthy development
of the ego would thus depend on a properly adaptive response in the face of
this loss, the use of a transitional object being precisely such a response. In
fact, Winnicott also describes a child who "malfunctions," so to speak, who
cannot establish a transitional object and remains in an anxious or traumatized state in the face of the loss of the mother. From a Lacanian point of view,
however, one would have to ask about the status of this transitional object. It
might seem that the child's anxiety is simply due to the loss of the mother
(conceived as a natural object in the world of the organism and its adaptive
relations), so that the loss of the mother can be compensated for by the acquisition of a substitute. Anxiety would thus be a response to this loss, for
which no compensatory substitute has yet been found. For Lacan, however,
if anxiety arises, it is rather because lack has not yet been instituted for the
subject. On this account, the "separation from the mother" is not the loss of
a natural object, suited to the organic needs of the child, and needing to find
a viable replacement; it is rather the first incarnation of a lack that opens the
field in which language will find its place. Far from being filled, therefore, or
compensated for by a substitute, this lack needs to be maintained and symbolically elaborated, which means in turn that anxiety itself is the sign, not of
a deficiency that needs to be repaired, a natural deficiency or "organic" lack,
but of a productive lack that calls for elaboration. This is why Lacan argues
that anxiety is the index of an Other that is too close or too full: it indicates,
not a lack to be overcome, but a lack that has not been fully established, and
requires elaboration in order to be secured. The clinical response to anxiety
will obviously be very different, depending on which of these accounts plays
the guiding role.

A peculiarity of this account, from a Lacanian perspective, is that "signal" anxiety seems to cover the whole of anxiety: in one case it is a "realistic" signal, while in the other it is a false or misinterpreted signal that leads to an inappropriate and defensive response. And yet Freud, for his part, distinguished "signal" anxiety from "realistic" anxiety; and while one might suppose that this is merely a terminological splitting of hairs, Lacan was always exacting about Freudian terminology. For what does it mean, in fact, to suppose that a "signal" should be understood naturalistically, on the model of a noise in the woods that indicates the arrival of a predator, and is sometimes mistakenly interpreted by a neurotic or defensive ego? If Freud argues that "signal anxiety" as such is distinct from "realistic anxiety," does this not mean that the very term "signal" must be detached from the arena of nature? Is this not why he distinguishes "signal anxiety" from "realistic anxiety"? How then can we suppose that "signal anxiety" should cover the entire field and be regarded as a message that is "correctly" received in one case, and "neurotically misunderstood" in the other? Can a "signal" be automatically understood as part of a purportedly "natural language," and would the reduction of neurotic anxiety, in the course of analytic treatment, amount to the restoration of this natural language—a clearer transmission of the signal? For Lacan, "signal anxiety" does not come in a natural and a distorted form, and if Freud distinguishes between two types, it is in order to show the difference between "realistic anxiety," which may indeed find its prototype in the animal world, where it functions adaptively, protecting the *life* of the animal (not the *ego*), and "signal anxiety" or "automatic anxiety," which belongs to the dimension of the ego as such, a domain that is distinguished from that of the organism, and understood from a perspective that is no longer adaptive or naturalistic. This indicates that when Freud speaks of a "signal," he has already placed himself beyond the horizon of animal adaptation, and entered a realm of language—the dimension of the Other—that breaks with animal adaptation and survival. As a result, to construe the "proper functioning" of the ego in terms of the organism and its survival would be to abandon the very field of psychoanalysis as such. The terminological details are never merely a scholastic matter, then, but point to a fundamental philosophical difference in orientation. Once again, it is always a good idea to read Freud. Without pursuing the question of language any further here, let us simply take up our thread again.

For some interpreters, "signal anxiety" is thus either realistic (the sign of a real danger to which the ego must respond by thought or action), or else it is neurotic (the sign of an internal conflict to which the ego responds in a maladaptive way). This account of anxiety is thereby tied not only to a particular understanding of the "threat," but also to an understanding of the ego in general: when it is functioning properly, the ego is in a relation of equilibrium with its environment, much like the animal in the wild, governed by the aim of survival in the face of danger, though obviously faced with a far more complex "reality" to which it must adapt.

For Lacan, by contrast, Freud's second theory looks very different indeed. In his first formulations, which are eventually subject to revision, Lacan organizes Freud's remarks about the ego by referring to the concept of the imaginary, with the consequence that the danger is neither a real external threat to which the human must adaptively respond, nor an internal conflict (in unconscious thought) that the ego seeks to avoid, but rather the threat of imaginary fragmentation. This first difference in the Lacanian position is decisive and quite far-reaching: in stark contrast with the preceding account, Lacan insists from the outset on the division that separates the human from the animal. This means that he will not speak of the ego in terms of its adaptive function, or by appeal to any analogy with animal behavior. If anxiety is the response to a threat, what is threatened is not the *life of the individual*, but the *imaginary structure of the ego*, and this ego is not an adaptive function, a center of conscious awareness, akin to something we might find in the animal (though perhaps more complex). Freud himself insists that the ego is not equivalent to "consciousness," and should not be construed in terms of what he had previously called the "perception-consciousness system." Lacan interprets this by claiming that the ego is rather an imaginary structure that characterizes human existence as such, distinguishing it from animal life, insofar as human beings are subject to a prematurity of birth that obliges them to fashion their first sense of integrity, not from their real organic functioning, but from the acquisition of an imaginary unity that arrives in place of the actual integrity that it does not yet have. In *Inhibitions, Symptoms, and Anxiety* Freud makes a similar observation:

> The biological factor is the long period of time during which the young of the human species is in a condition of helplessness and dependence. Its intra-uterine existence seems to be short in comparison with that of most animals, and it is sent into the world in a less finished state. [SE 20:154]

This is the basis for Lacan's famous thesis on the "imaginary body," according to which human life is constitutively detached from "natural existence" and subjected to an imaginary alienation which, far from being a contingent or remediable "error," is the necessary condition of ego-formation and corporeal unity—so that the very possibility of bodily coherence, locomotion, and motor coordination (all of which are impeded and inhibited by anxiety), far from being given by nature, depends on this imaginary unity of the body, whose organization and functioning should not be too quickly confused with the organism and its life.

Lacan thus refuses the naturalistic framework of interpretation, which means not only that the "ego" is distinct from the adaptive functioning of the perception-consciousness system, but also that the "danger" that is signaled by anxiety (the "objective correlate") must be different as well. Taking his lead from Rank's theory of the "birth trauma," Freud also hesitates on this very point. Agreeing with Rank that the first "danger" to which the ego responds is birth, he nevertheless asks how we should actually understand this danger. Freud writes:

> In the act of birth there is a real danger to life. We know what this means objectively; but in a psychological sense it says nothing at all to us. The danger of birth has no psychical content. We cannot possibly suppose that the foetus has any sort of knowledge that there is a possibility of its life being destroyed. It can only be aware of some vast disturbance in the economy of its narcissistic libido. Large sums of excitation crowd in on it, giving rise to new kinds of feelings of unpleasure. [SE 20:135]

The "danger" that characterizes anxiety, then, is not a threat to life, but a sudden experience of bodily disintegration, a "vast disturbance in the economy of its *narcissistic libido*" (emphasis added). The "threat" that is "signaled" by anxiety is therefore a threat, not to life itself, but to the unity of the ego, which is first and foremost the imaginary unity of the body.[22] "The ego," Freud

---

22. This argument has been made very clearly and convincingly by Richard Boothby, whom I have drawn on in this analysis, even if, as I claim, Lacan's own position turns out to move in a significantly different direction.

says, "is the actual seat of anxiety" (*SE* 20:140), and not the organism as such. Now this observation also accords with the distinction between fear and anxiety, since, as Richard Boothby has observed, fear poses an external danger, whereas anxiety concerns an excess of *internal* excitations (such as those the child feels when it is no longer contained within the amniotic fluid). As Boothby points out,

> Lacan's view of anxiety . . . specifies the meaning of the danger to the ego signaled by anxiety. Freud clearly found it difficult to determine the nature of the danger. In *The Ego and the Id* he remarks that "what it is that the ego fears . . . cannot be specified; we know that the fear is of being overwhelmed or annihilated; but it cannot be grasped analytically" (*SE* 19:57). For Lacan, the danger is readily interpretable in terms of an explanation of the unity of the ego that is lacking in Freud. Inasmuch as it is formed on the basis of a unifying perceptual *Gestalt*, the ego is liable to anxiety in fantasies of the fragmented body, or *corps morcelé*. [p. 143]

Even "castration anxiety" can be clarified this way, since in the course of the child's maturation, the organ which Freud says is privileged in the child's negotiation of sexual difference has this particular status, not as a real organ, but only in the imaginary. As Lacan puts it, for the girl nothing is lacking in the real of the organism, which means that the absence of the penis can only be registered with respect to the imaginary body, just as, for the boy, the threat of castration is to be understood, not as the danger of a real loss, but as a threat to the imaginary integrity of the body.

Anxiety is therefore not a natural or adaptive phenomenon, but rather the correlate of the imaginary structure of the ego, a structure that supplements and reorganizes organic life, and is unique to the human being, so that it should not be misconstrued in terms of the adaptive functioning of the animal in relation to reality (the organism and its *Umwelt*). This break between the human and the animal, which the philosophers have stressed in their meditations on anxiety and human "existence," is not limited to the philosophical domain, and it is perhaps no surprise that in *The Meaning of Anxiety*, Rollo May surveys some ethological research asking whether animals in fact have anxiety, and concludes that, while animals certainly have response that resembles anxiety (quaking in the face of a thunderstorm, or showing distress at the departure of a close companion), anxiety itself is a peculiarly human phenomenon, with features that distinguish it from these apparent counterparts in the animal world.[23]

If, for Lacan, the ego—the subjective correlate of our analysis—is thus radically different from the adaptive interpretation of the "perception-consciousness system," this also means that, when we turn to the "objective" correlate and the "object" of anxiety, we cannot regard anxiety as being in principle (when it is "functioning properly") a response to reality, based on a model of survival. On this point, the distinction between fear and anxiety is crucial. And indeed Freud has said that signal anxiety is distinct from realistic anxiety, not only in neurotic cases but in its very essence as a correlate of the ego, which means that *anxiety* properly speaking is not really an animal response at all. In the face of a real danger, the animal experiences *fear*. Anxiety as such—not only in its mistaken or "dysfunctional" moments, but in its very essence—would thus never be a truly adaptive response. Freud himself points this out: "On further consideration we must tell ourselves that our judgment that realistic anxiety is rational and expedient calls for drastic revision" (*SE* 16:394). The best

---

23. Rollo May, *The Meaning of Anxiety* (New York: Norton, 1977), p. 96ff.

response would be to run, or to stay and fight, but in either case, anxiety is not helpful, since it immobilizes us, or makes us nervous and disoriented. "If the anxiety is excessively great it proves in the highest degree inexpedient; it paralyses all action, including even flight" (394). When the animal is confronted with a danger, Freud says, "in this situation there is no place for anxiety," and in fact, "a terrified animal is afraid and flees; but the expedient part of this is the 'flight' and not the 'being afraid'" (394). "Thus one feels tempted to conclude that the generation of anxiety is never an expedient thing" (394).

What then is the distinction between "fear" and "anxiety"? If "fear" is the natural mechanism, the adaptive response that immediately turns itself into something else (motor action), what really is anxiety? Faced with the branching paths of this terminology, Freud dissects the phenomenon further. Anxiety is partly a feeling that generates a preparedness for action. The feeling itself is inexpedient, so when it functions well, it disappears into action, and should "transform itself without disturbance into action." When the affect isn't transformed into motor action, it remains as anxiety ("accumulated tension") and is inexpedient. But if, in the face of a real danger, "anxiety is never an expedient thing," how then can it be regarded as part of the defensive mechanism in the ego, an adaptive response in the face of a threat? Unless we wish to collapse the distinction between anxiety and fear, calling all anxiety "neurotic," and leaving only fear as adaptive, this question should indicate that Freud has opened a very different path. In short, an adaptive model may be appropriate in case of "fear," but anxiety as such seems to take us into another dimension.

We see here a gesture that will later be repeated in terms of the death instinct: Why does the subject awake in the middle of the night, troubled by a traumatic dream that does not fulfill any

wish, but breaks with the principle of pleasure, repeating a traumatic scene? If this is not merely an aberration, a deviation from
a natural norm, but an index of something essential in human
life, then something in the human relation to death, and something in the phenomenon of anxiety as well, must run counter
to the model of animal experience, and (like the unconscious
itself) disrupt the model of adaptation that seems to govern the
interpretation of this "response to danger."

We are thus brought to see more clearly the difference between two interpretations of Freud's "second theory." If, as Lacan
claims, anxiety is in some way uniquely human, then it cannot
really be grasped as a more complex version of animal adaptation, which for its part would be a similar but more elementary
"response" to the "stimulus" of danger. The peculiarity of the
human being in relation to animal existence—a peculiarity high-
lighted by anxiety—should rather lead us to understand anxiety on a different model. And if Freud speaks of a response to
danger *on the part of the ego*, should we not ask, more generally,
whether the ego itself can be understood in terms of its adaptive
function, on an analogy with animal adaptation, or whether the
ego is not a different sort of phenomenon? One thus begins to
see how Lacan's account of anxiety, in contrast with the previous interpretation, opens the door to a vast philosophical domain in which the peculiarities of human existence are at issue,
a tradition that culminates in Kierkegaard's *The Problem of Anxiety* and Heidegger's *Being and Time*, where anxiety emerges both
as an index of the uniquely human relation to death, and as the
opening toward a deeper understanding of temporality—one that
departs dramatically from the conceptions of time that we have
attributed to nature (evolutionary time, developmental chronology, linear historical unfolding, and so on). For this tradition,
as for Freud, anxiety cannot simply be inserted into the appara-

tus of evolutionary survival and adaptation, but serves as a fundamental marker of the peculiar nature of human being, and the uniqueness of our relation to death and time. This constitutive division is already evident, for Lacan, in Freud's remark (which is itself a traditional one) that anxiety is to be distinguished from fear, since the latter has an object and entails a "real threat," whereas anxiety is a relation to "no object," and thus entails a certain encounter with negativity, nothingness, and the void. From this perspective, the adaptive account, in which anxiety functions properly when it is "realistic" and serves to identify a real danger, and improperly when it arises from an internal conflict, does not really distinguish between anxiety and fear. If we stay with the model of self-preservation, anxiety should resolve itself into fear, and the distinction between the two should disappear when the organism is functioning properly. But clearly this is not Freud's model, according to Lacan, since it insists on isolating anxiety as a unique and constitutive dimension of human existence—not an aberration that appears only during moments of malfunction, but a key to the very structure of the human subject. This is why Lacan follows Freud in claiming that fear has a "real object," whereas anxiety has "no object," or rather takes "the nothing" as its object. It is this essential link between anxiety and nothingness that is eliminated from the adaptive explanation, in which the ego adjusts to reality. Thus, from the initial observation about the imaginary structure of the ego, to the consequences that bear on the human relation to the void, anxiety takes Lacan in a very different direction through the labyrinth of psychoanalysis.

For Lacan, therefore, the problem of anxiety is not an isolated problem or merely a local detail of the theory, but leads to a reflection on the ego in which a series of very elementary problems must be confronted, from the unique character of the human being and the unnatural structure of the body and space, to the peculiarity of the human relation to mortality and time, all of which are concealed, according to Lacan, when the ego is misconstrued in terms of its adaptive function in relation to reality. In response to the adaptive interpretation of the ego, Lacan could not be more emphatic:

> These propositions are opposed by all our experience, insofar as it teaches us not to regard the ego as centered on the perception-consciousness system, or as organized by the reality principle . . . Our experience shows that we should start instead from the function of méconnaisance that characterizes the ego in all its structures, so markedly articulated by Miss Anna Freud.[24]

The difference between Lacan's account of the "threat to the ego," understood via the imaginary, and the account of a more adaptively oriented ego psychology, in which neurotic anxiety is the sign of a maladaptive response to reality, based on unconscious conflict, is not a small difference, then, but leads to a substantial philosophical parting of the ways, in relation to the nature of the ego as such, the very difference between the human and the animal, and the philosophical tradition in which Freud is consequently situated.

This brings us to one further observation, which is especially pertinent for readers who are interested in grasping more precisely the actual corporeal dimension of anxiety, and indeed the very status of "affect" as such. For in saying that anxiety is connected with the imaginary structure of the ego, Lacan stays

---

24. Jacques Lacan, "The Mirror Stage as Formative of the Function of the I as Revealed in Psychoanalytic Experience," *Ecrits: A Selection*, trans. A. Sheridan (New York: Norton, 1977), p. 6.

very close to the Freudian attempt to explain anxiety in its most intimate, mechanical workings. He does not speak of anxiety as a "thought-like" process (whether this is linked to the "perception-consciousness system," as in the case of "realistic anxiety," or to the activation of an unconscious conflict, as in the case of neurotic anxiety); he rather regards anxiety as an overflow of internal excitations that cannot be contained by the imaginary integrity of the body. If desire animates the body and structures its possibilities, this overflow of *jouissance* has a very different function. As Freud himself says, the "danger" at birth is not a threat to life from the standpoint of the baby, but rather an awareness of "some vast disturbance in the economy of its narcissistic libido." The "conflict" in anxiety is not a matter of conscious or unconscious *thought* but rather a matter of the *discontinuity between the real of the organism and the imaginary unity of the body*. This is what Freud means when he speaks of an "overflow of excitation," and this is why Freud's second theory, in which anxiety is construed as a threat to the "ego," can be integrated to some extent with the first theory, in which anxiety is the result, not of an external threat, but of an internal *libidinal surplus* that cannot be contained by the economy of the bodily apparatus. One begins to suspect that the canonical account of Freud's "two theories," in which the second amounts to a convenient rejection of the first, has organized the reception of Freud in a fundamentally misleading way, so that the continuous problematic that leads Freud in his theoretical development cannot be properly grasped. In any case, it is clear enough that the standard account of Freud's "two theories" is itself the product of an interpretation, and not an innocent or neutral description—an interpretation in which, as we have seen, both halves of the theory are diminished. Lacan's account not only provides us with a different view of the ego, the body, and anxiety, but also entails a reorganization of the canonical account of "Freud's development."

This discussion of the imaginary does not mean, of course, that "unconscious conflict" is simply irrelevant to the phenomenon of anxiety. But "unconscious conflict" and "thoughtlike awareness" concern the symbolic order of representation, and we should not immediately conflate the bodily disturbance manifested in anxiety with the order of representation that is involved in the idea of the unconscious. The unconscious is certainly *related* to anxiety, but anxiety, understood as an affect, must be distinguished from the order of the unconscious. Harari will stress this point when he takes up the famous Lacanian thesis in *L'Angoisse*, that "anxiety does not deceive." As a symbolic system, the unconscious is always subject to displacement and substitution: it is designed to deceive and censor, and this is why it calls for interpretation in some respects. But anxiety does not deceive, and it cannot be interpreted. Anxiety can only be put to work, "administered in small doses," as Lacan says, in the course of an analytic treatment.[25] In Lacanian terms, then, anxiety is not a symbolic phenomenon, but is situated at the border of the imaginary and the real, and we cannot simply jump from anxiety to the level of "unconscious thought" or "unconscious conflict," without explaining more precisely the series of steps

---

25. In *Seminar XI* Lacan writes: "Anxiety is that which does not deceive. But anxiety may be lacking." (A patient who hallucinates may not be anxious, for example, but when the hallucination begins to disappear, anxiety may well arise. In Heidegger too, anxiety may be lacking, and even if anxiety provides a crucial passageway for *Dasein* on the way to Being-towards-death, the inauthentic mode of being can predominate, in which *Dasein* flees from anxiety into the world of the "They.") Lacan continues, saying of anxiety that "in my experience, it is necessary to canalize it and, if I may say so, to take it in small doses, so that one is not overcome by it. This is similar to bringing the subject into contact with the real" (p. 41).

by which the imaginary structure of the ego is related, both to the real of *jouissance*, and to the symbolic order and the functioning of unconscious thought.

One final step is now necessary if we are to see what organizes Harari's discussion in this book. Our account of Lacan's treatment of anxiety has thus far focused on the imaginary body, without exploring these steps; but as we shall see, Lacan's later remarks on anxiety, elaborated in the 1962–1963 seminar that concerns us in this book, are precisely an attempt to go beyond his initial account, in which anxiety is explained as the threat to the imaginary unity of the body. This seminar, then, would take a step beyond the formulations we have just outlined, by moving from the famous thesis on the "imaginary body," and articulating the relation between the imaginary, the symbolic, and the real. This is why we stressed the apparently minor terminological point concerning the difference between the "ego" and the "subject": for Lacan, what is ultimately at stake in the theory of anxiety is not the ego at all, imaginary or otherwise, but rather the status of the subject as such. As Lacan says in *L'Angoisse*, speaking of "signal anxiety": "The ego is the site of the signal. But it is not for the ego that the signal is given . . . . It is so that the subject—it cannot be called otherwise—may be alerted to something (2.27.63; W 158).

In short, the question of the *subject* is raised by the phenomenon of anxiety. Anxiety is not simply a matter of the *ego*, and in this sense Lacan takes a step beyond Freud in *L'Angoisse*, by claiming that the threat cannot be reduced to something at the level of the *ego*. Anxiety will now concern the very birth of the subject as such. This is the step that Harari's account will elucidate.

The phenomenon of anxiety thus serves as an illuminating guide, not only for distinguishing different schools of thought that have emerged from Freud's work, but also for understanding how these schools have in turn come to be imbedded in very different discourses and intellectual traditions, from the adaptive models of evolutionary psychology to the philosophical trajectory of phenomenology and existentialism. The seminar on anxiety makes a major contribution, not only to our understanding of Freud, but also to Lacan's own conceptual development. The fundamental issues that were first organized by his thesis on the mirror stage—the imaginary body, the dialectic of recognition in relation to the other, Lacan's use of Hegel, and his account of the object relation—all this is reworked in *Seminar X*, which represents a major reappraisal of his own previous work, grounded, as is always the case for Lacan, in a disciplined attention to Freud's own text.

Translator's Note

*L*acan's *Seminar on "Anxiety": An Introduction* is a transcription of Dr. Harari's seminar. Much can be said about translating speech as transcription. Suffice it to say that Dr. Harari both reviewed the transcription of his seminar and incorporated therein pertinent questions from seminar participants and his answers to those questions. The text contains, therefore, both written and spoken discourse markers. In addition, Dr. Harari's expository style and method have the character of Lacanian teaching; that is, originally, spoken to be heard. The translation attempts to keep pace faithfully with this double characterization. It is hoped that readers will hear the author's voice behind the text that served to guide the translator in her endeavor. I would like to thank Richard G. Klein for helping me regarding certain references in the text.

Quotations of all texts have been provided from standard English translations, wherever possible. On the rare occasions when relevant passages could not be located, translations have been made from Spanish versions cited by Dr. Harari.

Jane C. Lamb-Ruiz

Preface

I

This book has been designed along lines similar to my earlier work, *The Four Fundamental Concepts of Psychoanalysis of Lacan: An Introduction*, the first edition of which was published in 1987. I explain in the latter—which fortunately continues to receive a very warm and stimulating reception by my reader friends—that it arose from material presented during the course of ten classes I gave on the topic at the Centro de Extensión Psicoanalítica of the Centro Cultural General San Martín in Buenos Aires in 1986. This new book has the same origin and is also an introductory work. It covers nine meetings that took place in 1987 on Lacan's seminar *L'Angoisse* ["Anxiety"], his tenth seminar, and the one that preceded *The Four Fundamental Concepts*. It should be pointed out that this choice was not the result of a naive and empirical chronological approach to the two seminars, but was and is due to a diverse series of circumstances that make *Seminar X* special and necessary for its work on, and processing of, Lacanian thought:

(a) The seminar situates with rigor, precision, and a wealth of clinical underpinnings the object *a*, which Lacan called his "invention."

(b) It has been claimed, whether from ignorance or bad faith, that Lacan underestimated and even "scotomized" the consideration of the always slippery notion of *affect*, which the other psychoanalysis[1] is so inclined toward or affected by. The seminar demonstrates the inappropriateness of this criticism.

(c) Although several ideas are only lightly sketched in the text of the seminar, paths for their further development are also clearly signposted.

(d) In my opinion, *L'Angoisse* is one of the best presentations of the way in which the "key themes" of Lacan's teaching impact on analytical treatment, either by fruitfully subverting it or by widening its scope.

As can be observed throughout the book, I act on point (c) above by developing a series of articulations, schemas, graphs, frameworks, and even concepts, the scope of which goes beyond the boundaries of *Seminar X*, with the aim of helping readers grasp it more thoroughly. However, I am convinced—and hope my readers will concur—that this didactic desire has not been accomplished at the cost of debasing the notions it deals with. Lastly, I would like to stress again, at the risk of stating the obvious, that not everything Lacan dealt with in *Seminar X* is in-

---

1. With the phrase "the other psychoanalysis," I refer allegorically to the Lacanian "other." The phrase also implies a critique of other forms of psychoanalysis that have not been able to, not known how to, or not wanted to incorporate the crucial retro-foundational approach of Lacan.

cluded in my introduction. Beyond this perhaps evident fact, I would like to emphasize two points:

(1) All of the "guide lines" forming the backbone of the principal teaching in his seminar are dealt with.

(2) The book does not claim to be an alternative to *Seminar X*; rather it endeavors to be a path leading towards it.

II

L'Angoisse, like so many other of Jacques Lacan's seminars, has not been published—even now—in an official version sanctioned by members of his family. By virtue of the legal rights which they possess, the free circulation of these seminars continues to be prohibited *sine die*. Hence, to work on *L'Angoisse*, I made use of various versions in French and one translation into Spanish undertaken by a psychoanalytical entity in Buenos Aires so that its members could study the text. The flagrant differences between these versions, I believe, I have overcome by proceeding with an inter- and intratextual reading, not leaving the reason for my choices to chance or intuition. The diversity evident in these versions will not be resolved by the publication of an official version edited by Lacan's family members since, as becomes manifest in the few seminars that have been published, they bear the stamp of a university-style summarizing marked by highly debatable, univocal editorial decisions. Furthermore, Lacan's published seminars tend to omit or simplify obscure, doubtful, or contradictory sections. I would like to point out that my mission in this book has been to strive at all times for a texture radically different from those official publications.

III

Alejandra Cowes, a university graduate in psychology, drew up an initial manuscript from recordings of my classes with her characteristic ability and determination. I would like once more to express my sincere gratitude to her. Each chapter corresponds to one meeting, and relevant questions and answers from the classes have been incorporated into the text.

IV

I end with the wish that this *Introduction* can become a useful tool in the work of delineating the untransferable, singular, and efficacious characteristics of a Lacanian psychoanalytical clinic. This is not merely of academic interest but involves, especially, the ethical order of the praxis operant in mental heath.

Buenos Aires
September 1992

Introduction to the English Language Edition

It is with genuine satisfaction that I present my book to English-speaking readers. This is undoubtedly possible due to the growing interest in, and ever-keener comprehension of, the teachings of Jacques Lacan both in the United States and the United Kingdom, two countries with great psychoanalytic traditions. This increasing interest has transcended the arena known as "the humanities," where it was initially played out, and has returned to its own terrain of origin, psychoanalysis. This is owing to the fact that if "the Lacanian field" has substance and conceptual weight, it cannot be played out or judged outside of the clinical practice of psychoanalysis. Indeed, we should speak of a "Lacanian clinical practice" (as I proposed with the title of the book of mine that immediately follows this one). This practice not only furnishes a differential reading of and approach to what happens in the analytic cure; it also makes possible the isolation and study of issues that are veiled or unknown in other psychoanalytic approaches. Stated briefly, Lacanian clinical practice is expanding because it is efficacious. And the dominant tradition in British and American thinking, characterized by a profound respect for the pragmatic, could not leave by the wayside the psychoanalytical orientation that today entails, in my view, *the greatest advance in our discipline and its involvement in culture since Freud's unequalled body of work*. In this regard, Lacan's "return to Freud" is often cited. For my part, I prefer to pay attention to the clinical-theoretical operations at stake in terms of a retro-foundation; indeed, psychoanalysis was made to found itself "backward" through a type of causality very similar to the action of the two scenes that are necessary to give rise to the efficacy of the phenomena circumscribed by our discipline (as happens in trauma, to cite an exemplary case).

Furthermore, retro-foundation also implies difference, or better, return with a difference. In this sense, *Seminar X* on anxiety (*"L'Angoisse"* is the title in French) is a formidable witness to the permanent and sustained dialogue and debate that its author maintained with Freud's works, especially (though not exclusively) *Inhibitions, Symptoms and Anxiety* and "The 'Uncanny'."

For my part, and in function of the "spirit" of those things that the Lacanian trajectory transmits, I have attempted in this book (while maintaining my distance) a retro-foundation of *Seminar X*. Stated differently, I have tried to extract and expound its logic, ordering, as far as I could, its developments, which are often characterized by a conceptual "back-and-forth" movement. Finally, I also want to emphasize that the origins of this book, described in the Preface, qualify it as a useful tool for all educated people seeking to approach the works of Lacan. I did not "suppose knowledge" on the part of possible readers, in order to widen the path of access to a work that—and I dare to maintain this—is one of the most important of the twentieth century. (Perhaps the twenty-first century will do justice to the place that civilization still owes to Lacan.)

Secondly, I wish to note that the English version of this book would not have been published without the initiative, support, and warm encouragement of the editor of the series in which it appears, my distinguished colleague and friend, Judith Feher Gurewich. To her go my sincere thanks for honoring me with her trust, respect, and consideration.

At this juncture I will wield a commonplace to make my next point, which concerns the idea that each language organizes the experience of its users in a singular and untransferable way. This makes it impossible to pour all the semantics of what is said in one language into another. Although this is true in general terms, it is even more so when one tries to do it, as is the case here, while moving from a Latin language to a Saxon one. Indeed, the complications arising from this translation were much greater than the ones encountered in translations of my books into French and Portuguese. In this regard, I would like to emphasize the difficulties related to the translation of the word *jouissance* (and the verb *jouir*), since its meaning is lost by translating it as "enjoyment" (and "to enjoy"). Even less remains, of course, were one to translate it as "pleasure," since that word is antithetical to it. I assume its denotation is clarified by my explanation in the book, but I would like to point out that since it is untranslatable, it appears in the book unmodified, in its original French form. (For the Lacanian reader, this decision will not be something new, as he or she will be familiar with various works in English opting for the same solution.)

As for *fantasme*, I have preferred to use the word "phantasy" in the translation, as it refers to the clear differentiation made in this regard by the Kleinian school. Kleinians, it will be recalled, distinguish "phantasy" from "fantasy," which is conceived of as a product of the imagination. Thus I pay homage to Melanie Klein, emphasizing her intuitive anticipation (with regard to Lacan) of phantasy as a nodular structure of the psyche.

Another clarification should be made with regard to "subject": at times I connote with this term the subject of the unconscious; at other times, indicated generally by the pronouns "he" and "she," I refer to the empirical subject commonly but erroneously referred to as "person." Read with a minimum of care, the differentiation can be made relatively easily by the reader. Also, given the emphasis, the focus, of Lacan on the analysis of language, at times I have had to include puns or portmanteau words, which, I hope, have been useful in illustrating, rather than obscuring the material.

In resolving these issues and many others of similar scope, I have had the invaluable help of a permanent dialogue, and almost line-by-line discussion, with the translator, Jane C. Lamb-Ruiz. I thank her for her dedication and the sensitivity to and capacity for the "spirit" of languages that she brought to this book.

Finally, I want to emphasize, especially to those who have not yet taken a look at the remarkable psychoanalytic teaching contained in this book, that the "Lacanian field" requires the art of patience, reflection, and reading "with one's head up" (as Barthes would say). For putting all of this into the following pages, my last thanks go to you. And who are you? My new friend, the English reader.

Buenos Aires
February 1998

The Lacanian Clinical Field: Series Overview

JUDITH FEHER GUREWICH

Lacanian psychoanalysis exists, and the ongoing series, The Lacanian Clinical Field, is here to prove it. The clinical expertise of French practitioners deeply influenced by the thought of Jacques Lacan has finally found a publishing home in the United States. Books that have been acclaimed in France, Italy, Spain, Greece, South America, and Japan for their clarity, didactic power, and clinical relevance will now be at the disposal of the American psychotherapeutic and academic communities. These books cover a range of topics, including theoretical introductions; clinical approaches to neurosis, perversion, and psychosis; child psychoanalysis; conceptualizations of femininity; psychoanalytic readings of American literature; and more. Thus far, the series is comprised of eleven books.

Though all these works are clinically relevant, they will also be of great interest to those American scholars who have taught and used Lacan's theories for over a decade. What better opportunity for the academic world of literary criticism, philosophy, human sciences, women's studies, film studies, and multicultural studies finally to have access to the clinical insights of a theorist known primarily for his revolutionary vision of the formation of the human subject. Thus The Lacanian Clinical Field goes beyond introducing the American clinician to a different psychoanalytic outlook. It brings together two communities that have grown progressively estranged from each other. For indeed, the time when the Frankfurt School, Lionel Trilling, Erich Fromm, Herbert Marcuse, Philip Rieff, and others were fostering exchanges between the academic and the psychoanalytic communities is gone, and in the process psychoanalysis has lost some of its vibrancy.

The very limited success of ego psychology in bringing psychoanalysis into the domain of science has left psychoanalysis in need of a metapsychology that is able not only to withstand the pernicious challenges of psychopharmacology and psychiatry but also to accommodate the findings of cognitive and developmental psychology. Infant research has put many of Freud's insights into question, and the attempts to replace a one-body psychology with a more interpersonal or intersubjective approach have led to dissension within the psychoanalytic community. Many theorists are of the opinion that the road toward scientific legitimacy requires a certain allegiance with Freud's detractors, who are convinced that the unconscious and its sexual underpinnings are merely an aberration. Psychoanalysis continues to be practiced, however, and according to both patients and analysts the uncovering of unconscious motivations continues to provide a sense of relief. But while there has been a burgeoning of different psychoanalytic schools of thought since the desacralization of Freud, no theoretical agreement has been reached as to why such relief occurs.

Nowadays it can sometimes seem that Freud is read much more scrupulously by literary critics and social scientists than by psychoanalysts. This is not entirely a coincidence. While the psychoanalytic community is searching for a new metapsychology, the human sciences have acquired a level of theoretical sophistication and complexity that has enabled them to read Freud under a new lens. Structural linguistics and structural anthropology have transformed conventional appraisals of human subjectivity and have given Freud's unconscious a new status. Lacan's teachings, along with the works of Foucault and Derrida, have been largely responsible for the explosion of new ideas that have enhanced the interdisciplinary movement pervasive in academia today.

The downside of this remarkable intellectual revolution, as far as psychoanalysis is concerned, is the fact that Lacan's contribution has been derailed from its original trajectory. No longer perceived as a theory meant to enlighten the practice of psychoanalysis, his brilliant formulations have been both adapted and criticized so as to conform to the needs of purely intellectual endeavors far removed from clinical reality. This state of affairs is certainly in part responsible for Lacan's dismissal by the psychoanalytic community. Moreover, Lacan's "impossible" style has been seen as yet another proof of the culture of obscurantism that French intellectuals seem so fond of.

In this context the works included in The Lacanian Clinical Field should serve as an eye-opener at both ends of the spectrum. The authors in the series are primarily clinicans eager to offer to professionals in psychoanalysis, psychiatry, psychology, and other mental-health disciplines a clear and succinct didactic view of Lacan's work. Their goal is not so much to emphasize the radi-

cally new insights of the Lacanian theory of subjectivity and its place in the history of human sciences as it is to show how this difficult and complex body of ideas can enhance clinical work. Therefore, while the American clinician will be made aware that Lacanian psychoanalysis is not primarily a staple of literary criticism or philosophy but a praxis meant to cure patients of their psychic distress, the academic community will be exposed for the first time to a reading of Lacan that is in sharp contrast with the literature that has thus far informed them about his theory. In that sense Lacan's teachings return to the clinical reality to which they primarily belong.

Moreover, the clinical approach of the books in this series will shed a new light on the critical amendments that literary scholars and feminist theoreticians have brought to Lacan's conceptualization of subjectivity. While Lacan has been applauded for having offered an alternative to Freud's biological determinism, he has also been accused of nevertheless remaining phallocentric in his formulation of sexual difference. Yet this criticism, one that may be valid outside of the clinical reality—psychoanalysis is both an ingredient and an effect of culture—may not have the same relevance in the clinical context. For psychoanalysis as a praxis has a radically different function from the one it currently serves in academic discourse. In the latter, psychoanalysis is perceived both as an ideology fostering patriarchal beliefs and as a theoretical tool for constructing a vision of the subject no longer dependent on a phallocratic system. In the former, however, the issue of phallocracy loses its political impact. Psychoanalytic practice can only retroactively unravel the ways that the patient's psychic life has been constituted, and in that sense it can only reveal the function the phallus plays in the psychic elaboration of sexual difference.

The Lacanian Clinical Field, therefore, aims to undo certain prejudices that have affected Lacan's reputation up to now in both the academic and the psychoanalytic communities. While these prejudices stem from rather different causes—Lacan is perceived as too patriarchal and reactionary in the one and too far removed from clinical reality in the other—they both seem to overlook the fact that the fifty years that cover the period of Lacan's teachings were mainly devoted to working and reworking the meaning and function of psychoanalysis, not necessarily as a science or even as a human science, but as a practice that can nonetheless rely on a solid and coherent metapsychology. This double debunking of received notions may not only enlarge the respective frames of reference of both the therapeutic and the academic communities; it may also allow them to find a common denominator in a metapsychology that has derived its "scientific" status from the unexpected realm of the humanities.

I would like to end this overview to the series as a whole with a word of warning and a word of reassurance. One of the great difficulties for an American analyst trying to figure out the Lacanian "genre" is the way these clinical theorists explain their theoretical point of view as if it were coming straight from Freud. Yet Lacan's Freud and the American Freud are far from being transparent to each other. Lacan dismantled the Freudian corpus and rebuilt it on entirely new foundations, so that the new edifice no longer resembled the old. At the same time he always downplayed, with a certain coquetterie, his position as a theory builder, because he was intent on proving that he had remained, despite all odds, true to Freud's deepest insights. Since Lacan was very insistent on keeping Freudian concepts as the raw material of his theory, Lacanian analysts of the sec-

ond generation have followed in their master's footsteps and
have continued to read Freud scrupulously in order to expand,
with new insights, this large structure that had been laid out.
Moreover, complicated historical circumstances have fostered
their isolation, so that their acquaintance with recent psychoanalytic developments outside of France has been limited.
Lacan's critical views on ego psychology and selected aspects
of object relations theory have continued to inform their vision
of American psychoanalysis and have left them unaware that
certain of their misgivings about these schools of thought are
shared by some of their colleagues in the United States. This
apparently undying allegiance to Freud, therefore, does not
necessarily mean that Lacanians have not moved beyond him,
but rather that their approach is different from that of their
American counterparts. While the latter often tend to situate
their work as a reaction to Freud, the Lacanian strategy always
consists in rescuing Freud's insights and resituating them in a
context free of biological determinism.

Second, I want to repeat that the expository style of the
books of this series bears no resemblance to Lacan's own writings. Lacan felt that Freud's clarity and didactic talent had ultimately led to distortions and oversimplifications, so that his
own notoriously "impossible" style was meant to serve as a
metaphor for the difficulty of listening to the unconscious.
Cracking his difficult writings involves not only the intellectual effort of readers but also their unconscious processes; comprehension will dawn as reader-analysts recognize in their own
work what was expressed in sibylline fashion in the text. Some
of Lacan's followers continued this tradition, fearing that clear
exposition would leave no room for the active participation of
the reader. Others felt strongly that although Lacan's point was

*well taken it was not necessary to prolong indefinitely an ide-
ology of obscurantism liable to fall into the same traps as the
ones Lacan was denouncing in the first place. Such a conviction was precisely what made this series, The Lacanian Clinical Field, possible.*

1

Affect, Signal, Matricial Framework

Jacques Lacan's *Seminar X*, which bears the French title of *L'Angoisse* ["Anxiety"], follows, as do the others, a very rigorous route, as much in its expository thinking as in its logical and temporal concatenation of two key moments in his teaching. In this sense, it is useful to point out that this seminar precedes *The Four Fundamental Concepts of Psychoanalysis*, already a classic, and the first of the seminars for which a version was established and published.[1] Also, *Seminar X* came immediately after the *Identification* seminar. This fact must be taken into consideration when noting that the topics in *Seminar X* do not emerge as free association. Lacan is careful to point this out clearly when he begins the seminar in November 1962. He indicates he will take up again a series of problems pending since the previous year. We will not go into the seminar on identification except to point out that it marks the systematic begin-

---

1. Jacques Lacan, *The Four Fundamental Concepts of Psychoanalysis*, trans. Alan Sheridan (Harmondsworth: Peregrine, 1986).

ning of Lacan's leaning on topology. Undoubtedly, *the question of identification lent itself to topology, as the topological surfaces considered in the seminar make it possible to think about certain conditions in which the internal and the external interplay in a very singular manner.* In *Seminar X* Lacan proposed going beyond the naive psychoanalytical considerations usually understood as projections and introjections. He responds to the classic conception of the subject interiorizing outside objects or expelling certain aspects of him- or herself to the outside, with topologies that are neither intuitive nor imaginary and where the inside/ outside pair loses all obvious value by being put into question. Now, the seminar on identification where topology began to function—the usefulness of which was foreshadowed in allusions such as those in the Rome discourse, where there is an early reference to the torus—could only leave certain issues pending.[2] At the beginning of *L'Angoisse*, the proposition is to deal with these deferred issues; this was the manner Lacan found suitable *to articulate identification with anxiety.*

To approach anxiety as the central theme of *Seminar X* was, moreover, a propitious, strategic manner of answering the objection of excessive intellectualism that then—and even earlier— had been leveled at Lacan's teaching. The accusers claimed— and there are still those who do claim—that the decisive concern for analysts was to be found in affect. Doubtless Lacan did not focus on the evanescent "affective aspects" from which what is now traditional criticism arose through authors such as André Green in his work *Le discours vivant*, known in Spanish as *La*

---

2. Jacques Lacan, "The Function and Field of Speech and Language in Psychoanalysis," in *Ecrits: A Selection*, trans. Alan Sheridan (New York: Norton, 1977), p. 105.

concepción psicoanalítica del afecto—el discurso viviente.[3] For Green, Lacan's body of work leaves aside the status of affect. Green considers this issue crucial for psychoanalysis, a discipline that shapes an environment where the "the heterogeneity of the signifier" prevails. As is known, psychology tends to make a supposedly simple division: psychoanalysis deals with affect while other schools, for example the Piagetian, deal with the cognitive. In this way the old distinction between feeling, thinking, and willing is maintained while, by the same token, psychoanalysis is absorbed into psychology. From this presupposition, many have attempted to make a hybrid out of the supposedly diverse kinds of cognitivism and affectivism, which has resulted in a series of sterile hybrids of which Green's is one of the best known.

It is important to point out the position Lacan grants *affect* in *L'Angoisse,* insofar as anxiety, for authors like Green, enters completely into the territory of affect from an almost phenomenological point of view: *anxiety affects the subject.* The Lacanian position, however, implies a focus on *not just any affect but the one that analytical practice is most interested in.*

Indeed, the presence of the term *anxiety* can be found from the very beginning in Freud's undertaking. For example, it can be observed in passages where Freud attempts *to differentiate between anxiety neurosis and neurasthenia,* or when the question of *anxiety hysteria* arises, sometimes—though it is not easy to accept this confirmation so easily—as a synonym for phobia. This is why anxiety is not just another affect, nor can it be a basis for a possible "theory of affects," giving rise to what Lacan called "the catalogue method"; that is, an enumeration—as a para-

3. André Green, *The Fabric of Affect in the Psychoanalytic Discourse,* trans. Alan Sheridan (New York: New Library of Psychoanalysis, no. 38, 1999).

digm—in which a series of apparently more or less organized feelings are put together, although the series hides an absolute discreteness. Similar lists tend to be made about instinct. As can be observed, there must surely exist as many instincts as authors theorizing about them, and with affects a similar thing happens. Confronting this panorama, Lacan produces a strong assertion, the kind he used to use to *amaze* and move people. "We are psychoanalysts," he states, "and not psychologists"; therefore, chaotic, jumbled, and juxtaposed theories of classification are not part of our field of practice. What interests us, on the contrary, is what Freud saw as central and decisive: anxiety. Lacan articulates this with a clinical reference that can be cross-referenced with a passage from *The Four Fundamental Concepts of Psychoanalysis*. He asserts that anxiety is important, no more or less than *to discover under which conditions and to what extent the analyst can bear the anxiety of the analysand*. In the following seminar he points out that *the anxiety of the analysand should be administered in doses by the analyst*. The recommendation implies that the analyst should not act as some kind of inductor—the analyst as anxiety-provoking by definition—nor as an anxiety domesticator. Frequently *the obstacle comes from the analyst naming or giving a name, which confers an imaginary meaning, to what is happening to the analysand*. This reduces anxiety almost immediately, but at the same time what was being said through it is suffocated: this is a vain undertaking because the return of the repressed will demonstrate the fallacy of proceeding with the analysis in this manner.

When we say that something wishes to be said through anxiety, we are expressing an idea from Freud to which Lacan delivers rightful value, pointing out that it is to be found at the beginning of his work: *anxiety is a signal*. The mere fact of pointing this out implies considering it as *something referring to an-*

other order. Thus, it is not a self- or auto-referential phenomenon but, on the contrary, has a condition of retransmission to
another field. *Anxiety does not represent itself.*

Seminar X was delivered at the beginning of the sixties, at a
time when the European and especially French cultural atmo-
spheres found themselves pregnant with the existentialist thinking that had flourished in the post-World War II period. To focus
on the issues raised by the notion of anxiety did not imply disdaining all the authors who had tackled the issue from a philosophical standpoint. So Lacan then took up the topic—almost
inevitably we could say—from an existentialist slant. But he did
so the better to differentiate himself from these postulations.
Seminar X does indeed take as its own points arising from philosophical discourse: it simulates and pretends to belong to it, then
immediately distances itself from that discourse. This is an intelligent way for psychoanalysis to utilize issues relevant to it,
even if they arise on philosophical terrain.

Lacan's initial approach in the seminar refers—and it could
be no other way when dealing with these kinds of existential
conceptions—to a *seminal* text, *The Concept of Anxiety* by the
Dane, Sören Kierkegaard. Not only would Lacan quote him at
the end of his seminar, a year later he would work through the
philosopher's work in his text *Répétition.* Kierkegaard had been
claimed on many occasions as the direct precursor of contemporary existentialism. Lacan went further during the seminar,
saying *the Dane was the most daring researcher of the soul prior to
Freud.* The Kierkegaardian philosophical tradition, which locates
the starting point of all thought in existence, has a crucial position implicitly in *Seminar X.* But Kierkegaard is not the only
philosopher to whom Lacan refers. Martin Heidegger, Gabriel
Marcel, Léon Chestov, and Nikolai Berdiaeff are also mentioned
in the first meeting of the seminar. The list is heterogeneous, as

these authors are comparable neither for their formulations nor—as Lacan says—for what is "usable" for psychoanalysis. Nevertheless, the developments in two of these texts are "used" in a major way for *the psychoanalytical appropriation of what is deemed pertinent.*

The influence and use of Heideggerian concepts can be observed in many passages of Lacan's work. Throughout his teaching, Lacan never stopped professing a profound respect for the work of the German philosopher. Also, among the "no less great," as Lacan expressed it, he placed his fellow countryman Jean-Paul Sartre, in spite of their extensive differences. Based on the concepts of both thinkers, Lacan drew up a small schema to orient his audience.

It seems odd that after working with the complex topological surfaces in the *Identification* seminar, Lacan turned to such a simple diagram as the one below. Maybe he was merely trying to make himself understood in the first meeting of the seminar, which we are looking at here. In this sense, the schema is valid. Referring to key notions in Sartre and Heidegger, he makes this diagram:

Cure *(Sorge, souci [care, concern: Trans.])*

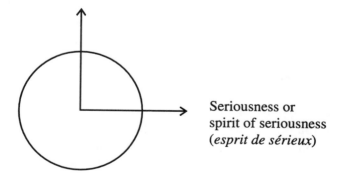

Seriousness or
spirit of seriousness
(*esprit de sérieux*)

Seriousness (*esprit de sérieux*), as defined in *Being and Nothingness*, is opposed to anxiety as a concept. Sartre writes, "Anguish [*angoisse*, anxiety] then is the reflective apprehension of freedom by itself. In this sense it is mediation, for although it is immediate consciousness of itself, it arises from the negation of the appeals of the world. . . . Anguish [*angoisse*] is opposed to the mind of the serious man who apprehends values in terms of the world, and who resides in the reassuring, materialistic substantiation of values."[4]

Lacan chooses not to define anxiety at that moment; he limits himself to referring to something that can be supposed by experience: we all suffer. This lack of definition makes it so the Lacanian conception does not bear any relation to those of Sartre or Heidegger. Furthermore, not providing a definition makes it possible to remain in what presumably would not be taken into consideration: something like a *direct experience* of what anxiety implies. In a vector diverging from, but not opposed to, the Sartrean one, Lacan locates what he defines as *souci* (care or concern), which is his translation of *Sorge*, a basic concept in Heidegger's thinking. Translated in a Spanish version of the seminar as *preocupación* (preoccupation, worry) but more often as *cuidado* (care), the edition in Spanish of *Being and Time* uses what we think is a more appropriate term: *cura* (cure). Lacan seems to have chosen this word as he refers repeatedly to the analytical *cure*. In his book, Heidegger defines cure as coming from the being of *Dasein*, correlative to "the fundamental finding oneself of anxiety."[5] Thus, what is trans-

---

4. Jean-Paul Sartre, *Being and Nothingness*, trans. Hazel Barnes (New York: Philosophical Library, 1956), p. 39.

5. Martin Heidegger, *Being and Time*, trans. John Macquarrie and Edward Robinson (New York: Harper and Row, 1962), p. 228.

lated in *Seminar X* as *souci* is none other than *cure, a word that successfully replaces the obsolete term* treatment, *which carries with it the risk of an entire medical ideology.* In speaking of the psychoanalytical cure, Lacan is paying greater homage to Heidegger, expressing with another word what in the seminar on anxiety appears as *souci*; both are unmistakable allusions to the issues of *Sein und Zeit*. What should be pointed out in Lacan's schema— which looks like a clock with little arms, doesn't it?—is that while Heidegger concerns himself with *Sorge*, the concern or preoccupation coming from meeting what anxiety witnesses, Sartre enlarges upon a worldly determination of *seriousness*. Seriousness was also a notion used by Kierkegaard, so that the Sartrean allusion is rooted in tradition, or at least in a salient precursor. Without going further into philosophical texts, this all serves as a warning that the Freudian theme, far from original in all respects, arises from a context from which it must differentiate itself in order to acquire autonomy. Anxiety is, by all accounts, a theme that has interested many great thinkers. Also, Freud's developments of the theme extend a previously delineated field of representation. It is from here that irrupts the famous Freudian tripartite title, *Inhibitions, Symptoms and Anxiety*. At some point the meaning of the triple articulation repeated in other texts such as "Remembering, Repeating and Working Through," where tripartition can be seen in the title itself, should be examined. Why did he weave issues in this way? Undoubtedly a recurrent textual structure is at play here, but what we want to point out is that among the three elements correlated in *Inhibitions, Symptoms and Anxiety*, there should be something that makes their articulation possible. What is surprising, as Lacan points out, is that "*everything is talked about in this essay except anxiety*." The Lacanian invitation to reread this text is not an idle one. It ties into another crucial text for us, "The 'Uncanny'." In this work *Freud does develop a theory of anxiety*, albeit inchoate, through the analysis of a particular modality, *the feeling of the uncanny. The affect known as* Unheimliche *should be included in the orbit of anxiety.* Paradoxically, from its singularity as nucleus, now the species called anxiety can be understood in general. Thus the Lacanian approach stops at first to analyze what is presented in *Inhibitions, Symptoms and Anxiety.* Questions arise about the title itself, so we can first ask whether there is homogeneity between inhibition, symptom, and anxiety. If there is not, why is the conjunction used in this manner? Second, if these concepts do not belong to a homogeneous order, does this necessarily imply that they are heterogeneous? If they fit together, do they have a causal relation or one of reciprocal exclusion? These are only some of the questions that elementary logic poses from a first reading. It seems to us that Lacan, to make the terms clearer, implicitly uses the schema of the divergent vectors marking the difference between *Sorge* and spirit of seriousness (*esprit de sérieux*) by placing it "upside down" on the clock.

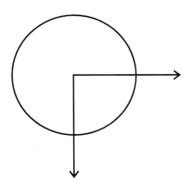

If we eliminate the circumference, we are left with two co-ordinates on which to place inhibition, symptom, and anxiety. We reiterate that Lacan does not specify in *Seminar X* the rotation made between the reference to Sartre and Heidegger and his situational reading of Freud's tripartite idea. However, an indubitable relation to the earlier schema appears clearly in the drawing of the later one.

The intention is to situate the three elements at play inside a matrix where there is a certain order in which the elements do not imply one another. The concepts are arranged here along a scale with respect to the coordinates.

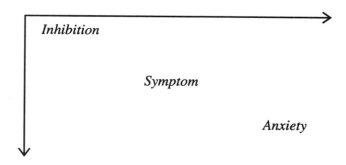

Once this order is established, it grounds the meaning of the vectors, the horizontal one alluding to *difficulty* and the vertical one to *movement*.

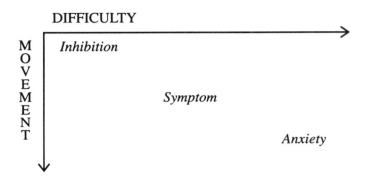

DIFFICULTY

M
O
V
E
M
E
N
T

Inhibition

Symptom

Anxiety

Once again, Lacan wisely *uses psychoanalysis for psychoanalysis*. Right at the beginning of *Inhibitions, Symptoms and Anxiety*, Freud gives various examples of analysands who can be said to be suffering from an inhibition. What is happening to them? Let's take the example of someone who is suffering from a motor inhibition, which has an impact on his capacity for movement. (A classic case is the astasia-abasia of Elizabeth von R., as told in the *Studies on Hysteria*, who could not even stand up.) Lacan points out that this is not a chance reference but rather that, if Freud chose it, he was thinking about something related to *locomotion, using it for its allegorical value*. Thus, this is a phenomenon that has something to do with movement—which is a property of every function, and especially of *stopping or halting movement*. Nevertheless, if we adhere to phenomenology, that is where the problems begin.

Freud observes the implications of phenomenological considerations insofar as they lead to dead ends. Returning to the case of inhibition impeding a function as vital as movement, what boundary is there between this affliction and a symptom? Where does the criterion of differentiation come up? It could be said that an inhibition subtracts or diminishes a function, whereas a symptom generates something new. This way, someone may be inhibited as regards his capacity for movement from one place to another or to ingest food, whereas the symptom consists of a series of add-ons or aggregates: for example, rituals carried out by a subject to get to sleep. Obsessional rituals, by their complexity and number, show strikingly that something seems to have been added on; in this way *the symptom could be considered as a torturous complexification of a function.* Nevertheless, this presumed difference collapses almost immediately.

Such classifications are useless when unconnected to structure and limited to a phenomenological description of what appears at first sight. For example, don't we know that anorexia—in addition to being an inhibition in descriptive terms—is a serious symptom that seals off the alimentary function? And how are we to think of erectile impotence? Obviously, it is an unaccomplished function; is it an inhibition? But is it not also a symptom? Here it could come from a hysteric substructure. What we see is that *strict attention to description can result in either interpretation.* Freud, with habitual astuteness, confronts us with the sterility of these approaches, which seem to be argued convincingly, and tears them down. This rhetorical device is common in his work and has exemplary effectiveness. The presentation and demolition of arguments is a particularly sharp way for Freud to lead the reader toward greater comprehension of what he is saying, and it also strengthens the likelihood the text will persuade the reader. The presence of these strategic detours leads us to a short digression, which we think is wholly justified.

The third section of "The Unconscious" essay, part of Freud's *Papers on Metapsychology*, is subtitled "Unconscious Emotions." It clearly appears to be an affirmation of what the chapter is about: that is, the feelings that belong to the unconscious. No sooner do we begin reading than we observe that Freud's discourse is directed at demonstrating the nonexistence of these feelings or affects. So the title would then have to be redefined, for example, as a question: *Unconscious Feelings?* The answer to this is that there are none.

The example also serves to demonstrate the punctilious manner in which Lacan read Freud. *The text does not say that there are no affects, but rather seeks to demonstrate that there are no affects that are repressed affects. All the affect does is to affect.* This indicates the nonpertinence, for example, of the theory of deep anxiety; let us agree that it is not necessary to turn to Melanie Klein to confront ideas such as this one. To consider deep anxiety would be to consider the presence of a kind of double-bottomed mind in which what appears as manifest conceals an anxiety that does not reveal itself to us. This conception of the psyche is like a knapsack where anxiety is hidden away from perception. To think in terms of deep anxiety also implies the possibility of *a model of the unconscious that is coextensive with the conscious mind so that each conscious phenomenon is correlated to another in the double bottom.* Everything the subject says could then—as Kleinism suggests—be interpreted due to the stable relation it maintains with what is contained in the unconscious.

```
                 |         |          |
                 | A       | B        | C
Conscious    - - -|- ----- -|- ---- - -|- --
                 |         |          |

                 |         |          |
                 | A'      | B'       | C'
Unconscious  - - -|- ---- - -|- ---- - -|- --
```

This approach merely sets up a one-to-one correspondence between conscious phenomena and hidden meanings. It confers authority, in the final instance, to interpret anything all the time. *Everything becomes interpretable, since the one-to-one reference always "gets" to the imaginary, which is viewed as "latent."* It is against this widely touted conception of the other psychoanalysis that

Lacan directs his undertaking, based on a close reading of Freud. *Anxiety affects the subject.* Undoubtedly there are defenses against it; one of them is the *phantasy*, as we shall see further along. But the French master's point in no way presupposes coextensivity but rather responds to Freud's stipulation by saying *there are unconscious formations.* The allusion to formations implies that there is *an effect of the unconscious suffered by the subject.* Suffered here means *"run over" by a signifier that is shown to come from another discourse, that is, the discourse of the Other.* The formations of the unconscious demonstrate the existence of a place that reflects or thinks, away from the ego, and that irrupts in an unexpected way when the subject speaks. The obvious experience of this is the *lapsus,* a formation that does not give us good standing with regard to the pompous prestige of our egos. Here there is a call for interpretation, but this is not about correlation with some hypothetical unconscious signified. It rather points to *a gap in the chain of discourse.* It is not necessary to have recourse to anything of a presumed deep nature, anxieties, or other affects. There is a chain, and what can be repressed is arranged along it by omission. But to repress does not mean to send to some depth where what is omitted would remain, waiting to astutely appear at the least expected moment. *What is repressed is merely what returns.* The contrary of this is to conceive of the unconscious as a doubling of the conscious mind; that is, like a character who makes an untimely entrance on stage. In fact, this fallacious theory arises from the representation that everyone has his or her own ego that is "transported" to some deeper level. This conception completely rejects *the legality proper to the unconscious, which is organized according to rules that are different from the ones of the conscious ego.*

Freud's strategy in "The Unconscious" makes it possible to discard the idea that there are unconscious feelings. *There are no affects; there are* Gedänken, *unconscious thoughts.* So, anxiety is something that the subject suffers and feels; the subject is affected in act. It is present phenomenologically and there is no need to infer or conjecture it along the lines of "If such and such occurred, you would suffer, therefore it's this or that type of anxiety." Such observations are not what psychoanalysis is about; they are *a kind of presumed prevention, constructed using imaginary universes.* Here the work is with the *times of anticipation* into which the subject slides, erecting a consistent and homogeneous world around what is foreseeable. When the moment of the act arrives, anticipation crammed with feeling is what stops the subject from working according to its desire. Here we will digress extensively to show that *it ill behooved Lacan to discriminate phenomenologically between inhibition and symptom in organizing his schema on the Freudian tripartite idea.*

The *matricial framework* Lacan would obtain by placing the three terms in the field marked by difficulty and movement shows a pattern in which one can observe six empty spaces where he would later articulate other concepts.

DIFFICULTY

Inhibition	×	×
×	*Symptom*	×
×	×	*Anxiety*

(left axis, top-to-bottom: M O V E M E N T)

This is a simple, two-dimensional model. However, this does not invalidate it, despite the ideological terrorism of some who, claiming to follow Lacanian teaching, invalidate from the outset any use of schemas due to their imaginary dimension and validate only topology. Obviously, there can be problems with these schemas;[6] they do have value for the place where they were generated and in the specific context in which they were produced. Problems arise when they are removed from the texts to which they refer. Also worth pointing out is that, in diagrams such as the one of the "clock," Lacan was not intending to make any points about structure. He was rather making schemas in a didactic manner to show a series of relations in function of the axes of reference. This was in order to try to account for the "affective" occurrences that the subject can encounter in drawing closer to desire. Thus, such an "innocent" matricial framework like the one we are developing is invaluable in the intellection of a series of issues related to the concept we are examining. The logic of the schema is simple to read. The directional arrows of the vectors represent increasing difficulty and movement. The schema thus stands for relationships and relations. For example, what Lacan will call *emotion* (*émotion*), he will locate at a point implying *greater movement* beyond the point of stoppage or halting, which he called *inhibition*.

DIFFICULTY

M O V E M E N T	*Inhibition*	×	×
	Emotion	*Symptom*	×
	×	×	*Anxiety*

---

6. It should be pointed out that a table with a similar layout and number of terms in play can be found in Lacan's seminar of 1956–1957 entitled *La Relation des objets et les structures freudiennes*.

The use of this term means we still are within the bounds of phenomenology, so we should make no mistakes: *the episteme of degree* tells us little about a structural definition. *Lacan focuses in a decisive manner on the etymological root of the words he uses* as much with regard to emotion—a surprising term—as the concepts in the places of the other "x"s. This is a recommended way of dis-covering how the terms selected are inscribed in each *lalangue*. Words, as we know, are not untainted. They have a history and carry a tradition; these are not hidden signifieds (meanings) only accessible to philologists or those with keys to etymology. Reference is not beyond the words themselves; it is in them. As for emotion, the meaning effect arising from removal of the "e" should be pointed out: motion. This signals movement or impulse. In this way, *emotion contains an unquestionable reference to movement insofar as its etymological drift is put into act in the present*. This should be taken into consideration, though it does not imply that the subject that finds itself in this condition has the possibility of free movement. Here we should remember that we are thinking from the point of view of the logic of what is opposed to this function, that is, the ways in which it is stopped. In this order and according to the apprehension of psychologists, whoever "falls" into this state known as *emotional* is suffering from a certain decrease in motor aptitude. This is true of all the theories of emotion, however diverse. All of them say that the emotional subject loses a kind of rational control over a situation, as it finds itself "taken over" by emotion. We could say that the subject finds itself here in a state close to the symptom—as the schema shows. The symptom is understood here from the perspective of lack of control or lack of efficiency of the will. As Lacan points out, an even greater degree of this alteration is presented in the case of dismay (*émoi*).

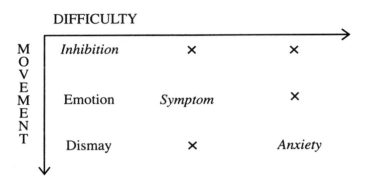

The allusion to a state of dismay seems a good choice for the translation of the original term *émoi*; *one who is dismayed, does not know what to do, and lacks action.* Dismay brings the suffering of the subject closer to anxiety. These, then, are the three states shown in relation to movement in the inhibition column.

Inhibition, in its gradation relative to difficulty, is increased by what Lacan terms *impediment (empêchement)*, which has a Latin root and is derived from *impedicare*, meaning to make an obstacle of, or to be trapped. Difficulty here is thus of a larger order than mere inhibition:

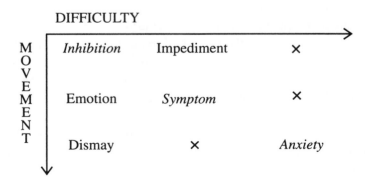

An even greater difficulty is found in the term *embarazo*,[7] which the Spanish word echoes etymologically as it connotes embarrassing, obstacle, obstruction, pregnancy, in the column that Lacan calls "from the subject." This situation, in addition to denoting greater difficulty, denotes the condition of reproduction and what the concrete state of the pregnant woman implies as regards the obstacle to be borne:

DIFFICULTY

M O V E M E N T	*Inhibition*	Impediment	Unease
	Emotion	*Symptom*	✕
	Dismay	✕	*Anxiety*

Independently of the resonances proper to biological pregnancy, everyone knows what a *situación embarazosa* (embarrassing situation) is. This comes from the very capture of the subject with regard to the difficulty of confronting and getting out of this kind of situation in a graceful manner. Also, as the French term is *embarras*, it punctuates the bar,[8] the one we know through experience, the condition of the barred subject ($).

The crucial question is how to read or intellect the symptom, which is what names the second column—interwoven as

---

7. Translator's note: the term is *embarras* (hindrance, confusion, unease) in French.

8. Translator's note: *barre* is a typographical term meaning slash. This term is used for the barred subject, or *sujet barré* in French.

it is in a series of relations of proximity, where similar class and specific difference, the very characteristics of any definition, come together in an Aristotelian sense.

Whereas similarity of type guarantees articulation at the level of isotopy, specific difference is what maintains the symptom with the minimum condition of singularity; however, that does not hinder close relations arising between them. Thus, "*to be impeded is a symptom*," Lacan points out, though he goes on to add that to be inhibited "*is a symptom put into a museum*." Putting into a museum carries with it the idea of something left over from what has been lived. With this simile, Lacan is thinking of a museum that has little to do with modern art galleries; the connotation here is what links the museum with conserving objects, witnessing and linking them to the past, that is, with a certain type of state of being—made dynamic, it is clear, through retroactive readings. In this way, inhibition appears at a significant distance from the symptom and even further away from anxiety. The museum-like condition is also related to something obsolete, a witness to what was. Hence, it does not have the same level of implication for the subject as the symptom does in terms of upheaval in movement and inherent difficulty. This is why, *when there is inhibition, there is not usually a demand for analysis as an inescapable alternative.*

The museum-like characteristic of inhibition is tied to what we have called the *sticky* jouissance *of the sign.*[9] The quality of the sign is due to the experiential presence of a one-to-one correlation where the subject sustains by believing, with regard to his or her inhibition, only what he or she asserts without the slightest opening for equivocation; when there is

9. Roberto Harari, *La repetición del fracasso* (Buenos Aires: Nueva Vision, 1988), pp. 143–151.

equivocation, analytical intervention can occur. In the vision of the world the subject displays from inhibition, *there appears, moreover, a relation of adherence or viscosity, a welding in which there is little likelihood that he or she will be "unstuck" by any question.* Many of the traces, which convert inhibitions into museum-like symptoms, are found in statements such as those that occur in the tango: "If I'm like this, what can I do?" Here is a manifestation of a kind of semblance of resignation with *jouissance*-related interests that can easily be replaced by a claim such as, "Yes, I'm like this. What of it?" A tinge of paranoia is present here that can even grow into boasting about an image, which phallicizes the feature. This, in turn, results in legitimizing the inhibition. For example, many *common phobias*, which are not recognized as such, have this museum-like dimension. They are presented by subjects along with *a rationalization founded on the sticky* jouissance *of the sign that converts inhibition into an issue of mere likes and dislikes.* A contractual agreement is hidden by it, which runs like this: "If nobody bothers me about my preferences, I won't anger others when they show their likes and dislikes." Hence the possibility of the pact: the one each subject can make with him- or herself with this sort of testimony about what he or she was, in addition to claiming the values of a parody of "freedom."

The allusion to the testimony of what once was takes us to the hypothesized "overcoming" of certain kinds of suffering. What was an infantile phobia can be replaced, presumably "overcome" by transforming it into a museum piece because it is dilated into a diffuse condition of timidity. *Now there will be no localized phobia, directed toward a particular phobiogenic object: the subject will not much fear something specific but rather will fear everything a bit.* In this way, it can be proven by turning to inhibition that what was "crossed" is not the particular neurosis of a child but rather *infantile neurosis*, the strong name given by Freud to assert that the neurotic circumstance is inevitable in childhood; that is why the neurosis cannot but leave marks, inhibition being one of the most frequent.

The framework we have developed in these pages is not yet complete. Two "x"s were not replaced; they remain unknown. Lacan does not fill in either of them, which is a good way of maintaining desire. We shall not advance his expository strategy; we shall limit ourselves to reminding readers of desire's proximity to the symptom and anxiety, both neighbors of the two unknowns. The specific difference will be given by its articulation in one case to dismay and in the other to unease.

As mentioned, Lacan sustains desire by not completing the scheme. This provides clarification for guaranteeing the name he gives himself and which, by extension, he applies to all analysts: *erotologists*.

Erotology is not sexology, since it supposes no sexual adjustment but rather, by taking into account desire, it takes it as an intrinsic dimension of the subject that in a redundant manner is called speaking. If it is a subject, it can be so by having been constituted as the effect of the interlocutory condition that generated it. *The subject is simply the effect of the signifier.*

The attention to the desire of this speaker makes it so Lacan, at a twist of the screw, reminds us—as we have already said—that there are *no unconscious affects but, rather, affects drift.* The emotion here, furthermore, is not synonymous with affect; the nonexistence of unconscious affects—since what is repressed are the signifiers that bind them together—is demonstrated by Lacan through a recurring bias of his, though here it is surprising and rich. The best text for considering the affect issue—in its dependence on "lines," and on the rhetorical "network" is, as he points out in *Seminar X*, Aristotle's *Rhetoric*.

As is known, the original *Rhetoric* tries to codify certain types of speech, advising and teaching its readers how to arrange arguments with locutions of persuasion. It is aimed above all at the orator focusing on a typical situation, such as a public trial. How is one to be granted the benevolence of the auditorium, the philosopher asks? Aristotle achieves a fundamental development in this regard. What is important is what is brought about by the rhetorical action. As the speech of the orator is shaped, feelings emerge in the interlocutory field from the listeners. To exemplify to what extent the Greek thinker approached the issue of affects pertinently, we can see a psychoanalytical reflection *avant la lettre* made by him around the issue of envy.

Despite the widely disseminated conceptions from the other psychoanalysis, envy does not reside in attacking, in trying to destroy what another subject has. This would appear to coincide with the traditional opinion holding that envy consists in seeking to harm the other, or in trying to get power over what the other might have, as one is in a weaker position. Since Lacan, we can count on a much more precise intellection of the issue. Envy does not reside in a motion that tends to ruin what the other possesses. *Another subject is not envied nor is the object he presumably has envied but rather it is the supposed ideal coupling between the other and what he appears to be deriving*—jouissance—*that is envied.* As such, envy is directed at this state of being as if hanging from the object in an idealized, idyllic relation. This is what Lacan demonstrates through a magnificent passage in Saint Augustine's *Confessions*, in which an older brother suffers when contemplating his younger brother being breast-fed by their mother. What does he envy? The breast? The milk? His mother? His little brother? Let us see now how Aristotle characterizes envy: "We can see on what grounds, against what persons, and in what states of mind we feel it. Envy is pain at the sight of such good fortune as consists of the good things already mentioned; we feel it towards our equals; not with the idea of getting something for ourselves, but because the other people have it. We shall feel it if we have, or think we have, equals; and by 'equals' I mean equals in birth, relationship, age, disposition, distinction, or wealth. We feel envy also if we fall but a little short of having everything; which is why people in high place and prosperity feel it."

The paragraph stands out because of its surprising punctuation. The first thing to point out is that one does not feel envy of someone who is really far away, but rather of a peer. Also, how can someone who has almost everything be envious? Is not he who lacks the most perhaps more envious? The issue is that the former cannot cease to lack something in order to get this all. We know that to say "all" is an imaginary postulate; there is no such thing. Lacan says of this that everything is some part and each part; in this sense, every one can be an-all, but this does not imply that there is a complete-All. Faced with this impossibility one envies the little that is sustained and that is lacking in order to possess the hypothetical All. We can agree almost to the letter with what Aristotle adds to this point: "Also if we are exceptionally distinguished for some particular thing, and especially if that thing is wisdom or good fortune. Ambitious men are more envious than those who are not. So also those who profess wisdom; they are ambitious—to be thought wise."

It is worth saying that each one of us goes after the phallic image that each one is lacking, the one that would refuse what Lacan in his algebraic notation wrote as $(-\varphi)$, *imaginary castration*. In ending the passage, Aristotle adds, "Indeed, generally, those who aim at a reputation for anything are envious on this particular point."[10]

---

10. Aristotle, *Rhetoric*, trans. W. Rhys Roberts, vol. 11 of *The Works of Aristotle* (London: Oxford University Press, 1971), 2:10.

As can be seen, Aristotle's postulations are oriented toward *conceiving of envy as an affect directed basically against equals or peers, based on small differences that are very recognizable to analysts.* This proposition is more than reconcilable with the teaching of Lacan and is at the antipodes of the Kleinian conception where what predominates is a destructive yearning based on the model of the breast-feeding infant who envies the maternal breast and its content as a partial object. What situation of greater subjective disparity can be imagined than the one Melanie Klein presents? A baby in a state of helplessness confronted with a mother who may or may not grant her milk. Here, says Lacan, we are not on the level of the supposed infantile omnipotence but rather on the one of the omnipotence of the primordial Other: the Mother. Envy, then, is something else.

Now, why introduce in this development the issue of envy? In order to announce that envy is a signifying situation that marks places topologically. With envy what is important is the one who is near, the one who occupies the next place, who, thanks to his or her specific difference, cannot fail to cause the fall, like sediment, into envy. This consideration does lead to reposing what in Freud is written *en passant* on *the narcissism of small differences*, which situates envy as the decisive element in the mother–child relation. To illustrate this phenomenon, it is not necessary to remind you that wars generally occur between neighboring countries, or even that civil wars are the bloodiest of all. How can people so alike, united by language, tradition, and history end up confronting each other in situations that are so difficult to conceive of? On the contrary, this is about facts that are perfectly conceivable, founded in the struggle for the little difference. In short, they continue to be issues that involve narcissistic image and the preservation of lack.

Our repeated allusions to Klein's conception of anxiety are not idle ones. It is important to discuss her slant on deep anxieties, the envy of a partial object, since *the Kleinian concept centers on anxiety*. Usually, it is thought of as a theory of object relations. Our understanding is that it is more akin to the conceptualizations of W. Ronald D. Fairbairn. Melanie Klein develops a theory of anxiety or, better yet, a theory of anxieties: paranoid and depressive (Herbert Rosenfeld would add "confusional" to the series). It should thus be pointed out that Lacan, proceeding with the as-yet-unfinished scheme, widens the Freudian path, helping us implicitly to formulate distinctions from the Kleinian orientation, which imply a different course.

The path of Melanie Klein and her followers locates affects— including anxiety—according to something like predefined evolutionary stages. In this manner, affects occupy a radically different place from the one of the sediments precipitated by and from the signifying chain. It is from here that these divergent points of departure have decisive consequences that are constantly felt in clinical practice. These are not playful musings, nor is this a mere issue of taste. What is at stake and in play is no more or less than the direction of the cure. In Argentina, twenty or twenty-five years ago, statements such as the following were often heard during clinical supervisions: "Patient x is very envious; what he cannot tolerate is for you to cure him. As envy is constitutional, the situation cannot be remedied." In this way, the other psychoanalysis arrived at the end of the analysis, a living stone from the Kleinian perspective, determined by something conceived of as biological. For this school, the analysand with his envious condition was incapable of being cured beyond a certain point, since it presupposed tolerance for receiving the milk by which the analyst would feed him. Envy would make the analysand give up, irreversibly, feeding at the breast of the analyst. This argument could seem laughable—phantasy-induced, in effect, rather than conceptual— but for a long time considerations such as this blocked knowledge of what happens in the phenomenon that Freud persisted in calling a *negative therapeutic reaction*. Various and complementary articulations are in play in the much-touted, little-understood "NTR." One of them centers on the libidinal fact of being able to continue in analysis, as Freud himself indicates. The primary factor in terms of magnitude is the extent to which the death drive is operant in the subject and the drive's consequent compulsion to repeat. When it seems the analysis is advancing, *a serious recidivism occurs—which we have called "a worsening"—of the symptom*. Here Freudian texts view that the relapse operates as a ratification that *the neurosis is a punishment*, or to be more precise, *a need for punishment for the subject*. And many find, when in analysis, that the best transaction in order to continue with one's life is to pay one's debts and for one's faults, with the neurosis as a bulwark. This is a seemingly dark prospect but Freud, as a good erotologist, did wonder what to do in order to conclude an analysis. The series of problems of the end in analysis also appeared as a logical derivation of the NTR. As he pointed out, at first he did not know what to do so analysands would continue in analysis, and then he did not know what to do so they would end them.

Theory, in its relation to clinical practice, is indispensable for an analyst in sustaining an analysis. To manage the treatment as a function of envy involves—though this seems, or is, a difficult assertion—a defect in the order of the analyst's ethics, which is the ethic of psychoanalysis. So that it is not about an option for being modern or for mixing tastes, as is the case with eclectic schools. *Though at first sight it may seem like an interference, the appearance of envy in the series of problems relating to anxiety is useful to set the boundary—with help from Aristotle—of the distinction between an instinctivist theory, which finds a "no beyond" of psychoanalysis in affect—a reigning conception in many circles—and the Lacanian conception that postulates affect as one effect of the signifier.*

2

Not . . . without an Object.
The Graph of Anxiety

The articulation of the object *a*, a decisive notion, is indispensable in sustaining analysis according to the Lacanian conception. Indeed, *the analyst attempts, or should attempt, to occupy the place of the semblance of the object* a.

Without going into detail about the notion of semblance for the moment, it is appropriate to locate immediately what Lacan called his "sole[1] invention" in psychoanalysis. It has been a proposal or discovery that is aptly named by his preferred qualifier: a theoretical invention. In the first place, as he pointed out, it is a way of including a new letter in algebraic notation that must be clearly differentiated from algebra *strictu sensu* in the ongoing work of our discipline.

With the aim of sustaining the place of the semblance of the object *a*, the analyst sustains a specific relation with his or her analysand, attempting to remain detached from the series

---

1. Translator's note: *unique* in French.

of problems proper to ties "between humans." *This implies not falling into any type of link-related psychology*, based on certain characteristics of double ties such as those experienced in various types of psychotherapy. If the analyst has a specific place, it is related to the object *a*. The question then becomes, what is this object?

The a, which does not connote anything as a letter, is so decisively important that it is not feasible to refer to many concepts, among them anxiety, without referring to it systematically. In this sense, the object a is the other basic issue of Seminar X, *apart from the one the title indicates.* Lacan even comes to assert at one moment that *the only subjective correlate that we can possess of this a is precisely anxiety*. This statement inaugurates a novel intellection of some problems raised insistently by psychology, and will allow us, via a detour, to seek to grasp the issue of the object *a*. Taking as a point of departure the "catalogue method," criticized earlier, the elucidation of some surprising relations becomes viable starting from *some classical, rather analogical classifications*. One of them has been amply examined: the elementary taxonomy of phenomenological inspiration that differentiates between *nervousness, anxiety, and fear*. The classification is the following:

Nervousness

Anxiety

Fear

Without a doubt, this type of differentiation is easily intelligible, as it is supported by a considerable degree of simplicity and can be understood intuitively; what it proposes is fascinating. Indeed, psychologists usually point out that a certain feeling of ill-being and disturbance, located strictly in experience, not involving the body, is what is known as *nervousness*. It coincides, moreover, with the customary psychiatric consideration, which, as is known, is very descriptive. Now, if nervousness has to do with the body, and with its disturbance to some degree and in some way, this creates another order. It might concern some organ, such as the heart, or a system, such as respiration, but the essential thing is that the body is involved in this phenomenon. Here we find what is usually and mistakenly called a "component" or an "equivalent" of anxiety: nervousness has been changed—through the participation of the body—into something different without resolving the issue of whether anxiety is one item and its corporal "equivalent" another one.

Nervousness

Anxiety

Fear

What ties nervousness to anxiety, in phenomenological terms, is a basic fact: the presumed absence of an object. The subject is nervous or suffers anxiety *without knowing from what or why.* Both kinds of suffering, in spite of their differences, share the bias of indefinition, of not knowing to what they are attributed. For the phenomenological intellection alluded to, this is a capital point: the fact that provokes nervousness or anxiety cannot be located. The fact here is that, *should one manage to locate the object so eagerly sought, another dimension is reached and one is in the presence of fear:*

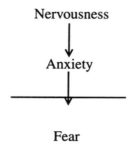

Nervousness

↓

Anxiety

↓

Fear

The object of reference can then be rationalized as belonging to the "external" world. In this sense, a certain degree of relief is found given that the threatening focus is circumscribed, and tactics or strategic maneuvers can be thought up to avoid the object more or less successfully.

Fear makes it possible to draw a boundary. The two preceding concepts, on the other hand, remain imprecise and indefinite, that is to say, they are in a situation of defenselessness that Freud used the term *Hilflosigkeit* to designate: *a state of psychic and motor helplessness where the subject has no resources to confront what affects him or her.* Ways of doing so do, however, appear when there is *fear*, for example, a *phobia.* In this neurosis, there is a localizable empirical object and an obvious avoidance tactic, which, generally, fails because it *must* fail. The point is that classification, in short, is easily understandable; anyone can apprehend or approach it without greater knowledge and therein lies the problem. *These taxonomies only produce tautologies.* The obvious is said, what is already known in an imaginary way, and it is here that the uncritical transparency of this kind of formulation can be seen. In this sense, we are all psychologists and *the assertions of psychology merely confirm what is marked out on the intuitive level of the doxa.* The fact of the matter is, however, that here we are moving onto psychoanalytical terrain that brings with it a break.

The psychoanalytical conceptualization usually postulates utterances that cannot be taken at face value and can provoke revulsive, pejorative, hilarious, or indignant effects, among others. What often comes into play is the rupture or breaking up of commonly understood or conventional meanings. As regards the foregoing classifications, we are trying to break with the empirical truism implying that we are only confronted with an object in the case of fear. This is where an unusual Lacanian aphorism irrupts: "*Anxiety is not without an object.*" This assertion is surely a new one. Anxiety comes to be something different from a reaction by the subject to something that is lacking, which is not in front of him or her. Undoubtedly, this is the kind of thing analysands commonly say: "I don't know why I am anxious since there is nothing that brings it on." Statements such as this one are made sincerely by subjects suffering from anxiety. The issue here is: *to reproduce the lack of object in the theory is to copy fallacious phenomenological evidence into it. The psychoanalyst, on the contrary, keeps in view the processing of what is said.* And a good way to achieve this is to put Lacan's strong assertion to the test.

Let us pause here and examine the meaning of his formulation. We can observe that the aphorism does not say that anxiety has an object but rather, elliptically, it uses a singular operation which is a "not" followed by a "without." Herein is ciphered the special logical statement of one form of negation, which we put in between the classical series from which we started:

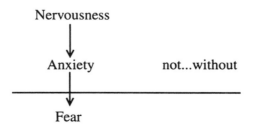

These two particles "not . . . without" structure the aphorism in a way that accounts for *the obscure, imprecise condition of the object at hand.* In this manner, the object is characterized as something that is very far from being obvious or evident.

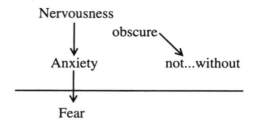

This obscurity is similar to what Lacan expresses when confronted with the ambiguity of an especially suggestive discourse, pointing out that "it will not be without intention." What intention is meant is not clear, though one suspects that there is one. Therefore, the use of the "not . . . without" is directed at taking the first term as a position with regard to the obscurity—and not the obscurantism, of course—that the aphorism testifies to. But there is also another trait leading to *a condition that we could call extraordinary in the sense of something beyond the conceivable or hoped for in the usage agreed upon:*

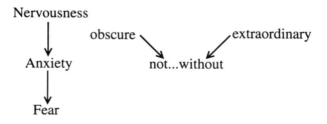

Lacan's use of the rhetorical operation "not . . . without" remains inscribed in other patterns of his teaching. For example, in the seminar of 1958–59, *Le Désir et son interprétation*, popularized by J.-B. Pontalis's summary, a definition of the masculine and feminine positions that rounds out this formulation can be found in the last pages: "he is not without having it (*il n'est pas sans l'avoir*)." The phrase alludes, of course, to the phallus and the masculine condition, and allows the presence—as an absence—of castration to come through. Such an assertion is supplementary to "One could say in an analogous formula that the woman *is without having it*. . . ."[2] This punctuation of a previous "not . . . without" is further proof of the difference between a psychoanalytical and a philosophical path. The point here is that *we are not involved in an opposition between being and nothingness, but rather in one between being and having.* And this is simply the one Freud postulates in Chapter 3 of *The Ego and the Id*, when he is discussing the topic of identification: *the subject has, or if he or she dispenses with having, the subject is, through identification.* In this way, returning to what Lacan points out in *Le Désir et son interprétation*, which he takes up again in *L'Angoisse*: the man is not without having it (the phallus), since phallic identification has a precise corporal localization, which does not occur in the woman, who does have it, through an identification with the phallus that invests her whole body.

Having presented the terms through a "not . . . without" regarding the object of anxiety, the fallacious phenomenological, psychiatric, psychological perspective is now broken. Let us

---

2. Jacques Lacan, "*Le Désir et son interprétation*," seminars of November 1958–January 1959, and of January–February 1959, transcription by J.-B. Pontalis, *Le Bulletin de Psychologie* (Groupe d' Études de Psychologie de l'Université de Paris) 13, no. 5 (January 1960):329–335. Italics in the original.

now leave this break or rupture aside and return to it once again in later passages.

Our guide lines, perhaps with a different texture, attempt to follow the pattern of *Seminar X*. The diagrams and schemas presented here for didactic reasons attempt to account for some of the relations that seem plausible in our reading of *L'Angoisse*. To grasp some of the more significant among them, we will draw a diagram and begin by *positioning anxiety in relation to the neighboring phenomena of desire and* jouissance. The drawing can be started in this way:

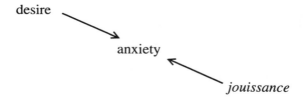

Anxiety appears in the central position and as such fulfills a function of being in the middle, compressed, as it were, between desire and jouissance. *It is situated as the signal that appears when the division between those it borders starts to be erased.* Desire and *jouissance* threaten to become mixed up and anxiety operates as a warning: it is the signal of something that believes itself to be sufficiently divided, differentiated in psychic life, but that at a certain point tends to erase its boundaries; that is why it is a "*border or edge phenomenon.*" It should be noted, since we are trying to construct a schema of relations, that *in the algebraic notation Lacan proposed, desire is written as a lozenge* (◊); *indeed, one way to read it is as "desire of."* This desire is then ar-

*ticulated, on one side, with what is known as the desiring subject
or barred subject ($), which is suffering the anxiety signaled by
the ego.*

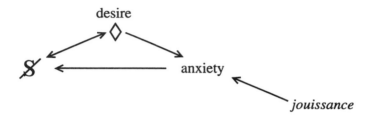

In turn, *the desire of the barred subject is barred in reference to what causes it: the object* a, *which the phantasy formula
accounts for* ($◊a). In the diagram, the relations can be repre-
sented thus:

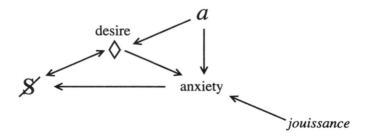

The *a*, as we have said, is *the subjective correlate of anxiety*
through which a new vector arises pointing towards the central concept. But, also, desire refers in particular to one of the
nodal points of Lacanian teaching: the postulate of *the Other
as "symbolic memory," as distinct from the other as similar or
proximate.* This virtual place, which makes it possible to con-

ceive of *desire as desire of the Other*, must occupy a place in the schema that bears witness to its relation with the notation of desire and with the object *a*, which also comes from this place.

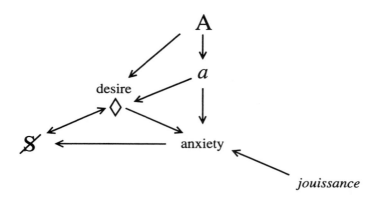

One of the indicators, *a "patent feature," of the object* a *reveals it as one form—among others—of manifestation of the Other, making itself present through this object.* As can be noticed, the interweaving of relations of anxiety becomes increasingly more complex. In Freud, to think anxiety implied a concept that later was changed, especially by some in the Kleinian school. Lacan, on the other hand, rescued the concept of *castration*, the Freudian proposition that had been discarded or, better said, foreclosed.

The castration complex as a nodular concept was much more than recovered. As we have said, *castration in Lacanian notation, went on to be written as* $(-\varphi)$. *The concept of object* a *cannot be thought without reference to castration.* At the same time, anxiety is not conceivable without its primordial relation to the same concept.

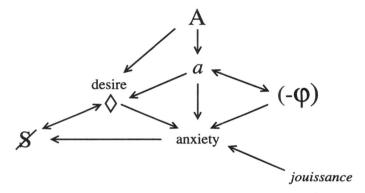

Lacan would come to say that *the object a appears where* (-φ) *is lacking*. This statement should always be borne in mind because in many cases it is difficult to distinguish between them. The fact that *a* alludes in the final instance to castration is inseparable from the relation that unites it to anxiety, as can be seen in the diagram. (This matter will be taken up in the next chapter.)

The lozenge, as is known, has multiple uses in Lacanian teaching. Another formula he uses is the one on the drive: ($0D). *In this formula, the barred subject is articulated to demand (D). We* should also take the drive into account in our schema.

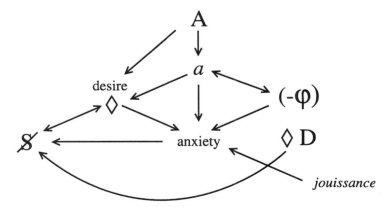

Demand plays a central role in neurosis; thus, what the *neurotic* tries to do is *get him- or herself to be asked, get him- or herself to be begged—though as Lacan points out—without paying the price that the demand entails.* This is a fine clinical observation: if the analyst knows how to hear that the one who is making the demand is not doing so to get what he or she is asking for, but rather for something else, it will be a crass error to respond to the demand since that will squelch the desire it masks. In some translations of Lacan's work into Spanish, such as for example the *Seminar XX, On Feminine Sexuality, the Limits of Love and Knowledge. Encore,* a choice was made to translate the French *demander* by *pedir* (to ask for) instead of *demandar* (to demand or beg). Demand has obviously nothing to do with an empirical and periodic request for something specific since *the translation by "demandar" also retains the legal nuance connoting a vindicating exigency for some "damage."* Thus, demand is introduced through the *signifier (Sig.) that is articulated—thus barring it— to the Other,* the latter's place being also linked to desire.

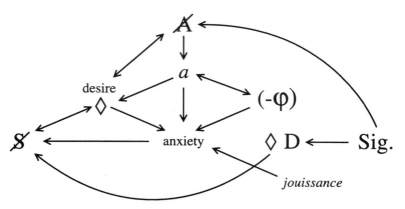

Due to the signifier, something occurs that would not likely happen among animals: deception. Deception is, of course, a subtle variety of what Lacan accounts for. We can deceive by showing what is true as false, something an animal cannot do; at the most it can deceive in the most elementary way, pretending or calling for camouflage, or even erasing its tracks. In such an order, it will draw a boundary: "An animal does not pretend to pretend. He does not make tracks whose deception lies in the fact that they will be taken as false, while being in fact true ones, ones, that is, that indicate his true trail."[3] This is an interesting fragment from "The Subversion of the Subject," where Lacan also draws *a clear distinction between tracks and the signifier* that merits further discussion. (We shall take up this perspective in Chapter 4.) Some semiologists have recognized this capacity of deception as exclusive to human beings. Umberto Eco, for example, formulated this in an extreme manner by saying that semiotics does not deal with the all-embracingness of the Symbolic but rather with studying "everything which can be used to lie."[4] This noticeably reduces the scope of the Symbolic—by demonstrating its nonexistence in animals, for example—which is salutary since, on the contrary, one might fall into *pan-symbolism* such as the neo-Kantian philosopher Ernst Cassirer did. Lacan's position is different: the signifier implies something with more set boundaries, maintaining a relation to anxiety mediated by a dichotomy that we shall now explore. The dichotomy makes a fundamental distinction illustrated by another Lacanian aphorism of the kind his teaching contained. Although one always runs the latent risk of making use in an

---

3. Jacques Lacan, "The Subversion of the Subject and the Dialectic of Desire in the Freudian Unconscious," in *Ecrits: A Selection*, trans. Alan Sheridan (New York: Norton, 1977), p. 305.

4. Umberto Eco, *A Theory of Semiotics* (Bloomington: Indiana University Press, 1975), p. 31.

echolalic manner of these conceptual condensations, it is worth reiterating them. We shall analyze the one asserting that *the signifier deceives but anxiety does not.* We are thus faced with the certainty/deception dichotomy.

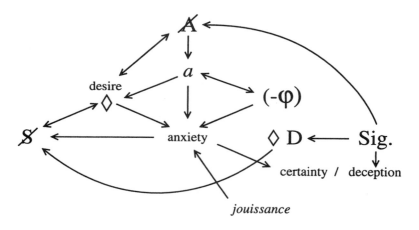

Hence, anxiety supplies certainty. Without going into a series of supports of a philosophical nature, such as Hegel's sense of certainty or parallel philosophical speculations, it is worth noting that *certainty, for our purposes, is what is irreducible no matter how many signifiers are articulated to it. The subject has no possibility of converting it into an element that can be smoothed out and apprehended in and by the signifying chain.* To make an issue metonymic implies displacing it over a network; this way, the affect can be placated. The functionality of the signifier "manages to," as it were, reduce the level of anxiety as can and does happen in the cure. Now, when Lacan introduces this characteristic, he immediately adds this clarification to it: *certainty comes to the subject through action.* At the same time, *action is what subtracts certainty from anxiety, "appropriating it for itself."* Insofar as the subject is involved in an action—not just any action but the kind that is impulsive and unstoppable—it is one step ahead of anxiety, avoiding being entrapped by it.

Two fundamental variants of action postulated by psychoanalysis shall be incorporated into this schema. But before examining them, let us refer to the two vacant spaces in the matrix of relations presented in the previous chapter. These spaces will be occupied by the two concepts in question: *acting out* and *passing to the act*.

In the *matricial framework with the two entries, acting out* is located in the slot next to anxiety, given its greater degree of movement relative to the symptom. *In this sense, it implies a summons to interpretation, carried out in a very noticeable manner.*

DIFFICULTY

M O V E M E N T	*Inhibition*	Impediment	Unease
	Emotion	*Symptom*	✕
	Dismay	*Acting out*	Anxiety

Lastly, to complete the remaining unknown, passing to the act is situated in the coordinates. *Passing to the act is that manner of action that stands out, and whereby the subject falls away, identified with the object a, in an ultimate attempt to avoid anxiety.* This act is located at the most extreme point on the difficulty axis, as can be seen.

DIFFICULTY

M O V E M E N T	*Inhibition*	Impediment	Unease
	Emotion	*Symptom*	Passing to the act
	Dismay	*Acting out*	*Anxiety*

Matricial Framework of Anxiety

Once these two modalities of action are located on the network of relations woven around anxiety, we proceed with the diagram by returning to the concept of certainty.

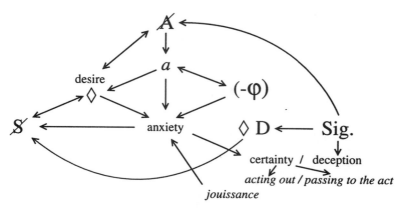

Certainty thus acts as a hinge between anxiety and the two types of action that psychoanalysis is particularly interested in. Why is this so? Because one can appreciate in them the singular relation of the subject with the Other, established to resolve certain issues that we shall later examine in detail.

There remains one additional relation to be represented in the diagram. This is the one that accounts for a subject that will come to be, that is, a *presubject* that the signifier works to split in order to bar.

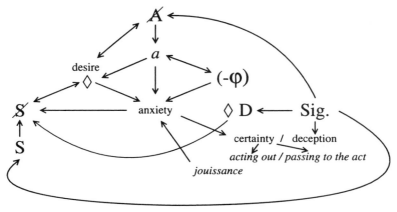

The Graph of Anxiety

Through the efficient action of signifying, the circuit of relations is closed, though in a temporary manner. It is possible to continue articulating new ties among them, for example, with *the concepts of the demand of the Other and the* jouissance *of the Other*, though for our purposes the ones we have seem sufficient. Discerning each of these relations in itself represents an arduous task. In *Seminar X*, Lacan tackles one by one these issues, which are by no means linked together in a single, linear way since they cover a complex tapestry of forward and backward relations. In the schema we have drawn up—why not give it the status of a graph since it satisfies the requirement for one?—as can be noticed, there appears no privileged order. Anyway, should anything have to be put into a hierarchy, it is the object *a*. This is perhaps due to its multiple, axis-like determinations and its neutral notation, with no effects of meaning. To summarize, *the graph of anxiety, as we propose calling it, will serve as the vectoring guideline for the purpose of defining the relational frame of anxiety.*

Towards the beginning of the seminar, Lacan points out that the ideal of all teaching is simplicity. He provides a series of reasons accounting for *this yearning for simplicity and the singular, both on the part of the teacher and the learner.* What is the reason for this? It is in these passages that Lacan introduces by way of explanation one of those Freudian concepts that his reading isolates and privileges, and that acquires a theoretical and clinical status undeveloped in Freud's texts. The concept is the *unary trait,* postulated in *Group Psychology and the Analysis of the Ego,* and translated in the new Spanish version as *unico rasgo* (*einziger Zug*) (only trait).[5]

Through the unary trait, the subject can be incorporated as One in the Real. And it does so through the signifier that preexists it. In this way, One can be counted and with it a way is opened to distinguishing between two decisive concepts that psychoanalysis differentiates: *the countable One and the unifying one.*

The concept of the unary trait is crucial to understanding what is at play in the countable One. In Freud's chapter on "Identification" in *Group Psychology,* one reads: "The identification is a partial and extremely limited one, and only borrows a single trait from the person who is its object."[6] It is not some kind of global imitation but, rather, the unary trait is enough to sustain identification. Hence, among other things, the yearning for the simple and

---

5. Translator's note: the term *einziger Zug,* unique trait or specific trait, is later elaborated by Lacan as *trait unaire,* translated as "unary trait," the trait that makes the subject a unit or one.

6. Sigmund Freud, *Group Psychology and the Analysis of the Ego,* vol. 18 of *The Standard Edition of the Complete Psychological Works,* trans. James Strachey (London: Hogarth Press, 1953), p. 107.

the partial. Taken from the level of the symptom, it is feasible to see how, for example, Freud's patient appropriated the loved one's cough. She mimicked her father's symptom while punishing herself by being sick for wanting a forbidden object. Stated differently, the cough officiated by being the unary trait as punishment but, at the same time, the partial identification allowed the patient to "be" the father, her loved object, rather than have him.

The unary trait is the conceptual instrument through which Lacan intellects the mode in which the ego ideal is structured. It is around the countable One that the *parlêtre* will be e-numerated, through the operation of the successor, of n + 1, as one more among subjects, capable of being named and differentiated from the unifying one.

The unifying one is the narcissistic stopper that can be represented and shown through the figure of the sphere. This total and complete one involves the *well-disseminated concept of the mirror stage.* The one appears at this stage. As Lacan observes, the anticipatory image that characterizes the stage gives rise to a series of idealist theories. Evolutionary psychology talks about, for example, the child who is egocentric at the outset, constantly referring to himself in a unified manner up to the point when he breaks the thick shell separating him from the outside world and manages to connect with the other. Theories such as these belong to subjective idealism since they originate with the hypothesis of a subject who constructs and segregates the world around it. *In all idealism the object appears later through the action of an omnipotent ego that organizes it. The condition of unification is, in this case, given from the beginning. For Lacan, on the contrary, unification is made possible exclusively through the mediation of the other, due to the identification of the ego with its mirror image: i(a).*

The mirror image stage has, as is known, *an empirical correlate of affect: the jubilation of the child facing its own image in the mirror, contemplating itself as a whole.* The Lacanian conception is far from being evolutionary, since it does not even propose that at the beginning there are dispersed pieces that consolidate into one at some moment. Indeed, *the imago of the fragmented body (corps morcelé)* that Lacan also postulates— verifiable, as he himself says, in artistic expressions such as the paintings of Hieronymus Bosch or in the innumerable types of schizophrenic and hypochondriacal suffering—has no initial stage but rather, starting from the unification determined by the mirror, a possible corporal fragmentation is created in the imaginary retroactively. *Only the appearance of the one-unifier can account for the viability of its loss.* There is no prospective intelligence or destiny of each fragment, preestablished since the beginnings of the *infans* with an aim to later juncture. This would imply presupposing knowledge supposed of the species, the first step in conceiving a perfect organism with each piece fitting into the whole with divine harmony.

By focusing on the unary trait and the one-unifier, we find ourselves at a decisive point in Lacan's teaching: that of *the constitution of the subject. This is an issue touching directly on anxiety as it is located in the interstices, in the furrows, which the constitutive process cannot but provoke. The countable One, it should be noted, is related to symbolic identification marked by the trait and which refers to the field of the Other.* For its part, *the one-unifier is related,* as we have indicated, *to imaginary identification:*

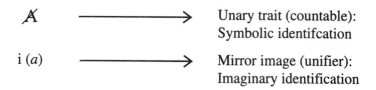

A   ⟶   Unary trait (countable):
                            Symbolic identifcation

i (a)   ⟶   Mirror image (unifier):
                            Imaginary identification

This distinction, which seems to meander away from the central topic of *Seminar X*, is used by Lacan to arrive at anxiety by an unlikely path. *He will conceive, thus, the constitution of the subject that does not end in a presumed completeness provided by the mirror image. Lacan locates the subject in the field of the Other, which is a prerequisite for the creation of the subject. On the opposite side, he will locate the subject to come (which comes to be).*

Once both terms are located, the Other (A) and the "non-existent" protosubject (S) are necessarily divided, since *the subject will be shown as barred*—a quotient by virtue of the unary trait that comes from A—as long as the Other can show itself with some inconsistency and not complete, that is to say, *also barred:*

That the Other be shown as inconsistent in the field of the up-to-then protosubject implies that it is lacking something—that, moreover, it desires but without knowing it.

Furthermore, one more datum should be included here. In this operation of arithmetical division there is a leftover or remainder that is not assimilated by the terms that have managed to be constituted. *What remains fallen away on the side of the Other, as a "residue," is simply the object a, "the proof and sole guarantee of the alterity of the Other":*

A	S
$\cancel{S}$	$\cancel{A}$
a	
Side of the Other	My side

This is an interesting paradox, since the operations on both sides involve an interchange that breaks completely with an entire tradition of classical epistemology, which, to this day, for example, positivism cultivates. This tradition supposes that a subject exists opposite an object in the world, and that therefore the object is the one that finds itself at the disposal of an observer who can, or cannot, get to know the object. This is where psychoanalysis makes a fundamental break with science understood from this perspective. *He who knows, the subject of science, Lacan says, is the same as the subject of psychoanalysis,* that is, a barred subject that pays for its own constitution through the loss of an object.

It is in and from the field of the Other that the barred subject and the object *a* arise. If with the lozenge, we articulate both terms, we indicate that the phantasy, according to its formula ($\cancel{S} \lozenge$ a), is written precisely on the side of the Other.

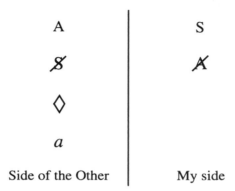

The phantasy is usually heard clearly, as a constant, in the analysis of neurotics. They can be conventionally terrible and flagellating, full of variations and turns that are *not* spoken easily. Insofar as they imply the sexual life of the subject, many times they culminate in a masturbation. *The neurotic, as Lacan pointed out so well, borrows his or her fantasies from the pervert, who passes to the act.* Nevertheless, this does not imply that "at the bottom" every neurotic is perverse, since there is no continuity between structures. What we do want to have stand out is that, within our purview, the action of having phantasies also comes from the field of the Other. What remains then on the side of the subject?

From the field we recognize as "our own," the barred Other is inscribed, the one that has a discourse we call the unconscious. That is to say that, on this side, the unconscious remains as something, impossible to attain, Real, which illustrates a structurally fruitless search. It is worth noting that Lacan's way of thinking of the constitution of the subject made it so the object *a* and the phantasy were immediately apparent, with anxiety operating in the interstices of this constitutive process. Lacan was trying, it seems, not to limit anxiety to being a mere psychopathological or clinical phenomenon. It is about something correlative and inevitable in the meandering constitution of each subject. One might even say that *he assigns an existential aspect to anxiety* above all in the sense of ek-sistence (remaining outside of), of presenting itself in a condition that shows the nonrecovery of the *parlêtre* with himself. So *anxiety in this way accounts for the subject not being a unified one, irrupting with its certainty and permanence.* It does not deceive; indeed, the subject is made viable through manifest imprecision with which the subject must locate itself, in a mandatory manner, *in a state of vacillation or fading.*

Regarding the constitution of the subject, Lacan provides in *Seminar X* the first specifications about the object *a*, which we are still far from being able to measure at this point in our presentation. We shall first turn to another important issue, proposed in the Freudian text "On Narcissism: An Introduction." In this essay, Freud alludes to the theoretical fiction that is postulated by the pouring of the libido, in the sense that it constitutes a back-and-forth circuit whereby at one moment it covers the ego and at another the object. However, such a process has legitimate limitations. Freud was not thinking of a system of communicating containers in which all the libido could come and go, continuously transforming itself from object to narcissistic libido and back again. Far from absolute transformation, *there is always a remainder, a leftover, a reserve of libido that stays put and does not move and for which conversion into a libidinal object is impossible. There exists thus, Lacan remarks, a mirror image (narcissistic image) that is limited. This limit, rigorously speaking, is imposed by castration.* Turning again to algebraic notation, the concept can be formulated in this manner:

Castration, given its particular condition, location, and the anxiety it carries as the signifier of the difference of the sexes, is organized in such a manner that it cannot be "moved." *As for its writing, let us remember that this is the phallus, preceded by its negativization: (-φ). This operation included in the notation means that castration is maintained, and that not-all can be specularized, insofar as castration marks a limit.* Doubtless, we find ourselves here with another reference to the condition of lack, which should be taken into account in the opposition between the two terms.

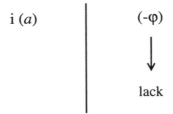

In any case, it is necessary to clarify that *this lack is not an empirical one. In referring to castration, we are putting ourselves in the series posited by Freud on the losses that all children suffer.* Weaning and stool are overly obvious examples of objects that are lost. Especially in the second case, Lacan refers poetically to stool and not to feces. Choice here is pertinent; this is a piece of matter that suddenly and like a ball is separated from the body and falls away from it. *This condition of suddenness, as of that*

moment, also involves anxiety. Up to here, the psychological comprehension of what happens operates admirably: we agree to lose what was possessed. With castration, however, everything is more complicated. In the cases just mentioned, it is very easy to represent and apprehend the situation of loss insofar as something is lost that up to then had been present, and anxiety would be the same according to the imaginary presupposition that one always tries to keep what is possessed. Freud himself asserted this; it costs us, he taught, to give up the libidinal positions that are sometimes reached. Nevertheless, this should not be understood in a psychological mode, with the issue residing in the subject's "resistance to change," as we will later go into in more detail.

As for the series of losses in which castration abruptly irrupts, *it is unlikely to think of anxiety as correlative to the successive losses.* In the case of the breast and the stool, the way this is taken into the imaginary is impeccable: anxiety for breastfeeding, on the one hand, and anxiety for the loss of a part of one's own body, converted into a gift of love through a sort of symbolic exchange, on the other. (This point will be gone into further in Chapter 8.) The fact is that with castration, the problem is more complex. It is not about, of course, emasculation, not even with the concrete threat of the "look out or I'll cut it off," even if this is really said. What is in play is a condition different from what might have been expected on the terrain of what is visible. *The condition of castration is the lack that Lacan calls the central one of desire.* This condition of lacking has such weight that it even comes to determine, through retroaction, its presumed chronological oral and anal antecedents. If breastfeeding has to do with the breast, and stool with the expulsion of fecal matter, *castration is related to the phallus.* But the problem is that *the phallus in question has nothing to do with the penis, nor with the possibility of "physical" castration.*

Though it seems obvious, it is decisive that we remind you, once more, that *the penis is not the phallus*. The phallus is a signifier that slips what we "find" in empirical form according to libidinal occupations: thus, *one could speak of phallic incarnations—significations—of which doubtless the dominant one is the one related to the penis*, but this should not be confused with the phallus, which is encountered much more frequently than might be imagined.

The distinction between phallus and penis allowed Lacan to understand with acuity certain issues, for example, a widely held prejudice about hysterics and their negativism regarding sexual intercourse, which makes them into something like belonging to a species of castrating monsters. This is usually said about some woman who is said to be "very castrating," a term that has passed successfully into the domain of pop psychology, because it is about producing certain situations based on the promise of an act of coitus that in the end never occurs. The "eye clinic"[7] provides an interpretation of these cases, saying there is a resentment against men that makes it so that she cannot consummate the coitus. The instruction would seem to be that she is not allowed to use his penis that is so envied. Another cliché asserts that hysterics fear the damage that a penis would cause to them. *Lacan demonstrated that the refusal of the hysteric is not directed at the penis but rather at its detumescence. Why? Because the moment of detumescence is the moment when it can be seen that*

---

7. I propose this designation to take account of a clinic, the referent of which is the visual, the descriptive, the world of appearances, and from which, I believe, psychoanalysis must keep its distance. As determined by the notable genius of Freud, psychoanalysis operates on the materiality of the word, that is to say, in what one could denominate as a clinic of discourse, of hearing, of latency.

the penis is not the phallus. Here we need to think of the phallus in priapic terms, according to what is implied in a phallic monument: something rock-like and unmovable. On the contrary, the moment of detumescence implies outstanding proof of the inexistence of the phallus as something totalizing, put in the margins and always erect. It is clear that not going through the detumescence test allows the hysteric to feed hope for survival, at all costs, of the phallus. As can be seen, this notion is very different from the widely held, accusatory, almost paranoid conception of the hysteric in her relation to some supposed verification of penis envy, which is absolutely mistaken under these circumstances. Beyond this ingenuous apprehension, this is about sustaining the unmovable phallus up to the last instances where the presence–absence dialectic cannot be crystallized.

The way in which Lacan conceives what happens with the hysteric is, in clinical terms, an immediate consequence of the theoretical distinction between phallus and penis. So what happens in detumescence? Is there presence or absence? As that is where the fall in sustaining the phallus can be seen, there lacks what would make it possible to avoid the existence of castration. *But the real problem—Lacan asserts with a rhetorical flourish worthy of Gongora—arises when lack lacks:* that is where anxiety appears. Something that should not have been exposed, as something meant to remain hidden, becomes present. Anxiety, however, is far from being without an object; to clarify this crucial aspect of the issue, we must contemplate as we move ahead what Freud called the *uncanny.*

3

To Lack Lack, a-Thing, Acting Out, and Passing to the Act

The concept of *lack* can be read in many ways and can be approached in even more ways in Lacan's teaching. That is why it runs the risk—and often the danger—of being bastardized. It is often pointed out, uncritically, that the main problem of the analysand is that he or she "does not tolerate lack." Before approaching the issue clinically and in detail, it can be said that this is far from being so.

If anxiety is not without an object, the fact that it arises when lack lacks indicates something very far from a simple nonacceptance of lack on the part of the subject. What is Lacan implying with this new aphorism, that *lack is lacking*?

To begin, let us look at some of the meanings given to the concept of lack, which, as we have said, has multiple ones in the teaching we are discussing. There are many different ways of thinking about this aphorism in general terms, but at least three can be defined for our purposes here. One of them will concern us to a greater extent, since it is the one that leads to dealing with the issue of anxiety.

The first way, already mentioned, of conceiving lack—with the avowed intention of sustaining ambiguity—we can call the following:

To lack lack

(1) To refuse castration

This is, as we said, a relatively classic, traditional idea in psychoanalysis. It is deduced, almost literally, from the same Freudian texts insofar as they bear witness to castration as a condition to be avoided. Nevertheless, *the most minimally informed reading shows that castration is normalizing, and that it will be the complex corresponding to it—along with its concomitant anxiety—that will make it possible to "overcome" or dissolve the Oedipus complex.* This overcoming inaugurates the period of latency and in turn installs the superego as the heir of the oedipal sexual definition, allowing access to culture. Culture here is understood to be divestment of the libidinal relations and exclusive type of relations maintained with the "parental order." As can be observed, starting with Freud himself, castration is in no way a terrible fact to be avoided. If it does connote something that is essentially persecutive, painful, and unpleasant, it also carries with it the opposite trait. From the point of view of acceding to culture, it does have a normalizing effect. In this way, *it is not feasible to deny the salutary, beneficial effect of this modality of lack; there is no reason to allege the eluding of castration as an omnipresent movement. However, in some pathological cases, an etiological factor explains why castration has been rejected; this is unmistakable.* And here is where a point of definition arises: *castration does not necessarily imply anxiety.*

Due to the insistent use of the verb "refuse," a clarification must be made. If it is true that psychoanalysis has very precise labels to characterize the defining operations of the structures in play (repression/foreclosure/denial), we have selected the word "refusal" to define this circumstance in a general sense in accordance with our expository aim. It is not by chance we have chosen to name a theme, firmly rooted in Freud, in such a manner. As of 1923, the year *The Infantile Genital Organization: An Interpolation into the Theory of Sexuality* was published, castration began to rely on its reverse: the phallus. When Freud conceives of the first term, he does so by referring to the second and vice-versa. Hence, the Lacanian notation we have already pointed out: (-φ).

The second way of thinking about the situation in which lack arises is to refer to the well-known notation Lacan used to account for phantasy (*fantasme*):[1]

To lack lack

(1) To refuse castration

(2) $(\mathcal{S} \lozenge a)$

Here we must bear in mind that *the phantasy functions in the psyche somewhat like a bottle cap. In some way, it protects the subject from the encounter with the register of the Real.* The phantasy is found in a place where its stability and persistence—and its apparent immediate and volitive summoning—guarantees the subject a situation in which *lack is veiled or made up*, to use a term from cosmetics. Keeping this in mind, it should be pointed out that it would thus not be overly rigorous to think that lack is lacking. The issue is that the *object a, according to Lacan's development of the idea, has no reason to indicate or comprise a lack*

---

1. Translator's note: the unconscious fundamental *fantasme* as defined by Lacan.

in itself. There is what we can call *semblances of this* a, which, expressed minimally, is merely an algebraic notation with no referent. *The a is not a partial object and in this sense should not be confused with the ones that are known as the breast, the piece of feces, the gaze, and the voice, since these are "stand-ins" or semblances. The object a is not to be confused with them because it is first of all a writing.* Partial objects can be ascribed or attributed to the object *a*, but partial objects as such do not in themselves indicate either a lack or a lack of a lack. In *Seminar XI* Lacan comments on this issue very subtly when saying that it is to be expected that the object *a* appears as if aspirated, that is to say, occupying precisely the place of a *bottlecap*. This is what is demonstrated by the schema of the fishing net. The fishing net is reduced to a simple diagram in these passages where one of the most usual systems of the *a* in the phantasy can be understood:

The object *a* comes to occupy the opening of the fishing net. *It occupies the orifice while at the same time covering it.* The opening aspirates *a* and the *a* comes to block the opening. However, though this relation makes it possible to speak of a lack of lack per se, we should also point out that this relation masks or acts as a kind of makeup to preserve lack, thereby sustaining the stability of the phantasy. *It is the void caused by the lack that keeps the phantasy in its place.* Nevertheless, this does not imply that we not consider its other side, the side where *a* is one of the modalities of lack. This follows because *a* is a remainder or leftover of the

Other (A), particularly when the Other, logically, is written barred (Å), thereby accounting for its very condition as lacking.

To lack lack

(1) To refuse castration

(2) $(\cancel{S} \, \Diamond \, a)$

The place of the articulation of the subject—mediated by the lozenge—does not inevitably indicate a place of lack that provokes anxiety because it lacks. The contrary is practically always true: *the phantasy serves as an efficient device against anxiety*. In short, it is necessary to think of the object *a* with two different statuses, from two different points of view that must be elucidated.

The third way to consider that lack lacks is the one that Seminar X *is most concerned with in terms of its link to anxiety, that is, the uncanny or* das Unheimliche, *the formidable Freudian expression that Lacan maintains with all its clinical and etymological implications.* This is a basic fact for the psychoanalytical intellection of anxiety: *the uncanny provides the most apt elements to apprehend what the lack of the lack consists of:*

To lack lack

(1) To refuse castration

(2) $(\cancel{S} \, \Diamond \, a)$

(3) *Unheimliche*

Once more we recommend rereading "The 'Uncanny'." It is necessary to return to this work, which, at each reading, suggests diverse and even inexhaustible effects of Freud's teaching. He opens his essay with a long philological, etymological disquisition on the term *Unheimliche*. After providing an extensive and brilliant series of examples while maintaining in suspense a definition of the term, he ends by saying, with Schelling, that *it is those things that, destined to remain hidden, have nevertheless become manifest*. It is what irrupts when it should not have appeared; what should be lacking is the uncanny. It is, moreover, a *sudden irruption that does not last*. It is an experience that, at a particular moment, comes down on the subject, *leaving him or her petrified and stunned*. It is anxiety.

Unheimlich is, as Freud points out, a compound word. The negation prefix *un* precedes *heimlich*, familiar. *Un*, he writes, is the mark of repression, which is part of the term as such: *something that was familiar has become not-familiar, strange, and threatening*. Through the peculiar status of the unconscious, where opposites, far from excluding one another, either make up for, substitute for, or replace one another or are implied in pairs, the familiar and the not-familiar end up occurring together.

The allusion to the family included in the term *heimlich* is not casual. The family is also being spoken of here. It is the welcoming, warm nucleus where each person can feel secure and sheltered. Nevertheless, the family is also the place where the subject undergoes amongst the worst experiences (with regard to affects, or the effect of structure) that she or he will suffer. This is, Freud remarks, the experience of *the uncanny in anxiety*.

Faced with anxiety that is implied by the irruption of the uncanny, we can locate something else that is much cited in the "manuals" of psychoanalysis. It is known as a *signal-anxiety*, is presumed to be produced automatically, and seems to be the result of adaptation attempts. It is minor anxiety manifested with the aim—it is said—to cancel out massive *panic anxiety*. This is how, for example, Otto Fenichel describes it in *The Psychoanalytic Theory of Neurosis*. In our judgment, the term *panic anxiety* is not essential if the precise determination of Freud regarding the uncanny is taken into account; furthermore, to understand signal-anxiety in terms of adaptation reintroduces the myth of the homunculus "in the head." Therefore, *there is no homeostatically opposite pair as regards kinds of anxiety*. The key text in understanding anxiety in its various manifestations is simply "The 'Uncanny'," as Lacan points out so well.

In order to study the formations of the unconscious, Lacan, no sooner than having taught us to notice unexpectedly the effects of grasping the concept of anxiety in *Jokes and Their Relation to the Unconscious* (this is the text, for example, that the seminar *Les Formations de l'inconscient* of 1957–1958 draws upon), sends us back to "The 'Uncanny'," published in 1919. This comprises a remarkable effect of teaching. One is usually referred to *Inhibitions, Symptoms and Anxiety*, given that the title itself announces the exploration of issues linked to anxiety and our exploration of it here, and for the "formations" we would have expected Lacan to refer us to a text on symptoms. But his sight is set on other works, that is, *Jokes and Their Relation to the Unconscious* and "The 'Uncanny'," which would seem to bring us oblique answers. This is because *he is following a strategy that is not immediately obvious*. Lacan, by choosing these works, accounts for his understanding of how one should think of psychoanalysis. As we have written elsewhere, do not expect Freud to show up for an appointment if it is to take place in a conventionally defined place. *One has to proceed very cautiously with Freud because when we believe that the texts will provide answers we expect they do not; they go to unexpected, unforeseen places.* Lacan acts on these circumstances with these references that are a constant surprise due to the effects of meaning they produce. The effects say much more than the references to the works one turns to, "knowing" beforehand what one will find in them in a frozen, preset manner.

The issue of the uncanny, the third modality for conceiving of what is at play and at stake when lack lacks, is in no way divorced from the other two. The refusal of castration and the establishment of the phantasy—along with its "fakes"—are decisive, insofar as they involve the concept of castration and the object a in elucidating *Unheimliche* in metapsychological terms. To do so, we turn tangentially to the issue of the mirror. Here we should remember that the part of the subject that is not in the mirror or specularized is $(-\varphi)$. Also, the a caps the opening in the net. In *L'Angoisse*, Lacan articulates in an intelligent manner how to distinguish the two notions. Clearly, *this is a logic of concepts that uses mathematical language as a referent for a reason*. The operations at play here should be analyzed in detail since even some Lacanian authors are somewhat confused about them. *Seminar X* asserts this in a very precise way: $(-\varphi)$ is in effect when a is lacking. Now, what does this mean in relation to the lack of the lack? To demonstrate, we can make a diagram like the one below, which looks like a *light bulb*.

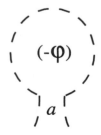

The object a, we reiterate, offers the alternative of masking lack. In this way it sometimes acts as a cap that blocks the regency of $(-\varphi)$, the imaginary consistency of which marks off the symbolic place of the opening. Also, it should be remembered that the a is in no way the object of desire.

$$(-\varphi)$$
$$a \qquad \neq \qquad \text{object of desire}$$

We shall now look at this point more closely. *The exclusive disjuncture applied to the relation between the object* a *and the object of desire arises from the necessity of emphasizing that they are two different concepts.* For Lacan, the object of desire refers to something that seems to place itself in front of the subject in function of his or her decision. This conception has given rise to a series of philosophical hypotheses. It is one of these in particular that Lacan is interested in dismantling: Husserlian phenomenology. We must not forget that by directing himself at Edmund Husserl, Lacan, by extension or elevation, was also pointing to other prominent figures in the French philosophical panorama of the time, such as Maurice Merleau-Ponty, a friend he respected, and Jean-Paul Sartre, whom we have already mentioned.

Phenomenologists stress the hypothesis of a thetic, intentional consciousness in their work. This consciousness is always a consciousness of something, pointing towards this or that object with a particular content other than, or distinct from, consciousness itself. In this design, the content could be the object of desire. That is why the object is present from the outset in a position of confrontation with the subject and in front of the subject.

Consciousness   ————————➤   Object

The object of desire is in front of a thetic consciousness. In a more convoluted manner, expressed in cognitive terms, Husserl would say that thinking proposes its object. The *noema*—the unit of thinking in Husserlian terms—is precisely what generates the intentional object. Needless to say, this is once more the terrain of the most old-fashioned idealism: the subject as immanent generator of the world despite claiming it is transcendent. To refer to an object of desire in these terms implies locating oneself in the primacy of the Imaginary. We are here in the presence of a being who places objects before itself, bestowing prestige on itself for creating itself in the mirror, self-specularizing, as it were, while constructing its own private world. The prestige arises, among other things, from the fact that in this situation the ego can only be vainglorious about its freedom in carrying out a project for which it will also seek universal validity. This type of formulation will oblige authors like Sartre to foreclose on psychoanalysis and its crucial discovery: the unconscious.

Sartre postulated bad faith at work in the place of the unconscious. This indicated to him that *knowledge—textual knowledge—of the unconscious as such was inexistent and therefore he rejected it.* Consciousness monopolized knowledge and knowledge allowed the subject to know. But the subject becomes misunderstood due to the resources of a "badly intentioned" consciousness, spurred on by bad faith. This is what was being said from the vantage point of philosophy and at a certain time it held a certain consensual sway among "vanguard" intellectuals. Now, minimal experience of analysis as an analyst or analysand indicates that the unconscious is very different from this supposed bad faith.[2]

---

2. Could this be why Lacan refers to the Other as the "guarantor of good faith?"

This is not about answering—in the manner of an exemplar—the infatuated, subjective position that makes feasible the phenomenological one. What we are doing is to point out how this *frame of mind forecloses the object that causes desire by confusing it and substituting it for the object of desire.*

The notion of cause leads us to Lacan's wise revision of it in *Seminar XI, The Four Fundamental Concepts of Psychoanalysis.* In posing this question, as he points out, an intellectual atmosphere of imprecision is always generated almost immediately. That is because *to postulate a cause and the effect it provokes makes it impossible to provide an account of an intermediate step. A hiatus is thus created.* In what we are dealing with, the cause appears as a category of eminently psychic order. It pertains to the sphere of the created in the sense that it cannot be "extracted" from the laws of the world. Lacan remarks that as the function the *a* fulfills with regard to the cause has been whitewashed, great confusion and opposing philosophical developments related to the theory of knowledge have arisen, which we will examine later on. Let us for now add to our schema of the light bulb the fact that *the object that causes desire is not the object of desire.*

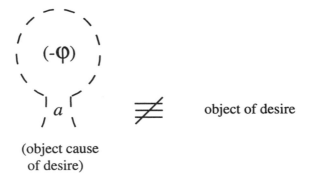

$$(-\varphi)$$

$$a \quad \neq \quad \text{object of desire}$$

(object cause
of desire)

This way, far from arising as a product in tune with the dictates of intentional consciousness, *the object* a *is in the position of originating the desire.*

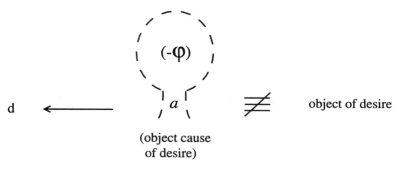

To strengthen this relation, it is appropriate to separate the causal link from the previous exclusive disjuncture. The object *a* does not appear as proposed to the subject, summoned by desire, but rather, on the contrary, it is what is located in the imaginary, *behind, as it were, desire itself and causing it.*

As can be observed, this postulate is not compatible with thetic consciousness. Desire is not something originary, autonomous, and independent that launches into a search for the object best suited to it. *The object* a, *"from behind" desire, imprints, imposes, and directs the itinerary of desire.* Considering the logical structure of this situation, it is clear that desire can only be

the desire of the Other, inasmuch as it is not an intuitive emanation arising from the deep reaches of corporeality or something of that ilk. *The barred Other produces a leftover from the
constitution of the subject that, proposed as a, originates desire.*

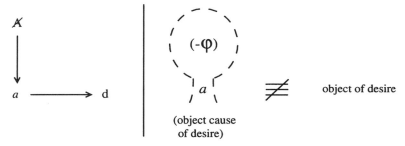

(object cause
of desire)

The subject's only choice will then be to seek this object of
desire that presumably is located in front of it. The subject will
think or postulate, through the effect of structure and as the subject of the representation that everything begins from the originary
strand of desire; every subject—from the ego—believes firmly that
he or she is de-subjected. *Thus the object a, while pretending to be
in front of desire, makes it possible for desire to be maintained through
the distance in effect.* However, when this is not the case, the rule
of castration is violated. Under these circumstances, the situation
can be represented in the following manner:

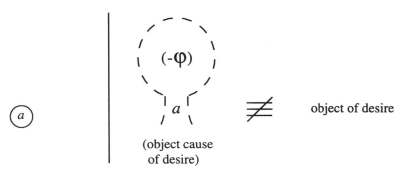

(object cause
of desire)

The circle, we know, is one of the traditional figures in Euclidean geometry. It may be the least adequate way of accounting for anything related to the discipline of psychoanalysis, and this even more so after Lacan's complicated topological developments that make using a simple circle to account for anything happening to the object *a* seem almost heretical. It does, in fact, help to illustrate pedagogically a specific constellation.

In this regard, we conceive of the circle more as a circumference marking the boundary of an empty space that would be covered by the *a*. For the time being, we will take it to indicate the existence of a lack with defined contours, that is, a lack with precise boundaries. In other words, it is an orifice made by a perforation. From this apparently innocent figure of the circle, topology arises. In fact, this figure, created by a perforation, can be conceived, for example, as an erogenous zone, since as it is in contact with the object cause of desire, it takes a journey whose route is determined by the fact that it borders on an orifice that opens and closes.[3] Furthermore, Freud tells us that *every erogenous zone, and by extension all the problems related to the drive, are redefined in function of castration*. The contour defining what accounts for the orifice, as it remains in this manner, therefore refers to *castration*:

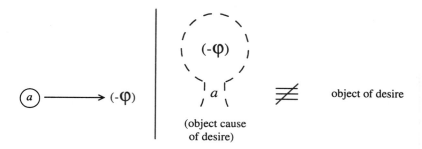

(object cause of desire)

object of desire

---

3. Lacan, *The Four Fundamental Concepts of Psychoanalysis*, p. 188.

Consequently, *the perimeter around the object a as the possible stopper of this opening is simply the (-φ) of castration that in the case of the stopper lacks as lack.* Nevertheless, there is one decisively important point that up until now we have not included in our presentation. We are referring here to the concept of *the Thing that is basic in accounting for the uncanny.*

The Thing, *das Ding,* comes up early in Freudian thought, in the "Project for a Scientific Psychology," published in 1895. It is first presented in passing in a lateral context. Nevertheless, Lacan's perspicacious reading reveals the huge implications of the topic Freud conceptualized only loosely.

The "Project" alludes to a *complex of perception* at work in the suckling infant, described in a two-part design. The first is determined and lasts longer than all feasible alternations. It can be drawn in the following manner:

What Lacan points out about the Real can be predicated from it: *the Real always returns to the same place.* The remainder of the complex of perception, on the other hand, is the one that undergoes transformation.

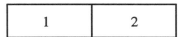

The argumentation is similar to what can be said about a stable subject and its attributes. The subject (1) is the one that remains while the predicates (2) change. *This opposition meets two conditions overall: one of endurance, stability, and even immobility in a certain sense and one of instability and flexibility.* And it is in the unalterable part of the complex of perception that Freud locates what he calls *das Ding: the Thing that configures the first hostile exterior with which the* sapiens *is confronted.*

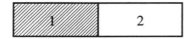

The place of the Thing can be occupied by what Lacan calls the *Primordial Other*, that is, the *Mother*, in the form of the *real Other*. Of course, this is not the empirical mother but rather the one that is produced as the unavoidable effect of structure. Though this throws out the argumentation of various psychological schools related to a kind of puericulture that sacralizes the purity of "maternal instinct," what psychoanalysis postulates and shows is exactly this. In this regard, one reads the following in the "Project:" "Let us suppose that the object which furnishes the perception resembles the subject—a *fellow human-being*. If so, the theoretical interest [taken in it] is also explained by the fact that an object like *this* was simultaneously the [subject's] first satisfying object and further his first hostile object, as well as his sole helping power."[4] Years later, in the *Introductory Lectures on Psychoanalysis*, Freud maintained that our discipline should not be confused with any psychology of the individual à la Adler—against whom Freud was also aiming his polemic—where each subject, impelled by his or her will to power, tries to make "little arrangements" to compensate for his or her inferior organism. Psychoanalysis is concerned with disentangling the feasibility of *how a subject can arise from a structure as absorbing and marking as the family structure*. It is not about a preconstituted being who comes to have relations with others but, rather, in a situation in which all the circumstances seem to occur for this not to happen, subjects do break away. This particular condition is what makes

---

4. Sigmund Freud, "Project for a Scientific Psychology," vol. 1 of *The Standard Edition*, p. 331. Italics in the original.

Lacan emphasize the question, what is there at the beginning? The *Desire of the Mother, he answers, and this consists in reintegrating her own product.* It is here that the Mother appears before the *infans* as *das Ding.*

The relation of the mother with the child situated in the place of the phallus is one of absorption or, as we say, the movement is directed in accordance with an intention of reabsorbing its own product. In this situation, *the Name of the Father should act to separate or break away, introducing a cut between the Thing and the child.* This circumstance can be detected in the protophantasy that tends to come up with analysands when they produce significations about a presumed imaginary return to the mother's womb.

The protophantasy of return to the mother's womb has nothing to do with a fetal psyche or anything of the kind. In fact, this is about a return to the nets of maternal desire, which is very different from a return to the fetal state. Until further notice, it is impossible to talk seriously about the psyche of spermatozoa, the ovum, embryo, and the like. What can be observed is that the place of the "embryo" does exist, from the Other. So, in this sense, *one can see a fetal psyche conceived from the place of the Mother.*

The issue now is to locate the Thing in relation to the decisive affect, the uncanny; that is to say, how does *das Ding* give way to the irruption of anxiety in this series of relations? To introduce the rule of *das Ding*, it becomes necessary for the border around the orifice, which the *a* managed to obstruct partially, to be suddenly and completely stamped out. This is the condition for the manifestation of what was destined to remain hidden. *If the a suffocates by covering or capping, the dilution of the border puts* a *and* (-φ) *aside, behind the abyssal opening:* das Ding.

We then say that *the lack of a border endangers the stability of castration.* For example, it should be pointed out that what comes to the fore in a symptom, which is not to be disdained, such as a phobia of heights, is actually a phobia of "lower depths." It is the abyss, like *das Ding*, that is calling. The subject who suffers from vertigo perceives a call to which he or she is about to answer, throwing him- or herself into the void. Beyond the vertigo itself, it is what summons one to jump into space, which is characterized specifically by not having any defined borders and being a void. The reverse of the object *a*, when the borders that it tries to cover are erased, is its hidden opposite side, that is, *das Ding*.

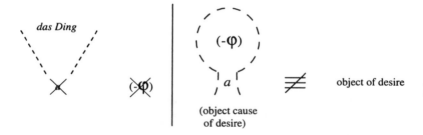

The link between the object *a* and the Thing determined why Lacan, many years after *Seminar X*—for example, in the seminar *D'un discours qui ne serait pas du semblant,* as well as in a series of classes held somewhat later entitled *Le Savoir du psychanalyste*—referred to the *a*-Thing.

The concept of a-Thing, *at other times written as "Ha-thing," marks once again that the link between the terms is required to account for the production of the threatening effect. The object* a *does not have in itself an* unheimlich, *persecutive character but does imply the unfocused, unlimited, imprecise appearance that the a-Thing has. Das Ding is totally indefinable and is as blurry as it is* tantalizing, terrifying, and like a stalker. It is for this reason that in phenomenology, anxiety is presented without a defined object. The subject says he or she is anxious without knowing from what, or who, or why he or she is suffering.

If one reads *Inhibitions, Symptoms and Anxiety* attentively, especially, as Lacan recommends, Appendix B of the essay, one can observe that anxiety can be something undefined. But it is, says Freud, *"about something,"* though the subject does not know what the "something" is. This is what makes possible the guarantee of the central thesis that has been shown as the starting point of the Lacanian development: *anxiety is not without an object.* The fact is that this object is not one that can be located quickly from a phenomenological point of view. It is not the fear of an animal, or of being closed in, or of heights. One thing is clear: if the conception of the object remains relegated to a naive type of sensory data, it is logical to say—as psychologists do—that anxiety is characterized by the lack of an object. But, on the contrary, if from the point of view of psychoanalysis we maintain a more faithful notion in which an object can well be something that is not an object in the first instance graspable as an object of the senses, *we can assert not only that anxiety is not without any object but also that the object in question is precisely what has been designated as the* a-Thing.

The object that provokes anxiety in the neurotic is the a-Thing, *that is, the desire of the Other, as the Other requires that the subject erase its borders, handing itself over to it in an unconditional manner.* Lacan points out that in this place is to be found, supposedly, a kind of *jouissance* that is reached through abdication. Such *jouissance* does not exist, but not because the *jouissance of the Other does not exist*, nor because one ceases to believe in it. The subject, from its limited, restricted, partial *jouissance*, as phallic *jouissance*, presumes the existence of total *jouissance*, of what assigns the subject no other location than the one situated in the field of the Other.

In clinical practice, it is very common for a neurotic analysand to suppose that some other person has knowledge about unlimited *jouissance* and that, from the paucity of the analysand's own *jouissance*, from the limitations on his or her own lost *jouissance*, he or she longs for the achievements and fullness supposed of this other person, who usually has a perverse structure. This person will do everything in his or her power to encourage this belief, demonstrating to the neurotic that he or she does know all about the recovery of the state of *jouissance* and promising the neurotic that, by following the road proposed by him or her, the neurotic will be able to escape the restriction imposed by castration.

The supposition about being able to attain the *jouissance* of the Other, possibly focalized on the perverse, is simply one of the "curative" fantasies of the neurotic who usually has no other *jouissance* than the *jouissance* of his or her symptom, since his or her sexual life is constricted and centralized around it, as Freud demonstrated. Now, the *jouissance* of the neurotic is phallic, which does not imply that the penis is involved in this but rather implies that the phallus accounts for the efficacy of its reverse: castration. *If "attention" is given to castration,* jouissance *remains localized in a precise way and it is thus partial.* But, in this position, the subject hypothesizes the existence of a total, maximizing *jouissance*. The *jouissance* of the Other—as Lacan calls it and which he introduces systematically in this seminar— also eventually takes on the inherent dimensions of *the ontological proof of the existence of God.* The mere fact of conceiving of it implies the existence of this *jouissance*, though no more so than in the thinking of the subject who postulates its existence, and from this, that it is "mental *jouissance*." The subject accounts for the *jouissance* of the Other by supposing it, rather than finding it, which in no way invalidates its efficacy.

There is an illustrious antecedent to this paradox in the history of Western thinking with the Stoics, who were precisely the ones to discover the notion of *material implication:* a true conclusion can be deduced from a false premise. And a false premise does not necessarily give rise to a false conclusion, though a true premise will give rise to a true conclusion. This creates a situation that torpedoes the logical equilibrium speaking beings long for. As for the *jouissance* of the Other, we reiterate, due to its nonexistence it does not follow that there is no belief in it. Now, this cannot be reduced to a simple question of erroneous belief or reasoning *since the place where the existence of the* jouissance *of the Other is presumed is the place of the Thing*.

The subject supposes that *das Ding* is to be found enjoying plenitude all the time or lying in wait for the moment in which it will appropriate the subject's flesh with great *jouissance*; *the very flesh, rigorously speaking, that the pervert offers politely, proposing to act as the faithful instrument of the* jouissance *of the Other*. The imaginary attempt to refuse castration can be seen in this invitation and, above all, the supposed limitation of desire.

For this point we must return to *the matricial framework of anxiety*, completed with acting out and passing to the act, which are surely not affects. Rather, both are expressions of *actions that sweep away the certainty of anxiety*. When the subject launches into these types of actions, he or she remains in a situation where *doubt is abolished* while appropriating certainty for its own uses. This is a major element in *Seminar X*, which is taken up in several passages. In the first meetings of the seminar some mention was made of this, as were others in the final meetings, which make it possible to define passing to the act, acting out, and their differences. Here it is worthwhile to take up these two items and their location in a partial cut from the framework.

symptom ⟶ passing to the act

acting out ⟶ anxiety

There is close proximity, as can be seen, between them and symptom and anxiety. It is worth pointing out that both concepts approach anxiety: they are *defenses against anxiety and attempts to avoid it.* Understood in this way, they again bring up a key thesis of *Seminar X:* the object *a* as the subjective correlate of anxiety, the object that causes desire, or, expressed another way, the object of the drive. Now, do *a* and anxiety reciprocally imply each other? If I think of anxiety, I think, so to speak, automatically of *a* through the necessary reference to the *a-Thing.* But we should underline here that the inverse proposition is not valid: *to think about the logical structure of the object* a *does not imply necessarily a reference to anxiety.* So this is not a reciprocal implication but a simple one. It is absolutely feasible to conceive of many of *a*'s relations without referring to anxiety. But what interests us here is the opposite: if we focus on anxiety, *a* intervenes unavoidably; consequently, and given its proximity to anxiety, acting out, as much as passing to the act, indicates operations through which the subject is related to the object *a.* That is why the fertile distinction Lacan makes between these two related phenomena should be examined.

To define acting out and passing to the act rigorously, *Seminar X* refers to Freud's clinical practice. Basically, the concepts are sketched out in the case histories of Dora and the young homosexual woman.

In principle, we can say the following about the destinies of the object *a*: *acting out is an attempt to make the object present, to locate it effectively, by creating a stage where it will appear.* By his or her action, the subject tries at the same time to maintain distance from the object *a*. There is a classic example of this in Lacan's work. In the same way that for Freud the analysands known as the Wolf Man or the Rat Man were decisive, it is feasible to observe Lacan's example of someone we can call "The Man with Fresh Brains."

In fact, the man was not Lacan's patient but rather Ernst Kris's and previously, Melitta Schmideberg's, Melanie Klein's daughter. In various seminars, and also in the *Ecrits*, Lacan builds "his" case. The "Man with Fresh Brains" was an analysand whose activity was especially intellectual in nature. Not without malice, Lacan asserts, "This subject finds himself greatly hindered in his profession, an intellectual profession which does not seem very far from our own."[5] Was he an analyst perhaps? This patient was suffering from a singular obsession: he believed that everything he might come to write could only be plagiarized material. He particularly feared stealing ideas from a much-appreciated colleague with whom he worked and spoke on a daily basis. As a witness—by conviction—and to a certain extent a judge of the "realism" of the situation, Kris chose to ask his patient to relate his thesis as well the contents of the book from which he asserted having taken it. From the "prolonged scrutiny," a paradoxical situation arose. Not only was the analyst telling his patient that he had original ideas but the analyst was also saying the patient's ideas had been plagiarized. The content

---

5. Jacques Lacan, "Réponse au commentaire de Jean Hyppolite sur la 'Verneinung' de Freud," *Ecrits* (Paris: Seuil, 1966), p. 394.

in question, compared to the postulations of the analysand, presented a "new light": what had happened was that the eminent colleague had frequently seized upon the ideas that the patient feared to publish, changed them ever so slightly, and used them without ever mentioning where they came from. The analysand, who believed that he had found unequivocal proof of his vocation as a plagiarist in the book, found himself, due to analysis, in the opposite situation.[6]

What the Man with Fresh Brains was plagiarizing, what he was stealing, Lacan tells us, was thus quite simply, *nothing*. But the allusion to *nothing*, in this context, implies a reference to *a*: the fragment that falls from the body, separating from it. What exactly did the analysand *do* once he had received the quasi-legal attestations of Ernst Kris during the sessions, which were "realistic" to the greatest degree but outside the analysis? He rushed off to the restaurants in a nearby street until he came upon one with a menu in the window announcing his favorite dish: fresh brains. This gastronomic excursion after his sessions was a sort of ritual. Lacan interprets this as the analysand saying to his analyst with this action, which can be qualified as acting out, simply what the analyst was making the analysand see: "he left him with fresh brains," just as the analysand was asking the analyst to reopen the "freshness" of his "analyst's brains." This was a subtle, trivial acting out, which in fact provided proof that Kris was conducting the analysis in a mistaken manner. *Lacan points out that the analysand places the object* a *on the plate. And by so doing, he places there as well his little piece of "original"* jouissance. By delivering this pound of flesh, by separating him-

---

6. Ernst Kris, "La psicologia del Yo y la interpretación en la téoria psicoanalítica," *Revista de la Asociación Escuela Argentina de Psicoterapia para Graduados* 17:135 (1991).

self from the object, the patient saves himself from identifying with it. *He maintains distance from it by staging it*, in this case, on the menus of the restaurants that made the object *a* letter. And this is where we find *the decisive aspect of acting out: it shows, it appeals to the gaze and calls for attention—doubtless in a provocative way—pointing out how its object cause of desire is outside.*

Acting out is *a message for the Other; it shakes the analyst's position, so that he wakes up and sees what he cannot hear.* The fact that this type of action shows, or is a showing, is thus inducing, aggressive, and challenging. But is this not "breaking the setting"?

In Freud's case history of Dora, the mistaken behavior that the patient has with regard to the married couple K.—friends of her parents—whereby she proposes herself as the object of desire of Herr K., as well as his wife, implies clearly, as Lacan points out, that she is acting out. It is *a staging*, where the showing and provoking condition before the gaze of the Other that we mentioned is particularly explicit. And there is, in this case, a crucial moment: the one at which Herr K. approaches Dora on the edge of the lake, blurting out, "You know that my wife means nothing to me." It is not our intention here to show in what way this short speech comes to sully Dora herself. The point is that her answer to this confession is a slap. The slap marks her passing to the act after acting out.

Passing to the act implies a withdrawal from staging, a cut where the story changes course. In the case of the young homosexual woman, Lacan takes into consideration a passing to the act produced under circumstances that, in our view, are a passing to the act followed by an acting out. He then explains in detail how the protagonist removes herself from the stage, in this case in an even more spectacular manner.

As will be recalled, Freud recounts that the young homo-sexual woman at a certain point puts aside—being an adolescent like Dora—her feminine concerns and any possible interest in men, and begins to court a lady of doubtful reputation, a *cocotte*, as Freud delicately puts it. This woman was being courted by the young woman in the manner of virile, courtly love, an amorous discourse that shows devotion by attempting to avoid any type of corporal relationship. *An exemplary mode of being able to give, according to Lacan, what one does not have.* But in the case of the young homosexual woman, courtly love takes on more drastic proportions: *it is offered like a gentleman who salutes the lady as proof of love and renounces giving what he does not have: the Phallus.* This is a circumstance that comes close to being, due to the intrinsic necessity of structure, a sacrifice. The challenge this kind of relationship with a woman of ill repute implied was accentuated by ostentatious walks through the streets of Vienna, including strolling in the vicinity of the young woman's father's place of work. The entire relationship with the *cocotte*, including the flowers sent, the walks, and the rest, was staged by a blatant acting out. The moment of challenge, however, came right at the very moment that, in some way, was sought in order to set up the supreme sacrifice. One day the attention-drawing couple ran into the father of the young woman, whom the courted woman did not know. The daughter observed the angry look on her father's face, which caused the older woman to inquire what was going on. Once this was made clear to her and before she could propose severing relations, the young woman threw herself off a platform, falling onto train tracks below and injuring herself. Identified with the object *a*—the gaze—the only solution the young woman had was to *attempt suicide, which is simply to follow the destiny of* a: *separated, fallen away.* In the attempt to give what one does not have (unlike what some analysts believe, that one gives what one has) the defining instant is the one in which there is violent and sudden yielding to the scene. The young woman throws herself off the platform in a suicide attempt, followed by an abrupt change of direction. She changes her relationship with the older woman and even with her parents. Lacan worked on Freud's use of the signifier *niederkommen* in the case history, which can be translated literally as "to let fall." This is precisely what happens to a subject like the young woman when faced with the devastating meeting with the object *a*-gaze that her father gives her. Since the principle of her position is to sustain an idealized relation with what her father "pushed" on her, she lets herself fall, literally, in an almost total identification with *a*. *Had the suicide been consummated, one could qualify the identification as "absolute."* This letting oneself fall explains the reason for a certain, usual modality of suicide: to throw oneself into the void out of a window is to defenestrate oneself, etymologically "out of the window." The subject does so *in an attempt to cross the opening, the boundaries, which separate the stage from the world and through which the subject returns to the fundamental exclusion where he or she feels him- or herself to be at the moment when desire and the Law come together in the absolute.* The result of passing to the act is the fall after which the *a* in the structure occupies the place of the *dejecture*. This term is just a condensation of what is rejected, left over, and what is fallen or falls away.

The state of dejection in which the young woman remained after her attempted suicide determined why, in spite of certain facts of the analysis that apparently indicated a change towards heterosexuality, Freud ended up directing her towards a woman analyst, confessing thereby an *impasse* about the possibility of success with her case and "letting her fall." The young woman had not changed the object of her desire except in an illusory way: she continued to be homosexual intimately without clashing with those around her, while she also temporarily accepted to "look for" a man.

The slap Dora gave Herr K. and the suicide attempt by the young homosexual woman are circumstances that made it possible, at the level of the quasi-direct relation with the *a*, at least temporarily, to avoid anxiety.

Now, in an earlier text, we emphasized the significance arising from the fact that the young homosexual woman was taken to psychoanalysis by her father, after her suicide attempt.[7] With this attempt, it becomes necessary to think that there was also a condition of showing and inducement at play. Here, too, the conditions for displaying the acting out also exist.

In this regard, let us remember that Lacan defined acting out as "transference without analysis." This will be useful to establish a valuable cross-correspondence in the manner of a word play.

Acting out = transference without analysis

We repeat: in *Seminar X* Lacan points out that if transference is not analyzed, the analyst, fallen from his or her place, sends the analysand directly towards acting out; thus, the message that could not be heard returns abruptly in a manner that can be seen. This argument gives rise to a particular combination with the following assertion: *transference* "is acting out *without analysis.*" Thus:

Acting out = transference without analysis
Transference = acting out without analysis

---

7. Roberto Harari, "Caída de un querer," in *Discurrir el psicoanálisis* (Buenos Aires: Nueva Visión, 1986), p. 191.

First, what can be understood here is the obvious and comfortable scholastic assertion: transference is analysis without acting out. On the one hand, what is pointed out here is not clear. Which transference is being referred to? In the case of the young homosexual woman, for example, there had been no consultation with the analyst prior to the defenestration. And on the other, what does acting out without analysis mean? In the same case, analysis had obviously not been set up as such as the moment of the *niederkommen*. The issue here is that *acting out is a wildcat transference, in the sense that it questions and overwhelms the place of the subject to a much greater extent than the symptom.* In acting out, we must take into account that *the subject is experiencing phallic* jouissance. Therefore, what arises from symptoms does not call for interpretation apart from the obvious technical detail signaling that *the symptom is not interpretable since it does not mediate transference.* If the Other is not being asked to assume the place of the Subject Supposed to Know, all the "truth" content in the world can be spoken and no change in the position of the subject will occur.

If interpretation proceeds from the Other—and that is what is done on a daily basis in clinical practice—it can work on the symptom. But Lacan's sharp approach to acting out underlines that it has a stronger power of demand than the symptom; it is a peremptory demand for interpretation, given the shattering it bears. The savagery implied by this (virtual) transference that is acting out without analysis asks the Other for symbolic restitution in a much more resonant manner than the symptom itself. *This implies the clinical reevaluation of all these types of defenses against anxiety, which are shaped by the trait of action, signifying action.* This is a capital point, making a basic difference in the Lacanian focus versus the one of the other psychoanalysis. Now is a convenient moment to stress that acting out is more than an obstacle to analysis: it can be asserted that *there is no analysis properly speaking if acting out by the analysand does not take place during the course of the analysis.* Thus, even passing to the act can precipitate entry into analysis, since it is proof of a much stronger and more articulated demand than the ones often still referred to as "unleashing mourning in the present," which is often used to explain the impulse to enter analysis. The Lacanian framework, on the contrary, provides insight into *one* of the entries into the analytical situation, which is characterized by a considerable increase in imperativeness and exigency, a fact clinical practice could not conceptualize previously.

4

Destinies of the a: Deception, Transference, Failure, and Mourning

We have pointed out that one of the outstanding features of *Seminar X* is that it does not present a *corpus* with a correlative type of exposition. Once issues have been presented and developed, they are not depleted, and do give rise to others. In *L'Angoisse*, we find one of the examples in which Lacan demonstrates—as we understand it—a sort of noncontemporaneity with himself. There are formulations that seem heterogeneous to one another, supposed contradictions that one has to know how to—be able to—tolerate in function of the wealth of postulations they contain. Obviously, extreme clear-mindedness and the formal logic of theorem-based argumentation do not appear to be contemplated. Themes are addressed in one place and then taken up later in another. The comings and goings in the seminar force the reader to accompany these movements. In this manner, our repeated loops around some delicate issues are an attempt, in our approach, to respect the direction of *L'Angoisse*. Our aim is to try to trace a course suitable to Lacan's developments; it is from this that we have drawn the order of argumentation presented in our work. *An order of exposition, an order of reasons, which do not necessarily strictly follow the original.*

In previous chapters we have shown various themes developed in the first third of *Seminar X*. We are now at a point where we can discuss the conditions for approaching the structures and the relations arising from them in the middle section of the seminar. This will imply returning to a somewhat abstract and more complex level than our previous chapter. To say this another way: we will now establish links with certain passages of Chapter 2, especially the *graph of anxiety*. Let us recall then the major characteristics of the relations it demonstrates that will assist us in our upcoming clarifications:

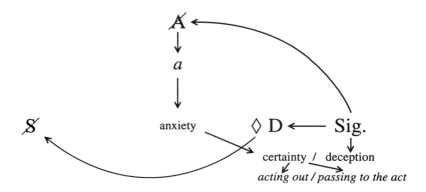

We must once more clarify the meaning of the elements in this graph. Let us refer to the pages where we developed them one by one. Acting out and passing to the act, let us suppose, were sufficiently explained on the basis of Freud's clinical cases. What we want to do now is to have this partial graph say more than it said the first time in order to extend the validity, in psychoanalytical practice, of its notations. Indeed, the graph is closely articulated to the clinic, given that it is not a magical construction of a logos feeding some metaphysical order.

To begin, we shall stop at the term *demand* (D), which, strictly speaking, belongs to the Lacanian lexicon. It is not found in Freud as a concept.

First, let us bear in mind that demand should not be understood in the sense of a specific request. Among other things, *demand implies the unconscious order at work.* We thus discard the naive, widespread conception, which understands demand as some kind of detoured desire extrapolated in a convenient disguise to the conscious level. An unconscious desire, according to this intellection, transforms itself in passing to the conscious mind into demand. Were this so, it would be impossible to understand why the series of problems raised by demand in neurotics is so decisive. And this is so defining that *there is psychoanalysis due precisely to the unconscious dimension inherent to demand, given that it makes possible the building of the clinical "setting" of analysis.*

To demand is not exactly to ask. Lacan makes this clear. What the neurotic is constantly demanding is something else. *He or she wants something to be demanded of him or her; the object that he or she seeks is a demand.* Time and again this situation arises. In *Seminar X*, Lacan adds that *the neurotic seeks to have a demand made to him- or herself, trying meanwhile not to pay the price that this implies; that is to say, he or she wants to give "nothing."* To account for this occurrence, we say that in the formula of phantasy (included in our graph on anxiety) the *a* is replaced by the letter corresponding to demand. The ($\lozenge a$) is converted into ($\lozenge D$), which is *the formula of the drive and the treasury of the signifiers:*

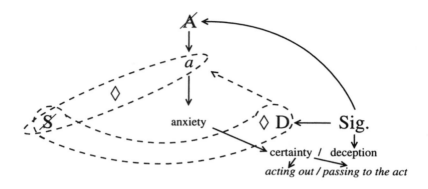

The replacement produced in the neurotic is crucial to understanding what can be called one of *the destinies of the object* a. For example, as we saw, a destiny is what was illustrated in the case of the Man with Fresh Brains, who scans restaurants looking for the object *a* made letter and served on a plate just after leaving the office of Ernst Kris.

In another example, the one of the young homosexual woman, a passing to the act—which implies the fall of the subject as object *a* to which she identified—can be linked to acting out, that is, a peremptory request for interpretation, for symbolic rearticulation. In the first case, the *a* is presented at some distance, it is inscribed on stage, as it were, and in the second, the *a* is at work in jumping into the world, off stage. Now *the neurotic*, through the substitution of demand for *a*—or in making demand his or her object—*carries or transports the object* a *to the analyst*. In this way, he or she manages to carry out *a displacement*, which allows the analyst to assume the place of object cause of desire. For this to occur, *the analyst must not make demands on the analysand. This process explains, in distinction to the process of the Subject Supposed to Know, why the very particular tie or link called transference exists.* If the analyst is capable of sustaining the place into which he or she is put—an especially difficult position—the analyst can be the object causing the desire of the analysand. Continuing with the Lacanian notation, we can write this in the following manner:

$$a \longrightarrow \cancel{S}$$

This way of writing the transferential relation refers to the *formula of the phantasy*, since its terms correspond completely to the formulaic, though the relation is not of the same order as the phantasy. *The analyst, in the place of the object a, provokes the barring of the subject, which means that the subject is positioning itself as subject of desire.* Indeed, this is the most elementary way of explaining what comes into play in analysis. The analyst is thus a *semblance of* a; we repeat: the analyst is not the *a* itself, but rather the analyst "resembles" its function. The *a*, strictly speaking, is nothing more than a notation, and as a semblance it manages to show, or attempts to show, in this manner, what the neurotic is asking for through the demand.

The neurotic, in his or her daily life, does get the effects he or she seeks with demand, that is, the neurotic begs to be demanded of, without perceiving its inducement. *The neurotic demands demand.* This is the effect observed clinically, which Lacan writes as ($\cancel{S} \lozenge D$). The fact is, the neurotic begs to be begged, while not intending—as we have said—to pay the price that supplication brings with it, or to respond to what it implies. The error that one way of handling the cure can fall into regarding this point is to think that what the analysand is demanding is what he or she is asking for expressly. Here we must make one simple distinction: *what the analysand is demanding explicitly is not what should be "satisfied."* If that were done, what would happen? The possibility for desire to continue circulating would become

blocked, obturated: it would be turned off falsely and momen-
tarily by a precise answer. What happens then? This demand
would be followed by another that would also require a precise
answer. Which, in turn, would give rise to another dissatisfaction. This would be beneficial, it is clear, since it reopens lack.

Though what we have just said may appear obvious and
elementary in a psychoanalytical framework, this error is the
cornerstone of many kinds of psychotherapy that are structured
around a peremptory requirement for resolving specific problems "of the present." The psychotherapeutic effect being sought
is strictly determined by the manifest demand of the analysand
who goes to resolve a particular issue that is "worked on" to the
exclusion of others. In this engineering of behavior, the only
"alternative," whatever the variety of therapy, is to pose the
issue in the dimension of an imaginary healing, that is, precisely
the one psychoanalysis seeks to avoid. To discuss a concept we
have already examined in detail, psychoanalysis seeks to arrive at the central question of lack and not to apply makeup to
it or cover it up with various meanings. This kind of demand
is directed toward plugging lack; what the analysand is asking
for neurotically is an imaginary cover for constitutive lack. If
the analyst falls into the assumption that his task is to occlude
lack in an imaginary dimension, he is giving up the role of
analyst to become an anxiety-provoking psychotherapist. And
that is why the classic recidivism of the symptom in all psycho-
therapies marks the healthy return of desire. Furthermore, and
to conclude, suffice it to write down the aphorism with which
Lacan accounts for "fundamental demand" up to 1972: "I demand that you turn down what I am offering you, because it is
not that."

Undoubtedly the issue of lack according to Lacan is not a
simple one. It is a polyvalent concept with several readings and

refers to different kinds of lack, as we have explained, even leaving aside the distinction made between *privation, castration, and frustration* in *Seminar IV*. Returning to the *destinies of the object a,* it should be pointed out that the neurotic destiny of the object cause of desire by which the object turns into demand makes Lacan think of a certain category that comes into play in one of Plato's dialogues, *The Symposium*.

The recourse to the concept of *agalma* is one of the pleasant surprises that the text we are commenting on affords us and appears in several places in *The Symposium*. In *L'Angoisse*, the question is touched upon tangentially, since it had been worked through extensively two years before in the seminar entitled *Le Transfert dans sa disparité subjective, sa prétendue situation, ses excursions techniques* of 1960–1961.

In Plato's dialogue, *agalma*, more than a concept, is a term that appears lost, spoken almost in passing. Its etymology is somewhat peculiar and tinged with imprecision. Lacan emphasized the importance of the term and has rescued it for psychoanalysis, making it into a concept. Before anything else, it is worth asking what the idea of *agalma* is. To do so, let us turn to a few passages of *The Symposium* to see how the term repeatedly refers to the condition of lack.

There are a series of speeches on nature and the implications of love, based especially on homosexual love. In one passage, Alcibiades, a handsome young man, speaks when it is his turn to participate in a game in which his companions at table had to praise whoever was seated beside them. Alcibiades, in a kind of drunken furor, as Lacan points out, makes a panegyric of the man who had been his peculiar lover, none other than Socrates.

Apparently Socrates was not particularly esthetically attractive, so that, in his eulogy, Alcibiades came to mention hidden qualities of attraction in the philosopher. He exclaimed of the man of whom he was still enamored, "I say then, that he is exactly like the masks of Silenus, which may be seen sitting in the statuary shops, having pipes and flutes in their mouths; and they are made to open in the middle, and there are images of gods inside them. I say also that he is like Marsyas the satyr. You will not deny, Socrates, that your face is like that of a satyr. Aye, and there is resemblance in other points too. For example, you are a bully—that I am in a position to prove by the evidence of witnesses, if you will not confess. And are you not a flute-player? That you are, and a far more wonderful performer than Marsyas."

In this quote one element stands out. In the comparison Alcibiades makes, he alludes to a grotesque exterior that hides, on the interior, an image of a god. Also, despite resembling Silenus or a satyr, Socrates used to seduce using resources beyond simple appearances. Alcibiades continues his encomium, pointing out to what extent he was overwhelmed by Socrates's words. And he says, "But I know him and will describe him, as I have begun. See you how fond he is of the fair? He is always with them and is always being smitten by them, and then again he knows nothing and is ignorant of all things—that is the appearance which he puts on. Is he not like a Silenus in this? Yes, surely: that is his outer mask, which is the carved head of Silenus; but when he is opened, what temperance there is, as I may say to you, O my companions in drink, residing within. Know you that beauty and wealth and honor, at which the many wonder, are of no account with him."

There is here an almost transitive projection between Socrates and his young lover, since the latter finds himself reciting the outside ugliness of his master by saying, "But when I opened him, and looked within at his serious purpose, I saw in him divine and golden images of such fascinating beauty that I was ready to do in a moment whatever Socrates commanded."[1]

What arises clearly in Alcibiades's speech is that what is at play is something hidden, inasmuch as its "exposition" is of a virtual order. This is about a lack, given that this allusion to what can "be seen" on the inside is an imprecisely attributed assumption accompanied by an assertion of the lack itself. Here is where analogy comes into action through recourse to the imaginary dimension. There is no such interior treasure. Apart from this, how does one obtain it, even if partially? *This interior* agalma *is what leads the analysand to ask himself the question about* a, *which, without his knowing it, inhabits him as cause of desire.* While Alcibiades, in his eulogy of Socrates (agalma is a noun coming from the action of the Greek verb *agallo*, meaning to glorify, exalt, and honor)[2] claimed the *agalma* to be inside his lover and master, using a comparison about the statues of satyrs in which effigies of the gods were hidden (*agalmata theon*), *the analysand wonders what treasures the analyst "contains," and through the transference displaces it onto the analyst, asserting, for his part, that he, the analysand, lacks it.*

As can be seen, this *agalma* has little or nothing to do with exterior beauty. There is no esthetic valuation occurring here but rather conditions set up by the analytical artifice. It is the fact that the analyst can put himself in the position of a semblance of *a* that determines that this comes to be, that is, that the emergence of the phenomenon of love becomes feasible as described by Alcibiades. *He, as the lover, loves the one that fulfills the function of being in the place of lack.*

---

1. Plato, *The Symposium*, vol. 3 of *The Works of Plato*, trans. Benjamin Jowett (New York: Tudor Publishing Company, 1937), pp. 347–350.

2. Translator's note: another ancient root is rendered in French as *rejouir*, which can signify to reexperience *jouissance*.

Maybe we should restate this: *love belongs to the order of deception*. In *The Four Fundamental Concepts of Psychoanalysis*, the seminar after *L'Angoisse*, Lacan works on this association in a detailed manner. If we agree that transference is deceptive, for whom is it so? Why, ever since the beginning of psychoanalysis and in various schools, does the apparent coincidence of transference being closely linked to deception appear? This question is very frequently eluded and an explanation like the following is resorted to: "What you feel does not involve me; you are feeling this in relation to your father." This is a classic maneuver to avoid the fires of transference that can achieve actual gains, and the issue is far from settled by these kinds of puerile "explanations." In the end, sooner or later, the inefficacy of this procedure reveals itself. However, *we should emphasize that a dimension of deception is inevitably at work in transference*. But not everything is limited to a mistaken object of love. What is fundamental is that *transference love—as Freud rightly pointed out— is true love, and love, in turn, is necessarily a deception*.

Deception-love functions as a hinge between two ideas arising in relation to it. If it is a deception, it can be considered so because it is directed towards an equivocated, inadequate representation. The second idea is to think that *love is a deception in and of itself*.

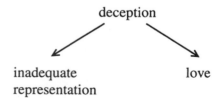

deception

inadequate
representation   love

Why is love a deception? Returning once again to Plato's dialogue: because it can be observed that when Alcibiades eulogizes Socrates, thinking to praise him, what he is trying to do is regain his lover. In this sense, the words are aimed at capturing the love of his ex-lover. *To love is wanting to be loved.* Now the deception in question is that one pretends that love is disinterested as to the continuation and obtainment of its effects and is an active procedure. The latter can be accepted in a limited sense: *love is active but with the aim of obtaining the passive aim sought, that of being loved.*

Love as deception has a relation of exclusion with certainty, bearing in mind that certainty is what does not deceive; anxiety as a certainty is located precisely on this level. This obliges us, finally, to pay attention to *the relation between love and anxiety.* If love is deceptive, a condition whereby the *agalma* is attributed to the other—to the treasure "it contains" on the inside, which the subject seeks in some way to appropriate—it only expresses itself as the possibility of being loved. The *agalma* could be reduced to the situation of seeking to obtain what love brings that is defined by capturing the love of the loved object. *It is clear that, in this dimension of deception, terms of reciprocity are dominant.* To love corresponds to—or at least it is an attempt to—be loved. The idea of disinterested love is a pretty, lyrical construction, but it is not in keeping with the most elementary clinical phenomena, and the demonstration can be extended to everyday life. So, *as to what happens in transference, one of the possible destinies of* a, *as in the case of acting out and passing to the act, comes into play in it.*

If, as we have agreed, acting out is transference without analysis, and the inverse, acting out without analysis is transference in a wildcat way, which in some way analysis, or at least consultation with the analyst, brings about, the transference modality of this destiny of the *a* requires additional comments. One is related to a topic widely covered in a previous book we have already mentioned: *La repetición del fracaso* [*The Repetition of Failure*].

Failure is one of the points Lacan stops to examine in the course of *Seminar X*. Of course, failure immediately brings to mind the *masochistic condition* at play in failure. In the various, interesting formulations he makes in this regard, the relations of anxiety to failure can be observed. Thanks to an easy representation of it from everyday life, one could naively understand that the subject experiences anxiety over failure. But here again, as is generally the case, the initial intellection of the problem has its traps. Lacan, in accordance with what psychoanalysis teaches, commits himself in a certain sense to inverting this approach to failure. And he says, *it is necessary that the dimension of failure exist as a means for reopening the situation of anxiety*. From its status as cause, failure is relegated to a simple instrument of anxiety since it is itself a hiatus, a hole. *What is unbearable, in any case, will not be failure but rather success, since it implies that "this is not lacking."* This point, in fact, is not so new for psychoanalysis. Freud postulated it in 1916 in "Some Character-Types Met with in Psycho-Analytic Work," a keen study of "those who fail when they succeed." In this short work, the theorizing centers in particular on the feeling of guilt. The subject could not tolerate success given the guilt it produces, so that the guilt condition is related necessarily to punishment. And it is clear that this is not pure speculation. Those who fail when facing success often appear in clinical practice. Lacan articulated to Freud's developments that failure in success answers to *the necessity of having to sustain the place of anxiety, that is, a middle term—middle median, as he said—between desire and* jouissance.

The tables of relations presented on earlier pages shall help us ahead to establish (according to what is presented in *Seminar X*) a sort of stratification that seems to be a mythical chronology. The argumentation has a myth-like dimension, in that Lacan repeatedly refers to *a subject that is not yet a subject*. (This does not indicate a fallacy, but rather a hypothesis on the conditions of originary production.) He postulates a *protosubject* as an ad hoc hypothesis, although its existence cannot be pointed out. The presubject, as we saw, is the one who is written as an unbarred S. Obviously, the ek-sistent, "complete" subject will be the S, subject of desire. Nevertheless, Lacan uses the S formulation that coincides with the notation that he usually uses to write the signifier. In *Seminar X, the S should be read as the protosubject, or more precisely, as the mythic subject of* jouissance.

The one the S designates is the subject itself of the initial moment of *jouissance*, which opens the way for the appearance, in the middle of the phenomenon, of anxiety in a previous relation regarding the later order, the one that refers to desire. The position that can be seen in this mythical chronology of *jouissance*/anxiety/desire corresponds to the beginning of our graph of anxiety, read from bottom to top:

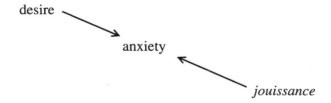

Consequently, *anxiety occupies an intermediary position, like a hinge, between* jouissance *and desire*. And failure? Failure is the efficient instrument of anxiety, given that success can have the same function as the one assigned to "satisfy" demand in its periodic manifestation: it can stop up and even asphyxiate desire. And here we find an interesting paradox: *the subject must fail, necessarily, so that its desire is not suffocated*. Maybe a condition of necessity is, strictly speaking, not the most adequate, though Freud's text does invite this reading since he refers to *the need for punishment as being equivalent to the unconscious feeling of guilt*. This point makes it possible to understand the action of a decisive instance in this subjective position: *the superego. It is the superego that leads to failure but not in the manner of failure through failure itself*. This has consequences for clinical practice and even ethical ones that become immediately apparent.

The analyst can, as he is often advised to do, push the analysand to win out over the rigors of his superego and allow him to work, leaving aside certain unjustified scruples and not being overly exigent of himself. In this picture, the analyst acts like a bellows blowing a teacherly air over the patient, proposing thereby a lesson in the art of living well. Faced with this "action," *the analysand has no other recourse to sustain his desire than to exacerbate the functions of failure*. This procedure also usually leads to something else: the analysand is left with no way out to sustain his desire than to pass to the act, manifesting itself in this case by giving up the analysis. When this jump off the stage occurs, the analyst alleges that the patient's superego has punished the subject with a categorical directive to leave analysis. He may even add that everything is due to the fact that the analysand "does not even allow himself to be cured." This may seem like a caricature but it can be seen in our area, and there continue to be those with an entire theoretical and clinical practice line that conceives of something like a sadistic superego continually mistreating the masochistic ego. These concepts are set up—as Enrique Pichon-Rivière would say—like a soccer field in the head where two teams are fighting for control, but in a very special way: one of the teams asks the other to attack it but does nothing to defend itself or attack back. This is a spurious manner of grasping some crucial phenomena of analysis where the fallacious "therapeutic ambition" denounced by Freud prevails.

In the seminar *D'un Autre à l'autre* of 1968–1969, Lacan discusses, in particular, the most usual aspect of *masochism*, which can often be seen in clinical practice. This is not the *erogenous masochism* postulated by Freud, that is, masochism consummated by and in perverse erogeneity. Nor does he mention the other variation, known in Freud's texts as *feminine masochism—which, obviously, is not exclusive to some "essence" from women but rather is generated by and in men's phantasies.* The masochism Lacan refers to in *Seminar XVI* is called *moral* masochism, which Freud had also called ideal. *Moral masochism is of fundamental import because it gives rise to a specific substructure: the destiny neurosis.*

Under this name, which has gained general acceptance, the subject, who appears to be in the clutches of a fatal destiny—Freud says—seems to be guided by dictates, reiterative and unavoidable fatalities that imply—and here Lacan says—*the restitution of this object a, which is the voice, in the Other. In destiny neurosis can thus be found a carryover, a displacement of the partial voice object as a.*[3]

Here it should be said that essentially the voice, of a superego kind, is operant in destiny neuroses. It is this voice that incites and insists on leading to failure.

---

3. We repeat once again: the writing of *a* in the work of Lacan means a yearning and achievement, in the sense of *making the order of writing autonomous with regard to clinical practice.* The notation is not written as a superimposition of clinical practice; the famous "complete interrelation between theory and practice" does not exist. It marks a constitutive shift between two heteroclitic orders. The concepts can be brought close to clinical practice but at the same time they maintain their irreversible autonomy. If this effect of structure were accepted, many would stop rending their clothes.

In a wider sense, it can be observed that *the superego leads ceaselessly to failure from the moment that it requires fulfillment premised on absolute, full, and constant* jouissance, *which is obviously impossible: Real.* Destiny neurosis, a singular phenomenon, brings to light a fundamental structure of the superego as voice, which is at work in a much broader territory than is traditionally mentioned regarding the voice hallucinations in schizophrenia (paraphrenia in Freud). The keen way Lacan accounts for this attempt to restitute the object *a*, incarnated by the voice, in the field of the Other, allows us to understand in what manner *a subject can keep on constructing the conditions of his own failure, and even for him to do so by taking into account that this attempt leads to the preservation of desire. Failure, summoning anxiety, will impede the dangerous drawing close to* jouissance, *which is, nonetheless, paradoxically sought.* Let us now move to another, convergent case.

The subject can have phantasies just like anyone, and often has, as analysts frequently observe, phantasies that the pervert carries out in passing to the act. The problem we want to point out is not the process of phantasy-making itself, but rather the possibility that the phantasy suddenly appears realized. This is an exceptionally rare occurrence, doubtless, and not because it is intrinsically unrealizable but rather because the neurotic does not usually do much with his or her phantasy. At that moment, the signal called anxiety appears, as a hinge, we said, between desire and *jouissance. The subject fervently desires something, but when faced with the threat of actually carrying it out, of the* Erfüllung *as Freud puts it, of the desire, anxiety is not long in making an appearance: desire has reached a terrain in which the approach to and of* jouissance *is unbearable.* The intermediation of anxiety functions to sustain desire, since it requires a differentiation between what is sought and what is obtained so that metonymic sliding along the signifying chain occurs once again, which is what desire does.

In this short description of *"failure seen in analysands,"* and though it may seem pointless to reiterate it, *the conception of* jouissance *as something situated beyond the pleasure principle* should be borne in mind. If pleasure tends to homeostasis, compensation, and equilibrium, *jouissance* is untamable in its tendency to increase tension. This distinction is fundamental in understanding the formulation of *Seminar X*.

There is another side—somewhat unrelated to what we have just seen—to the possible readings of the graph of anxiety having to do with the issue of *deception*. If *certainty* determined our more or less detailed handling of the notions of acting out and passing to the act, we initially linked deception to the phenomenon of love. This is a very obvious type of deception when we bear in mind the participation of the narcissistic dimension with its well-known capture in the mirror. But the graph describes another trait of deception, the signifier, as inevitable as the other one.

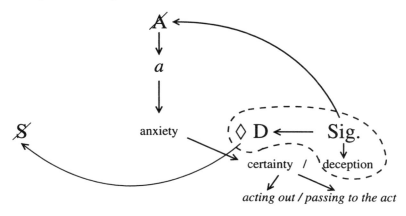

The graph shows that the deception of the signifier is closely related to demand. If the demand is deceptive, it can be so, strictly

speaking, through the effect of the signifier. To clarify this point, let us take up once again some very keen references by Lacan that consolidate his conception of the signifier, which we began examining in Chapter 2.

As we said, there is a cut where the trace ceases to be one, and is elevated to the category of signifier. This is where we pass from the animal domain to the domain of the speaking being. What mankind does can be illustrated by the joke cited by Freud: "Two Jews met in a railway carriage at a train station in Galicia. 'Where are you going?' asked one. 'To Cracow,' was the answer. 'What a liar you are!' broke out the other. 'If you say you're going to Cracow, you want me to believe you're going to Lemberg. But I know that in fact you're going to Cracow. So why are you lying to me?'"[4] This Jewish joke works on the capacity of the signifier to say something true by making one believe that it is a lie, in an attempt to deceive the Other, which it fails to do in this joke. *Through the signifier, the subject can make use of traces that are falsely false with the intention that the Other not find out.* In this manner, an "originary *not-known*" (*non-su* in French) is construed. This then determines the games of deception speaking beings engage in. In short, *the subject pretends pretense when he is speaking the truth, and this is the way that the subject reacts to the fact of being marked by the signifier.* This is obviously a circumstance that psychoanalysts must pay attention to even though linguists may not. The extent to which the action of the signifier goes beyond the action of a mere trace or notch can be perceived through the intelligibility of this process.

Similarly thus, the distinction between *the Lacanian signifier* and *the Freudian mnemonic trace* should be drawn. *The terms*

---

4. Sigmund Freud, *Jokes and Their Relation to the Unconscious,* vol. 8 of *The Standard Edition,* p. 115.

are not homologous and what Freud called representation is not equal to the signifier. In any case, one sporadically finds in Freud's texts a notion that we do think congruent to the Lacanian position: external associations. As will be recalled, these associations are made based on homophony, or as Freud puts it, "paraphasically similar cadences," that is, similarity of sounds. The term and its use can be traced in *The Interpretation of Dreams* or in *The Psychopathology of Everyday Life* in order to find out to what extent this conception is close to the Lacanian signifier. (The difficulty presented by hastily trying to homologate point by point the Freudian concepts with those of Lacan continues to be an incentive for a more rigorous reading of their texts.)

We were saying that the recourse to deception is the best verification about the way in which the subject reacts to the determinism imposed on him by the signifying order. It is therefore valid to postulate that the speaking being is more than the candid claim that he or she is only a "marionette of the signifier." *Freudian determinism does not imply a sort of resigned fatalism, the vision of a world of homunculi directed by the strings of parental or societal discourse, past or present.* This "game" with the signifier has an impact, in particular, on the terrain of the deception of love. Indeed, amorous deception is peculiarly related to the deception of the signifying chain. Thus, one could think of these terms as the relation between imaginary deception and symbolic deception. Here, however, is not the place to explore this more fully since it merits its own in-depth examination.

Once the *conceptual feasibility of the deceptions of love and the signifier themselves are laid,* the dimension of the register corresponding to anxiety must now be situated. It is very difficult to locate it in the order ruled by the signifier, since, were it there, it would be subjected to the possibility of deception, and by definition, *anxiety cannot deceive.* This characteristic of anxiety makes situating it in the register of the Real imperative. Furthermore, the relation between certainty and deception should be modified in the sense that the separating bar undergoes a thickening process transforming it into the Lacanian lozenge. In this new relation, *disjunctions and conjunctions, implications and disimplications between the terms can now be observed. The point is that though anxiety is without a signifier in terms of the analysand's imaginary volition, it is nevertheless obviously treatable through the symbolic operation of psychoanalysis.*

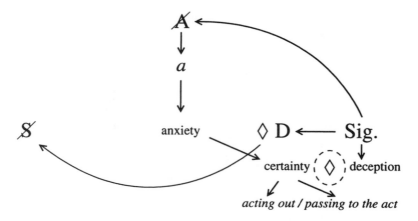

After examining in this chapter some of the topics developed in the middle part of *Seminar X*, such as the destinies of *a*, the clinical fact of failure and the deception of the signifier in its relation to demand, the time has now come to approach what we can call *the indicative function of anxiety*.

The problem of this function is related to the known Freudian reference about signal-anxiety. Here we should ask the following question: Accepting that this is a signal, what is it a signal of? And where does it appear? To whom is it manifested and to what request does it answer? These are at least four of the questions—not easily overlooked—that arise from an initial analysis of the issue.

The first point is that although defenses against anxiety can proliferate, anxiety is in itself also a defense. The post-Freudians argue, for example, that anxiety is a kind of wisdom of the ego, which chooses it among the defenses available against panic anxiety, which is what one is trying to avoid. Lacan answers by saying that *anxiety is a defense independent from the fatuous designs of the ego. This is related to his very lucid grasp of resistance.*

When reference is made to resistance in psychoanalysis, this is not about a wise ego determining it does not want to know anything; even if it is conceived as taking place in the sphere of the unconscious, to talk about this process is no more than transporting with preciseness a conscious operation to another level, in an imaginary way. Lacan said, simply, "*something resists.*" The other psychoanalysis maintains that the ego, through the symptom, resists being cured. While *Seminar X* observes that in such a case there exists *a desire that returns through the symptom, and that it resists because it keeps saying, it keeps making present.* The desire proceeds firmly, strong as a fortress. This intellection of anxiety as a defense calls for a distinction between the alternatives frequently presented in clinical practice. Although as analysts we know that *it is decisive to know how to "dosify" anxiety,* we should not turn a deaf ear to its call insofar as it sets up a touch of attention—a "signal"—about the possibility of suffocating desire. Lacan's recommendation in this sense is comparable to the one he provided about acting out, viewed as an obstacle to be avoided by post-Freudians, but reevaluated by Lacan as a violent form of the analysand's "saying." So: *signal-anxiety is of itself a defense.* Furthermore, the devouring therapeutic ambition that seeks the immediate and radical mitigation of anxiety contributes to suffocating desire.

Returning to the indicative function, it should be pointed out that the four questions can be located within a set of issues that should be postulated as the background to the entire *Seminar X*: this set considers that anxiety appears as a signal and hinge when the distance between desire and *jouissance* is shortened. In this sense, *if anxiety is a signal, it is the signal of the desire of the Other*, which crystallizes the first point to be considered.

Why is the desire of the Other signaled by anxiety? Lacan refers once again here to Hegel and his classic dialectic between the master and slave, developed in the *Phenomenology of Spirit*. What desire seeks, in fact—for Hegel—is recognition: the desire of desire. So the subject wants to be recognized by the other. This recognition never manages to become the one that is secretly sought, given that if I am recognized the other situates me as an object, since I am the one it desires. And I cannot bear myself as object, and now there is no mediation possible but a fight to the death for pure prestige, fought justly against the one whose desire I desired. *The lack of full recognition gives rise to a dialectic of hostility*. But Lacan adds that when reference is made to a desire for recognition things do not happen along homogeneous lines, as reciprocity is discarded from the outset. Desire, in his understanding, is not desire for recognition; if it were, recognition of desire would be dialectically feasible. The issue is that the desire of the Other goes along a different path from the search for recognition. Lacan explains this by saying that *what the Other seeks is to find itself in me, for which it solicits my loss*. This assertion has a tinge—and there is no reducing it—of a Kleinian approach, a Kleinian ambiance.

The research of the Kleinian school regarding paranoid anxiety is perhaps what is most worthy of consideration, since in anxiety, paranoia is definitely present. Hence, we infer that anxiety, known as paranoid anxiety, is due, as we have said, to the Other seeking to find itself in me, demanding therefore my own loss. The situation refers to what we have shown regarding the Thing, the Desire of the Mother as a location of *das Ding*. *The primordial Other seeks to meet itself at the price of losing its own product as such. So what the Other seeks in me is its lack.* And this is blatant, since precisely the opposite seemed to be the case: what is sought—it is assumed—is plenitude, integration, which is doubtless valid for the imaginary register. But everything is not resolved by this; *if the Other seeks its lack, it will not only find occlusion but rather it will also ceaselessly ratify its lacking condition.*

Lacan makes some lucid references to *mourning* that can contribute to a clarification of these relations. There are those who say—with no basis—that the theme of mourning has little or nothing to do with Lacanian teaching. Obviously, the Kleinian questions of mourning for the breast are not an issue in Lacan. Nevertheless, he does point out that *one mourns someone whom one has loved or hated, and that when that person disappears he or she stops implying the subject as lack. Mourning occurs because the "person" for whom one is the lack is lost.* As can be observed, this is very different from the classic assertion, "What it is, is that he was everything to me." Beyond the spherical plenitude broken by this absence, a certain modality of lack comes into play: the lack the subject constituted for the one who has died. And Lacan wisely wonders, why is the subject grieving? Why does he come to feel that life is not worth living if the loved one goes away? To have the distance necessary to ask this question, it is suitable to turn to some facts of anthropology, which provoke an effect of estrangement in the face of what is obvious from our perspective.

From the point of view of the ethnocentrism of the civilization we call European, a certain rite practiced in many societies, known as primitive societies, can seem bizarre. When one of their own dies, there occurs what we would call a celebration. Is this a maniacal defense mechanism or even hostility to the departed? And here Lacan punches us with his question: Why should I necessarily stay in the wrecked, destroyed state of mind of a lamenting survivor? By chance could this, this state, be what she or he has left me? *Why couldn't I, for example, be content about his or her having lived, about what she or he gave me, and so celebrate this along the lines of an homage?*[5] This entirely innovative reflection is far from, in extremis, the various assumptions regarding universal defenses against mourning. On the contrary, these are differential ways of channeling the hostility arising from the loss of the one for whom I will no longer be the lack. In this sense, *the melancholic, in lamentation, is accusing the departed.* Let us remember what Freud wrote in "Mourning and Melancholia": "Their complaints are really 'plaints' in the old sense of the word. They are not ashamed and do not hide themselves, since everything they say about themselves is at bottom said about someone else."[6] If the melancholic says, "I'm a mess," it should be understood as, "You're a mess." Sometimes we even hear something like, "Why did you die on me?" Now, these intellections extend to the terrain of mourning, which is the normal prototype of melancholy. It should be observed that Freud also does not stop wondering why mourning, a blatantly unbalanced, decompensated state, does not appear abnormal or incomprehensible to us. And he thinks, maybe a little hurriedly, in light of what Lacan would later say, that it occurs because we all know

---

5. Many years later, the wonderful film *Dreams* by Akira Kurosawa showed the funeral procession of a village "stopped in time," which was ruled by this (to us) surprising signifying constellation—made act.

6. Sigmund Freud, "Mourning and Melancholia," vol. 14 of *The Standard Edition*, p. 248.

that mourning is overcome in the course of time, by itself. But the issue is to ask why this is so about something that appears natural or spontaneous, that is, to reconsider the reasons for this supposed spontaneity that is observed in this reversible reaction to the lost object.

Going back, we say: *if the aim of the desire of the Other is to solicit my own loss, this fact indicates the crucial character of anxiety, insofar as it officiates as a signal in the face of the imminence whereby this loss becomes feasible.* To clarify our terms: that the Other seeks my loss does not imply that it attempts to annihilate me. This is not even about a relation of mortal combat between consciousnesses in the Hegelian mode; this situation is very different from the fight for pure prestige. Far from the master–slave dialectic, we say that *if the Other seeks my loss, it does so because it is trying to restitute its own object* a. *It desires a fragment of myself, which it can appropriate, and that is where the anxious condition appears, when facing the threat of loss of the pound of flesh.*

We have in principle resolved several of our questions. What does anxiety *signal*? It signals *the desire of the Other. Where* does it appear? It appears precisely in the ego. And if we turn to the seminal text, *Inhibitions, Symptoms and Anxiety*, we observe that Freud constantly refers to this instance as regards the appearance of the signal. Now, *to whom* does anxiety appear? It appears *for the subject*—understood, naturally, as differentiated from the ego. And we must stress: the subject is the recipient of the alarm bell sounded by the ego. And finally, the fourth question: *From what request* does it arise? The answer: *from the request of the Other*, from the moment it solicited my loss when it calls for me to constitute myself as its object *a*.

These formulations in *L'Angoisse* would be expanded upon a year later: indeed, during the last class of *Seminar XI*, there is a cryptic aphorism, like an exordium:

> I love you
> But, because inexplicably
> I love in you something
> More than you—
> The object *a* +
> I mutilate you.[7]

This brief preamble to Lesson 20 refers love to something other than the narcissistic dimension. It is about extracting, extirpating "bloodily," in the final instance, the object a. The reference to mutilation is, of course, allegorical; nevertheless, it can be recognized constantly in daily clinical practice in numerous situations. For example, the issue of the phallus in detumescense is a preoccupation, as we have seen, that defines the hysteric. This is the gambit that needs to be reviewed and becomes crucial in detecting how the subject proceeds when faced with the loss of the object and confronts it.

Lacan, in affirmations such as those in *Seminar XI*, teaches that *the object is constituted specifically at the moment at which it is lost; that is, when it is cut off as fallen, separated.* This is radically different from the belief that, in the first place, there is an object and, second, the object departs, which is how Kleinianism nourishes itself. For Kleinians, first there is co-presence of subject and object with which a relation is maintained, and then the problem arises, when the object is lost. Lacan maintains the inverse of this: the outline of the object can only be delineated and obtain quiddity at the moment of the loss.

In this regard, the classical example of feces is the most transparent and even obvious, but this also occurs with partial, leftover objects, such as in the case of the oral object. It could

---

7. Lacan, *The Four Fundamental Concepts of Psychoanalysis*, p. 263.

be argued that the breast object, present from the beginning—according to the Kleinians—is not present at a particular moment; that is, that at weaning, the object that already existed is lost. But here is where Lacan's question comes up: What is this about it already existing? And if it had already existed before weaning, where would it have done so? Furthermore, *is there not perhaps an entire dialectic dimension not only between the breast and the nursing infant but between the mother and the breast?* The answer is that *the object a, as such, is specified unequivocally at the moment that these dialectical relations are interrupted by a cut.* And, to clarify the formation of the *a*, he gives it a particularly explicit definition that goes against the naive conception of puericultivating psychoanalysis: *the a is—Lacan points out—a biceptor. It belongs neither to one nor the other; it is between one and the other.*

British and American psychoanalysis—and here we are not referring only to the Kleinian school—is widely influenced by the postulation of object relations. One of the basic threads of its theorization concerns the separation of the child from the mother. To take a more primary fact, we can focus on what happens at the moment of birth, a prototype of this kind of empirical, visible separation. What the British and Americans see as paradigmatic to the loss of an object—the mother's womb—Lacan analyzes as a *double cut.* One goes into effect on the mother and the other on the neonatal infant. Both cuts have a leftover, different for each one. The coverings, the expired placenta and the umbilical cord: here we have some things that cannot be situated. The placenta, for example, to whom does it belong? Whose is it? With the exemplar of the placenta, Lacan thinks of the condition of the object *a* as a biceptor, with one side gazing one way and the other gazing the other way, and accounting for how separation and loss are requisites for the constitution of the subject. *These are some of the reasons Lacan claimed the* a *as his only "invention" on the terrain inaugurated by Freud. The object* a, *in effect, subverts psychoanalytical thinking by pointing to an internal separation in the sphere of ek-sistence.* And this subversion as innovation does not only have repercussions on Kleinism. Someone such as D. W. Winnicott, for whom Lacan professed great respect, postulated the widely disseminated theory of transitional objects. In a certain sense, this conceptualization seemed to be an advance over the redundant thinking about a mother–child "symbiosis" (which some "integrators" wanted to see alongside the theme of Desire of the Mother in Lacan); in all, such a postulation is not resistant to criticism. Lacan's questions to Winnicott were aimed at questioning this transition. How is one to think of it? Transition between what and what? Between two exteriorities? In looking at these questions it can be seen that the postulate of a *transitional object* is neither very clear nor very far from the mirror object. Although Winnicott's clinical perceptions were very talented, his lack of rigor in conceptual operations is proverbial. However, following the *squiggling technique* that Winnicott used in the psychoanalysis of children, it is possible to verify Lacan's exposition on the biceptor dimension of *a*. It is in Winnicott's intuition-based clinical practice where suggestive coincidences in light of Lacanian demonstrations can be found.

Seminar X teaches that there is *a certain faculty of cut that favors the loss of what will later be objects* a. Why should we call ourselves mammals, Lacan points out, if not for the condition of becoming separate that the oral object has? In fact, there are other characteristics that could have differentiated our zoological variety—that we are mammals—from the others.

To "illustrate" the quality of the cut intrinsic to the object *a*, Lacan turns again to painting. In this case, he discusses two paintings by Zurbarán, representing Saint Lucia and Saint Agatha, each of whom is carrying on a tray the organs—eyes and breasts, respectively—of their patrons. Lacan observes that it is not the fact that these objects have been ripped out and off that produces an intolerable impact—they are in the end, objects-cause. But if anxiety, as a level, is prior to desire, its point is marked as such in the case of Oedipus when he was blinded: it is not the mutilating act that is important but rather that "an impossible vision threatened them from your own eyes on the ground." Also, in spite of these images, *we insist: this is about internal partition and not empirical separation.* Or to use a good neologism: *it is a "separtition."*

Continuing along the same line of thinking, Lacan asserts in *Seminar XI*, that *the gaze is outside insofar as it does not belong to an eye but to an all-seeing world.* Therefore, in summary, *the object a must be apprehended in all its possible movements.* Considering its destinies should in no way be made into either a reference to empirical, daily interchangeable objects or to the objects that American and British psychoanalysis discusses in its object relations theory, referring in a general and practical manner to interpersonal relationships, or at least to relations based on styles of behavior. *Lacan in no way refers to behaviors with an object. He refers to feasible localizations of the loss that founds the a in the marked—phantasmatic—relation it has with the subject.*

5

The Framework of the Division of the Subject by the Signifier

The questions arising from the issue of anxiety as signal deserve special attention beyond what was said in the previous chapter. The *indicative function* of this kind of anxiety, pointed out insistently by the other psychoanalysis, obliges us to specify the *topos* within which it occurs. We said that it appears in the ego, as a sign of alarm destined to be received by the subject. As a manifestation of the ego, it operates at the behest of another instance, that is to say, it is referential insofar as it is not directed towards the same place it is located. The subject is not the ego, and we must repeat this though it may seem obvious: Lacan makes a fundamental distinction between the ego and the subject that is shown in its notation:

$$\mathcal{S} \qquad / \qquad m$$

The subject, which is the subject of the unconscious, is written with a slash through it.[1] *The subject is divided between*

---

1. Translator's note: in French, a slash is *une barre*, as noted in note 8, Chapter 1. A letter with a slash through is said to be *barré*.

what it knows and what it says. The ego, for its part, is written with an "m" (the m of the *moi*). The ego is a place, which in no way shows individuality or the singularity homologous to the one carried by the subject, whose desire is unveiled during the analysis. *The ego is a product of identifications, a deposit—says Freud—of the occupations of the object, which have been given up;* that's why there is a preexisting *field of the Other* that the ego has produced as an effect through successive and crossed identifications.[2] The result of this could only be the most heterogeneous jumble. Here we have a paradox, since when someone says "I" it is supposed that he or she is referring to what is most proper to him or her, something unique. However, this is not so; the ego is what is most improper to the person uttering the "I." *The "I" is a production and not the most coherent one. Now, it is also from the field of the Other that the subject of the unconscious is produced.* Therefore both the subject of the unconscious and the ego share the determination that arises from this decisive, other terrain, despite differing as regards the effect it has on them.

Lacan frequently emphasizes the effects coming from the field of the Other. When he raises the topic of *love*—which we will examine more in depth further along—*he slips in some very surprising remarks of the kind he used to use to* épater le bourgeois.[3] His comments refer to the danger that anxiety ceaselessly warns of. The threat in question is that the Other tries to gain power over the subject by postulating the subject as what can make it, the Other, complete. This is how what the Other wants from me (which I do not know) is marked. It tries to gain power over the

---

2. Identifications that we should grasp in the manner laid out in Chapter 2.

3. Translator's note: "amaze the bourgeois."

subject, incorporate it, or, to use a particularly graphic expression, the Other tries to ingurgitate and/or swallow the subject. Various phantasies demonstrate this situation. As we have said, the risk of being imminently devoured is apprehended through *the protofantasy of the return to the maternal womb*. The problem is that this kind of protofantasy can—and frequently does—give rise to neurotic theories with great persuasive power, which have been widely disseminated. *The question then becomes one of distancing oneself from the neurotic conditions of production in order to elaborate conceptualizations that can be transmitted as doctrine based on a foundation*. Here we shall make a short detour.

Freud warned, wisely and indirectly, of the ways neurosis can forge extremely strong theories as long as they are not opposed from outside the neurotic terrain that nourishes them and makes them grow. In our judgment, he did so by referring to *infantile sexual theories. Why did he use the term "theory" when he could have chosen a word with less prestige in the scientific domain, if he was merely pointing out certain conceptions about infants?* Surely, this was a very strong proposition, meaning exactly that there are infantile sexual theories.

One sexual theory of childhood considers that all speaking beings possess a penis. Another, for its part, claims that children are born in the manner of feces, that they are defecated. Although Freud may have referred to phantasies, lies, ideas, illusions, or, to be more drastic, nonsense, he did insist on talking about *theories*. The validity of the term is revealed if we realize how extremely appropriate it is if one is trying to make an epistemological type of observation or criticism. Freud used this term to indicate that we should take great care in supposed scientific theories, given that in the last instance the way they differ from infantile sexual theories may only be one of degree and of "packaging." Theories such as these proliferate in the "psych" community, constructed on real blunders. We could mention in this regard the theory of fetal psychism and infanticide.[4] Curiously, these theories claim to be psychoanalytical when what they are doing is capturing the psychoneurotic phantasy at a certain point; instead of accounting for it, they erect a conceptual edifice upon which they start generalizing. *These theories have become principles that explain everything and act as a vision of the cosmos.*

The point about infantile sexual theories contains a recommendation by Freud worthy of being remembered, related to another epistemological trap to which official psychoanalysis usually succumbs. As the new "grand theories" emerge, claiming to explain everything based on a zero degree constructed on a phantasy—as is the case of infanticide, for example—so too does a certain equivocation based on pluralist aspirations stemming from the "contributions" of small, personal theories, which are then added to a "whole" dictated by the needs of individual analysts. Lacan's insistence on conceptual rigor is very often unpleasant, usually bothersome, and has repeatedly been dubbed authoritarian. It is clear that it is much easier to put oneself in the position of being tolerant while magnanimously reconciling the unreconcilable with the advantage—while pointing out how right everyone is—of becoming a model of comprehension, wisdom, and democracy for others. To escape the *narcissistic trap of eclecticism* is surely more uncomfortable but it is the only way not to block the possibility of acceding to the (semi) truths that might be within our reach. This is a basic point for understanding where Lacan is aiming his constant and lucid epistemological criticism: at purging the theoretical foundations of concepts. The objective is that each category bring with it more than the

---

4. Translator's note: in Spanish, *filicidio*, killing of the son.

sudden extrapolation—also in theoretical form—of everything the analysand conveys and brings to analysis. The only thing to be achieved, by doing the contrary of this, is for one neurotic theory to overturn another one like itself in the mirror.

One basic example of a possible neurotic theory, easily found in clinical practice, is the very high percent of analysands who believe that their coming into the world was not wanted, or at least they consider that they are not the way their parents desired them to be. It is common for them to say that their parents wanted them to be of the opposite sex. Starting from this empirical and statistical verification, one could suppose that a universal phantasy is at work here and, based on it, formulate a theory elevating this reoccurrence to the level of a concept. However, one must maintain the necessary distance to observe that, in any case, this complaint is an effect of the structure of what happens with a universal phantasy: the one of *the family novel*. As Freud pointed out in "Family Romances," this is a protophantasy that allows the subject to believe that he or she is not the child of his or her parents by rationalizing the phantasized situation with "likely" scenarios, such as mistaken exchanges of infants in the nursery. These fallacies are used to conclude that the parents the analysand was lucky to get—or unlucky, as the case may be— are not the real parents; his parents are surely remarkable ones. What is lucid and intelligent on Freud's part is the way he detects this phantasy and generalizes it, thereby showing an historical truth. He does not contradict his patients' beliefs in their illus- trious lineage—obviously, it is not a question of discussing with analysands what they say, as they are neurotics in analysis—but rather he agrees with them. Indeed, he points out that these patients are children of other parents, different from the present parents, since they have nothing to do with the idealized parents of the patients' childhoods. Now, at the moment of recounting the family novel, the neurotic's progenitors become unidealized, far from the marvelous appearance they had of yore. Here we have the "nucleus of historical truth" of the family novel that is a clear example of reducing a neurotic theory—an infantile sexual theory that is basically patented at the moment of adolescent de-idealization—to its conceptual and historical intellection. However, that does not mean that this is about canceling the phantasy as such only because it does not adjust in a reductive manner to reality—which reality, anyway? However, to elevate this phantasy into an entire construction on which to base claims of theory and psychoanalysis is to make quite a jump.

Far from a mere epistemological digression, these remarks on infantile sexual theory are related to the decisive issue of the relation of the subject to the Name-of-the-Father. Though the seminar on anxiety does not explicitly discuss it in a nodular manner, we think it underlies the entire seminar. When one can bear the symbolic debt, and recognize it, it is possible to articulate psychoanalysis. *In the analytical movement, the tie with the Name-of-the-Father is truly crucial, even dramatic.* To use this adjective is not exaggerated when we observe the constant yearning to construct theories from nothing. *Ex nihilo, nihil est:* from nothing, comes nothing. *The constructions, claiming to arise from zero, are as frequent as they are aberrant.* Some people have attributed these attitudes to certain personalities or conflicting and passionate relations readily found in the history of psychoanalysis, which they have tried to demolish from the foundations up. However, the reoccurrence of these attempts demonstrates that *this comes from an effect of structure and not from the people in play.* Of course, this is about knowing how to use the Name-of-the-Father, thereby being able to disregard it, but in act and not in self-engenderment.

After clarifying some of the epistemological problems arising from the issue of anxiety as signal and its use by the other psychoanalysis, we shall now turn to another series of problems we have faced since the first pages: the relation between *anxiety* and *fear*. Let us remember that psychology and psychiatry—which are, by definition, phenomenological—continue stuck to the criteria of a localizable object that—according to its appearance or nonappearance—gives rise to fear or anxiety respectively. However, with the aim of starting to transcend this obstacle fed by what is manifest, it is worth referring to the issue again using a schema that can situate it in global terms. The first series of relations to consider concerns behavior in the face of danger, as it is commonly understood. Thus, the subject find himself faced with an outside, objective danger that provokes fear. This feeling then gives rise to the reaction that is presumed to be the most adequate: flight. The succession of circumstances can be shown as follows:

$$\text{danger} \longrightarrow \text{fear} \longrightarrow \text{flight}$$

As can be observed, *this series almost corresponds to the diagram of a drawn bow*. An outside stimulus has an impact on the afferent neuron that connects to a central, fact-processing neuron and sends an answer—an efferent one—in the form of a motor reaction (flight implies motility in itself; going far from the situation of danger). This characterization is perfectly comprehensible and it is very attractive in examining these terms from a prima facie point of view, since we recognize ourselves almost immediately in this manner of observation.

Now, putting the distances aside, the series we mentioned here makes us remember another triptych that Lacan criticized insistently and in an extremely pertinent manner. This conceptual schema is the very basis for an entire current in the other psychoanalysis. Although it does not belong, strictly speaking, to the theme of the relation between anxiety and fear, it shares—

as Foucault would have said—the same episteme, so that the coordinates used to conceive of both sets of problems are practically the same. We are referring to the well-known schema of *frustration-regression-aggression*. The relations, which resemble each other, are thus:

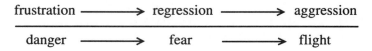

This frustration is owed, clearly, to an external situation. It is a way of referring to a certain state where something is missing from the place it was supposed to be. What happens with anxiety, where lack lacks, is very different. However, let us continue with the schema. The subject perceives that what it presupposed should have been there is lacking, in an imaginary sense. Something indicates that what is being sought is not there or that access to it is not feasible. *According to those who elaborated this theory, the feeling of frustration provokes a state of regression in which infantile standards of behavior are reactivated. Within the limits of a particular behavioral disorganization, some level of aggression is brought about that aims to attack the source, which, from the outside, sends noxious stimuli as indicators of the imagined lack.* This conception is so secure that it has even resulted in a test known as the Rosenzweig frustration-aggression test.

The frustration-aggression pair includes a causal, unidirectional relation whereby the frustration leads to the aggression after passing through the required intermediate state of regression. Aggression in the subject is thus apparently due to an appeal to "archaic standards of behavior." The resulting triad taking regression into account can come to explain—as a good deal of the other psychoanalysis has done—almost the entire etiology of psychoneurosis. The procedure to follow is simple: it is enough to locate the frustrating circumstance, grasp where the subject has regressed to, and, lastly, observe that through this, instead of dominating love, the subject manifests aggression above all else. In this way, a convenient map is drawn up for moving around the terrain of the etiology of psychic illness.

In the episteme shared by both triads, one can observe that in frustration, regression, and aggression, something is operating in a forced and irremediable way. Here we can ask, when faced with the frustrating situation, why does the subject not face it in a different manner, since the effect is "inadequate"? On the contrary, in the danger-fear-flight triptych, adequation prevails. The supposition here is that moving away from danger, occasioned by fear, adequately resolves the situation. Leaving aside this differentiation, one can see that in both cases the terms are monolithically welded together. That danger provokes fear, and that this leads to flight, is an obvious course. It seems spontaneous, logical, and even natural, though the final reaction might even be inadequate. (Why is this so and what ruler is being used to measure danger?) What does Lacan do to grasp what is at stake in a situation of fear? He uses an example drawn from Russian literature, specifically from Chekhov. *In this order, Lacan again follows Freud, for whom writers always had the advantage over psychologists in their fine understanding of the psyche.*

The story that Lacan quotes is known in Spanish as "El Miedo" (the fear). Apparently, this is not the best translation of the original Russian title, since he questions the French translation of the title, "Frayeurs" [frights; Trans.].[5] What is striking is that he does not know how to deal with the appropriate word

---

5. Translator's note: the title of the work is translated in English as "Panic Fears."

for the translation. Does this anecdote reveal an effect of structure? Alternatively, put another way, is the signifier missing where there is fear? The story begins with an anonymous narrator saying, "During all the years I have been living in this world, I have only three times been terrified."[6] He then goes on to recount the strange circumstances in which this fright arose.

The first time the narrator says he was traveling by trolley along a country road at dusk. Suddenly, something strange in the distance caught his attention: a little light shining in the bell tower of a village. There were no villagers around and it was impossible to climb up the tower because the entrance was nailed shut. That is when fear struck. "At first I thought that this was vexation at not being able to explain a simple phenomenon; but afterwards, when I suddenly turned away from the light in horror . . . it became clear that I was overcome with terror. . . . I was seized with a feeling of loneliness . . . as though I had been flung down against my will into this great hole full of shadows, where I was standing all alone with the belfry looking at me with its red eye."[7]

The second time, the character suddenly finds himself in front of "a huge black body" advancing down the train tracks, passing by him in a flash: "It was an ordinary goods truck. There was nothing peculiar about it in itself, but its appearance without an engine and in the night puzzled me. Where could it have come from and what force sent it flying so rapidly along the rails?"[8]

---

6. Anton Chekhov, "Panic Fears," in *The Schoolmistress and Other Stories*, vol. 9 of *The Tales of Chekhov*, trans. Constance Garnett (New York: The Ecco Press, 1986), p. 245.

7. Chekhov, "Panic Fears," pp. 245–246.

8. Chekhov, "Panic Fears," p. 248.

The enigma was soon solved: it was just a car that had come loose from the locomotive in a downgrade along the tracks. However, fright had been present.

On the third occasion, the narrator meets up with a dog upon returning from a hunt, a friendly dog that follows him, wagging its tail. This is not an unusual situation but the narrator could not figure out where the animal came from. As he walked along, the dog grew bolder. "Darkness was coming on, which completed my confusion, and every time the dog came up to me and hit me with his tail, like a coward I shut my eyes. The same thing happened as with the light in the belfry and the truck on the railway: I could not stand it and rushed away."[9]

Here, also, what is unexplainable takes on a different nuance since the narrator was at his own house with a guest, an old friend who had just lost his dog along the road.

The fright Chekhov describes, Lacan points out, is of a different order than anxiety. Indeed, there is no threat, no oppression; the subject is not "involved" in what is most intimate about himself, and "what affects him refers to the unknown that he faces." Furthermore, if we consider fear, as psychology and psychiatry do, as a response to a localizable object, the three examples provided by Chekhov's narrator fulfill the requirement. Fear appears in the face of an object. So where is the difference for Lacan if anxiety is not without an object?

The essential question here is that, though the objects in these cases are localizable, they did not pose any risk to the narrator. A faraway light, a loose freight car, and the unexpected company of a friendly dog. Although these are concrete objects, they are not dangerous, but there was fear. In addition, here is where the

9. Chekhov, "Panic Fears," p. 251.

danger-fear-flight triad begins to fail. To grasp what happened, we may start from fear, which unifies the three situations.

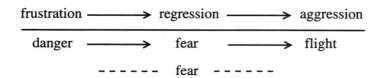

We still need to review one issue that is often mentioned as the "basis" for fear. It is often said that the subject fears because he believes the threatening object to be stronger than himself. That is why, the argument goes, children are frequently afraid. The explanation seems so simple that it finds instant believers. Children are afraid because they are small; as they grow, their fears will disappear. From this point of view, phobias would be interpreted as regressions, as so many manifestations of some type of childish behavior. We should point out that in the situations described by Chekhov, the characteristic of an object that was threatening and more powerful than the narrator was also absent. What is striking in the three accounts in the story is that the narrator did not find himself involved directly in a situation of physical or psychic risk. He does not find himself tense, oppressed, or implicated, which are features of anxiety. Indeed, he feels fear, fright. But this fright does not lead him to flee immediately but rather leads to a very distinct state: *paralysis*. Therefore, here we have another element that can be added as a counterpart to the trilogies.

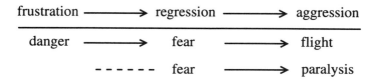

The narrator becomes speechless, overwhelmed, but in no way does he take flight after rationally assessing the forces related to a threat that does not even exist. The crucial point here is that the paralysis causes a crisis in the supposed adequation inherent to fear: the paralysis provokes an inadequate posture in the subject, a contradictory reaction caused by fright in the face of a strange object. But what kind of object is it?

What the three situations have in common, as we have pointed out, is a nondangerous object that causes fear by the mere fact of being *unknown:*

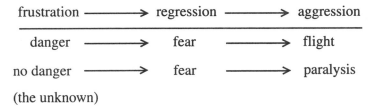

frustration ⟶ regression ⟶ aggression

danger ⟶ fear ⟶ flight

no danger ⟶ fear ⟶ paralysis

(the unknown)

Constant references to the unknown are easily found in the psychoanalytical milieu. Just as Chekhov's character tried to calm himself with the thought, "That phenomenon is only terrible because I don't understand it; everything we don't understand is mysterious,"[10] a good many analysts in Argentina—and in other latitudes—assert that one fears the unknown. This aphorism has been very widely disseminated. In addition, it is appropriate to respond with what we have demonstrated through the series of problems related to the uncanny. *Many times, what is most terrible for the subject is to fall into repetitions that are not deliberate; terror and the uncanny come from the fact that one repeats suddenly, and over and over again, something one cannot stop from reoccurring.* In the Chekhov story the unknown does ap-

---

10. Chekhov, "Panic Fears," p. 246.

pear to be pertinent but results in momentary paralysis. In any case, this demonstration undoes the assumption of "objective" adequation of fear, presented as the inverse of the inadequation related to anxiety. Lacan's argumentation is thus directed towards the persuasive construction of a parallel aphorism. *Starting from the basis that anxiety is not without an object, through an audacious inversion of the issue, he proposes the following: fear is without an object.* Or in a more attenuated form: *fear can be without an object.*

Doubtless, this proposition appears scandalous at first glance. Were the light in the bell tower, the freight car, and the dog not there? But we can agree that in none of the three objects, as we said, is it feasible to apprehend any characteristic that is the least bit dangerous: in themselves, they are innocuous. In the first case this circumstance is pathetically demonstrated when the unexplainable little light, in spite of the distance, becomes a frightful and paralyzing gaze. What Lacan is trying to bear witness to through his argumentation for the absurd, are the extremes that have been gone to in the effort to psychologically theorize what constitutes merely *a lived experience of the imaginary: the belief that anxiety has no object and that fear does.* This theorizing has the advantage of allowing one to think that from one state to the other there is the transition of an element that seems to involve locating the object. To find the object, thus, would be a form of defending oneself against anxiety. Hence, fear would provide a sort of relief to the anxiety-provoking situation.

Lacan's wise inversion of the terms used in classical psychology—and repeated by the other psychoanalysis—provides a link to lucid thinking about another problem that arose at the very beginning of Freud's undertakings: *actual neurosis.*

As will be recalled, the creator of psychoanalysis was confronted, at an early stage of his investigations, with *a series of psychopathological syndromes unlike the habitual psychoneuroses, which he ended up calling actual neuroses.* Unlike hysteria, then the major focus of his attention, Freud observed that these neuroses had their genesis in certain problems in the present, that is, inadequate sexual practices. In addition, actual neuroses would give way were such practices corrected. One of the most frequent types was *anxiety neurosis* that appeared intimately linked with *coitus interruptus*. From this, and in a manner that was perhaps daring given Freud's usual prudence in establishing unilinear causal relations, *he concluded that coitus interruptus determined anxiety neurosis.* Much direct criticism could apparently be expected from such an assertion. In this sense, every informed analyst wondered for a long time how it was possible for Freud to venture something so debatable, how he could have formulated such a risky hypothesis that begged the obvious question of what made the patient carry out this inadequate practice. Lacan, wisely, changed the way the question was formulated into: What is the nucleus of truth by which something insisted in Freud, so that he kept making endless reference to actual neurosis, and maintained, consequently, the causal relation between *coitus interruptus* and anxiety neurosis? This is the point to examine. What was Freud trying to emphasize? Specifically, that in the practice of *coitus interruptus* there is a defining knot that allowed him to think the articulation that occurs when the phallus falls, separated from the place of *jouissance*. In this condition, the subject ejaculates on his own, as it were. The status of an instrument that suddenly is separated from the condition of *jouissance* and acquires autonomy—by being put "out of play"—is thus transformed into one of the places that provokes anxiety.

Let us recall in this regard that for "human experience," *the phallus is more significant by its fall than its presence*, a fall that, obviously, also occurs in a "normal" orgasm and that is nothing but detumescence. In addition, as we have explained, nothing authorizes considering the hysteric, whose efforts are directed at avoiding confrontation with detumescence, as castrating. Rigorously speaking, *the "castrating" woman is the one who manages to be penetrated by a man, accepting the invitation of castration induced by the detumescence of the penis.* Because, otherwise, what would it be other than castration? The answers to this question are usually as common as they are naive: it is a fantasy, it is something symbolic, or even something imaginary. This is no more than a theoretical wild card that is rather rudimentary and confused. Lacan insists on affirming that the body is involved in castration, for it is the body that gives castration its support in the Real, since it is not about the mirror or signifiers. *The feces that separate and fall away from the body and the breast lost at the moment of weaning are thus constituted. With regard to castration, of course, no empirical organ is "cut"; nevertheless, castration has a real in detumescence.* It is the flaccidity of the penis that makes it possible to isolate the condition of the phallic object in its condition as missing object. That is why the issue should be conceived in a dialectical mode in which the phallic image, written as (φ), should be grasped in a necessary relation to its negativization: $(-\varphi)$.

This serves to highlight that this is not only about the empirical, full, and sharp presence of the *object a* in the manner of Saint Agatha, Saint Lucia, and Oedipus, but also *that anxiety is related, in this case, to the moment when* a *arises as lacking.* Thus a positivization of the object corresponds to negativization that finds its paradigm in detumescense in which the *object a* is carried by castration. It is for this reason that the phallus is the most difficult object to grasp, since its characteristic is to be an "obsolete object." Surely this disparity of the place of the phallus with regard to the other objects led Lacan to exclude it from a list he made of them when he returned to the issue the following year in *The Four Fundamental Concepts of Psychoanalysis*.[11]

One more relation marks the presence or nonpresence of the object. What was discussed about castration can help to clarify how fear can arise without a threatening object.

Let us consider now what Lacan develops under the name of *framework of the division of the subject by the signifier*. This may be an ostentatious name but it is appropriate in providing an idea of the relations in play between three phenomena and their functions that are already known to us.

The intention of the framework is to locate the relations between three fundamental experiences of the speaking being. The concepts in question are articulated on three floors:

Jouissance
Anxiety
Desire

In any case, this structure is the final reference of *the framework of the division of the subject by the signifier*. For purely didactic ends and because they shape concepts that have already been discussed, we are mentioning them before the terms to which they relate.

As will be recalled, *anxiety acts as a hinge between* jouissance *and desire*. It occupies the intermediate function—medium

---

11. In the case of the phallus it is not easy to distinguish $(-\varphi)$ from a, which is one of Lacan's objectives. We shall return to this in the following chapters.

rather than mediating—that impedes the other two from coming closer to one another. It is interposed as an edge phenomenon, as a gap onto the void (*béance*, in French), when the distance between them is shortened. The *Thing* that anxiety obeys—in the Lacanian sense of the concept—is what appears when the possibility of unification between desire and *jouissance* is attempted. There are several remarks to be made about this issue, not the least of which is distinguishing the different kinds of *jouissance*. However, that is not what we propose here. We are interested in *how the various "floors" go about structuring the signifier that divides the subject as three moments* (temps) *of operation.* First, we must place the terms in the following way:

		jouissance
		anxiety
		desire

So now, we have a framework with three rows and three columns. We shall analyze in detail the elements to be placed in the various spaces and the relations that arise among them. In the first space, the undivided, complete Other, A, arises.

A		*jouissance*
		anxiety
		desire

The position of the Other has logical preeminence. The subject, as we said, is made or constituted in this territory, which is far from being the emanation of an interiority or anything of that ilk. It is from this requisite that one can come to conceive of the emergence of a subject, which we enter initially in the framework as a simple S with no slash through it:

A	S	*jouissance*
		anxiety
		desire

Here, as we have already pointed out, we find Lacan making an ad hoc hypothesis. The subject, such as we apprehend it, is barred. In this sense, the S should have a slash through it: $. However, in *Seminar X*, as we have observed, there is one exception to this rule. *Here the S designates the presubject, or better yet, the mythical subject of* jouissance. Fundamentally, this name derives from the fact that in this place the protosubject finds itself subject to the Other under a condition where it would seem to be submerged in the *jouissance* of the Other— as an objective genitive. It is mythic because though it does not have "actual" existence, such an existence is a necessary presupposition as occurs in the *jouissance* of the A.

The protosubject—admitted as an unavoidable hypothesis— *gives rise to an irreducible remainder in arising from the place of the Other.* It does not emerge unscathed from this territory of division: "How many times does S go into A?" or $\frac{A}{S}$, but rather, it emerges having left a fragment, which falls away and is a remainder. In relation to this, what remains of the A, of the whole Other, will be the object *a:*

A	S	jouissance
a		anxiety
		desire

There is no need to reiterate the relations that link the object a with anxiety, as the framework indicates. *But here, this is what happens: when the division is made that flings out or splits off the remainder as object a, the Other that was complete becomes barred or divided through the operation of division.*

A	S	jouissance
a	A̸	anxiety
		desire

Consequently, *an Other with a lack, linked to anxiety, appears, which we should point out, in the final instance, is what should be called—as Lacan points out—the unconscious.* Now the especially interesting point can be seen in the following: the operation that flung out the object a as a remainder is written as derived—but not as a metaphor—of what was the mythic subject of *jouissance* at the beginning. But later, *it is from the place of the a—in its column—that the desiring subject arises, that is, barred,* since $ is equivalent to $\frac{a}{S}$:

A	S	jouissance
a	A̸	anxiety
$̸		desire

For now, the positions in the framework indicate that the barred subject and the object *a* are in the same area: in the field of the Other. On the contrary, on the side of the mythic subject of *jouissance*, the unconscious is to be found. This situation refers back to what we explained in Chapter 2, though now it has been articulated with three floors of reference, and it changes—as Lacan does—the order between *a* and S. Let us recall that if we write the lozenge between the barred subject and the object *a*, we find the known formula:

A	S	*jouissance*
a $\lozenge$ $\cancel{S}$	$\cancel{A}$	anxiety
		desire

That is, the phantasy is written on the side of the Other: ($\cancel{S}\lozenge a$). Further on, Lacan will attribute the following trajectory to the terms, in which the relations of determination between the desiring subject and the field of the Other can observed.

A ←——— S		*jouissance*
a →$\cancel{A}$		anxiety
$\cancel{S}$ ←		desire

This trajectory shows that the subject, in emerging through access to the Other, (A ← S), is the unconscious ($\cancel{A}$). From here, "all it can do is to make something of the A in which the metaphorical function matters less than the relation of a fall by which it will find itself related to *a*. *To desire, then, the Other, A, is never to desire more than a.*"

Once we have set up the terms this way, we should turn our attention to the situation of anxiety. This makes the relations it can have richer and much more complex. First, anxiety implies the appearance of the object *a* precisely where nothing was expected; it is where lack lacks. However, at the same time, one can think, when *jouissance* predominates, is there a larval form of anxiety? And in turn, when desire rules, is it not blocking anxiety? At the least, these are the questions that arise from observing the medium position of anxiety between the upper and lower level of the framework. To clarify these issues, a reading emphasizing the vertical relations of the terms over the horizontal ones should be used. In doing so, it should be pointed out that when Lacan refers to this chart as the framework of the subject divided by the signifier, he is not alluding to some historical occurrence that took place in some distant past when the genesis of this or that subject is presumed to have occurred. *The framework is not diachronic but rather seeks to point out the synchronic dimension of the division of the subject.* The relations considered in the framework continue to exist while the subject is sustained as such. *The framework allows Lacan to theorize two fundamental questions: masochism/sadism and the differences between the sexes.* Both questions have been continuously linked in the history of psychoanalysis according to a "theory," a neurotic theory that has judged sadism to be dominant in men and masochism in women. Without in any way subscribing to this blunder, we shall examine in a "cross-referencing" manner both ideas, while emphasizing Lacan's points regarding them.

The first question we should ask is why take for granted that masochism is necessarily the correlative inverse of sadism? Let us answer forthrightly: *if there is sadism and masochism, a cross comes into play with no symmetry to it.* In the seminar of

1966–1967, *La Logique du fantasme*, Lacan says the masochist *finds him- or herself identified with the object in the accentuated sense of the word and not "attenuated," as appears in some versions of the seminar in circulation.* Here the reference to the object is meant in a more colloquial sense, for example, the way hysterics usually make use of one of their habitual complaints about not being loved and that "they are treated like an object." *This object is one that is interchangeable with others and can be discarded.* This is what the masochist demands and great care must be taken to avoid believing that the masochist is someone who subjects him- or herself to the designs of the sadist. *The contrary actually occurs; the masochist demands to be treated badly*, sometimes in the extreme, as in the case of Leopold von Sacher-Masoch, who forced his wife, Wanda, to *sign contracts that were real commitments of servitude demanded by him as slave of his wife as master. Through these demands, the masochist tries to obtain a place in the Other, thereby reaching himself, like an abject wreck.* Reintroducing the theme of masochism through the example of the hysterical protagonist leads us to make some new points regarding what is known as feminine masochism, which, as we have said, is a masculine phantasy despite its name.

Feminine masochism is an interesting side issue in Freud's teaching, which opens the way to the intellection of the particularly intricate Lacanian issue of feminine *jouissance*. Of course, what *Seminar X* explores is very different from, and much less elaborated upon, than the passages on the same topic in *Seminar XX, On Feminine Sexuality, the Limits of Love and Knowledge. Encore*, where the "encore" in the title itself impels one to think about this issue. It can be translated as "even more" because *it is about the begging demand of the woman regarding* jouissance *through the use of a common word in the climax of orgasm*. By using the term *Encore, Lacan evokes a sense of complaint, petition, and impossibility*, thus initiating an illustrious treatment of the theme of feminine *jouissance*. We repeat that feminine masochism is imagined by the man as regards the position of the woman. When the masochist passes this to the act in its perverse variation, we find that the one who assumes this passive position of an interchangeable and abject object to be used is a man who supposes he occupies the position from whence the woman experiences *jouissance*. (We shall take this point up again later.)

However, the result of this demand to be an object, which can be found in latent form in what the masochist is asking for, is something else. What is it? Lacan observes *that it is not simply the* jouissance *of the Other—which is a phantasized intuition—but the anxiety of the Other*. The situation can thus be understood as follows: in spite of the masochist's servile appearance, he dictates to and imposes *his desire* on the Other and is basically seeking *the anxiety* of the Other, while *seeming* to require the abject position to open himself to the *jouissance* of the Other. *Through the contract, the masochist imposes more on the Other than on himself.* There is neither surrender nor any "do with me what you please" but rather, *the signifying articulation imposes precise rules of servitude with the aim that its fall awaken the anxiety in question.*

Now that we have examined the masochist side, we can ask what happens to the sadist, who, as we have said, is not his reverse. In appearance, the sadist seeks the anxiety of the Other; he openly mistreats others. But in fact—and Lacan discusses various excerpts from sadist texts in *Seminar X*, especially ones from *Juliette, The 120 Days of Sodom,* and, we add, from *Justine*—the sadist is seeking the object *a*, and finds it in what we could translate as "the skin of the idiot."[12] *If the sadist is aiming for the skin of the idiot, when he or she is in search of the object a, his or her objective at the height of the torment cannot be reduced to obtaining the anxiety of the Other. Rather, he or she is trying to get hold of that object a that is to some extent the reverse of the subject.* It is like "an inside-out glove that signals the feminine essence of the victim." Apparently, the skin is not what he is after but it acts as a meeting place, since the masochist is ceaselessly clamoring for letters to be inscribed or marked on him by his partner through flagellation. The tegument, the skin, however, is offered within certain limitations established in the perverse contract. And the sadist? Through the skin, he passes what is most hidden to the outside, thereby hiding the trait of his own anxiety.[13]

We say again: a game of counter-images was imagined between the masochist and the sadist. Lacan, on this point, contests the versions based on a classical Freudian focus, the one that supposes that sadism exists in principle and relegates masochism to a sadism against the person him- or herself, as well as the reverse that supposes that in the beginning, a self-destructive tendency rules that tries to play itself out through an outside support, where it is converted into sadism. But why did Lacan

---

12. Translator's note: the original French is *la peau du con*. In French, the expression to get somebody's skin, *avoir la peau de quelqu'un* means "to get them." The equivalent of the French slang term *un con* can be asshole in the sense of not very intelligent, though in French the denotation of the term is a woman's vagina.

13. We prefer this conceptualization from the class of March 13, 1963, to an earlier one in the class of January 16, 1963, since it reveals, in our judgment, a tentative and not so precise search for the differential formulations at stake. This is one of the seminar's merits; it is a work-in-progress and not finalized knowledge.

try to stress continuously the noncorrespondence, the non-reversibility between the position of the sadist and the masochist? First, he observes *that were this not so, one would be working with a logic of two terms in which anxiety would have to be inserted: latent in the masochist who tries to provoke it in the Other and also latent in the sadist, since the sadist veils it from himself through the encounter with skin.* Taking into account that *in Lacan, conceptualization tends to be carried out in a quaternary way,* the avoidance of opposing pairs acquires epistemological value since to use them—though they suit other disciplines such as linguistics—can easily lead to dichotomies such as projection/introjection (indispensable in Kleinism) or various pairs that attempt to account for an inside and an outside. Lacan says that projection is imaginary; introjection is symbolic. There is no symmetrical back and forth. Homologously then, the issue is not that the sadism/masochism "pair" is lacking a term for it to be understood correctly, but rather that two terms are missing. Lacan accounts for this when, arguing in favor of a quaternary way and of the functions of four terms or "squares," he says *that to go from one term to another "a quarter turn must be made involving no symmetry or invention."* This formulation strikingly anticipates what he will use to design for, and move between, the four discourses he discusses in the seminar of 1969–1970, *L'Envers de la psychanalyse.*

But this criticism of Freud, being partial, is unjust, since it is to him that we owe the precise intellection of the masochistic function, to which we shall now return, given its logical link with anxiety and the feminine.* Indeed, as regards feminine masochism, Freud points out that it is the most observable: "We have sufficient acquaintance with this kind of masochism in men (to whom, owing to the material at my command, I shall restrict my remarks), derived from masochistic—and therefore often impotent—subjects whose phantasies either terminate in an act of masturbation or represent a sexual satisfaction in themselves."[14] This brief passage provides various ideas. The first is Freud's empirical excuse in mentioning "the material available," when observation, like all observation, obeys a theoretical position. The second refers to the causal relationship between "masochistic persons" and impotence, which establishes a very valid clinical point. In the face of impotence, for a long time the other psychoanalysis maintained that a hysterical man is impotent like a hysterical woman is frigid. For us, this is another manifestation of the much-loved complementary reversibility, just another neurotic theory built from the Imaginary. Furthermore, the construction contains another attribute construed as obvious: if a man is impotent, he cannot penetrate; and if he cannot do so there might well be something inside the woman that terrorizes him. Here, for sure, is the argument about fear of the dentate vagina, and through this mythology everything is explained. Except that were the libido captured by a masochistic phantasy, the process of these imaginary theories would soon crumble. Fear of a dentate vagina and the negative of feminine hysteria are not what are in play here. *Feminine masochism determines impotence, since it locates in the phantasy the position regarding being tied up, bitten, whipped, denigrated, subjected to unconditional obedience, or punishment in whatever form.* All this can be "gotten" by the neurotic, though in a very relative manner, since the neurotic imagines it concomitantly to masturbation.

Feminine masochism does not necessarily lead the man to homosexual behavior but it does tend to restrict itself to the area of phan-

---

14. Sigmund Freud, "The Economic Problem of Masochism," vol. 19 of *The Standard Edition*, p. 161.

tasy, "separtited,"[15] *exogenous to the subject. It remains in the place of the Other, like a foreign formation, which is much more bizarre for the subject than a symptom.* The symptom can in the end be tolerated, theorized about, and accepted. The phantasy, on the other hand, is something that irrupts in the subject and whose confession is usually forced, shameful, and late. *The subject's sexual life is sunk down, rooted in what is so difficult to say.* We can ask ourselves, is the subject impotent? Is he a masturbator? However, let us not forget that in formulating these questions, we are being very descriptive at the most old-fashioned phenomenological level. In addition, based on this, nothing authorizes us to deduce that hysteria produces this state of "avoidance."

After listing some situations of the manifest content of the phantasies of feminine masochism, Freud adds, "Much more rarely are mutilations included in this content; when it does happen, great limitations are imposed on them. This is a decisive point since some theories posit that primary masochism is dominated by the death drive, the maximum expression of which is self-annihilation. However, the fact is that great care is taken to avoid mortiferous mutilation." In *La Sexualidad Perversa*, Michel de M'Uzan cites a pathetic case of masochistic perversion in which the phantasy is passed to the act. Though there is a physical risk and mutilations do occur, they are carried out under tight restrictions.

Freud goes on to dismantle the notion that any sort of regression takes place in masochism: "The obvious interpretation, and one easily arrived at, is that the masochist wants to be treated like a small and helpless child, but, particularly, like a naughty child. . . . But if one has an opportunity of studying cases in which

---

15. Translator's note: a portmanteau word from partition and separation: *sépartition*.

masochist phantasies have been especially richly elaborated, one quickly discovers that they place the subject in a characteristically female situation; they signify, that is, being castrated, or copulated with, or giving birth to a baby. For this reason I have called this form of masochism, *a potiori* as it were [i.e., on the basis of its extreme examples], the feminine form. . . ."[16] *It must be said that feminine masochism can only be spoken of in beings that are biologically men.* In this masochism, the subject, assuming the place of the object in an accentuated manner, ceaselessly clamors for the coming of the anxiety of the Other. And if this intellection also applies to the masochistic phantasy, this is because we speak of the Other as a transindividual instance, one that does not necessarily require incarnation in a partner.

The points we have just covered, as an effect of the teaching in *Seminar X*, allow one to understand how feminine masochism moves away from its usual meaning, which insists on attributing to the woman some sort of "essential" tendency to suffering. On the contrary, it is reduced to an issue concerning men. It is from this place that feminine circumstances may be presupposed, assumed as such, and made into phantasies by the neurotic when they are not put on the stage of perversion.

After elucidating the place of anxiety in the series of problems related to masochism and sadism—cross-referenced to the division of the sexes—Lacan continues outlining the relations drawn up in the framework of the division of the subject by the signifier. He thus goes on to explore a place where a primordial articulation is made, which we have yet to investigate.

16. Freud, "The Economic Problem of Masochism," p. 162.

6

Sublimation-Love, Jouissance, and Gut as Cause

The three levels of the framework of the division of the subject by the signifier are usually referred to in passages of *Seminar X* as *moments* or *times*. The use of these terms seems to suggest some—diachronic—relation of succession between the terms *jouissance*, anxiety, and desire. In any case, there is no evolution since no level is abandoned in order to have access to another: *these are not stages but rather a structure. The three moments are undoubtedly ordered by the relations among them in the framework.* Once each of the elements on each level has been elaborated, Lacan follows a tack that is perhaps surprising.

As we have seen, there remains an empty slot in the framework of the division of the subject by the signifier. Instead of placing something in it, as could be expected from what happened in the initial matricial framework, *Lacan invites us to expect a singular phenomenon: love.* He does this to observe in what way this very common experience is placed deductively in the triptych of *jouissance*, anxiety, and desire.

Love arises, then, as a fourth or quaternary term in a transitory manner out of what, up until now, has been a ternary structure. It does not occupy the empty slot in the framework, but rather the Lacanian strategy leads to processing it with another focus rather than just slotting it into a space arising from an operation of division. Suddenly, the itinerary of *Seminar X* takes an abrupt turn and proceeds by aphorisms.

The aphorisms in question can only be forceful and provoking, coming as they do from Lacan. Nevertheless, there is more to them than a wish to scandalize or play with words since *they are actual conceptual developments condensed into a single "kernel" proposition.* Easily remembered, unthinking repetition of them has made them into widely used topics. However, they must be broken into smaller pieces so the effect of the teaching they contain and are transmitting can be grasped. The first aphorism Lacan proposes regarding the place of love is the following: "*Only love allows* jouissance *to yield to desire.*"

Taking the developments in Chapters 2 and 3 into account, one can observe the function of *anxiety* as the medium element appearing on occasions *when the distance between desire and* jouissance *is shortened*, thereby threatening to nullify it. This aphorism accounts for the fact that in some manner *jouissance* can yield to desire. A certain explanation becomes possible, the one born from *the narcissistic phenomenon called love.*

When we refer to a narcissistic dimension inherent to love, we are talking about *constitutive deception*, as we discussed in Chapter 4: to love is to want to be loved. But does love also come from the place of the Other? If we turn to a founding text such as the Rome discourse, "The Function and Field of Speech and Language in Psychoanalysis," we find a suggestive maxim of La Rochefoucauld quoted by Lacan: *nobody would know what love is if he did not listen before talking about it.* This sharp sentence accounts for the *interlocutory dimension* that love necessarily possesses and from which there is no escape.

The forms, manners, and modalities whereby love arises and is established in the subject are inseparable from a certain discourse. *Love indicates culture, history, and hence, signifiers.* As a phenomenon, no matter how spontaneous it might seem and although it claims to be a sort of emanation from the inside blossoming in the most intimate part of the subject, love is a fact of the signifier and is made up of signifiers. It is not an ineffable gift, proper to the human or something that descends from a divine sphere. It is because the subject hears love spoken of that he or she feels it. He or she is capable of loving or knows how to love because of what has been heard. The mirror here is not enough. And Lacan adds a proposition to the first aphorism, which we could consider as subordinate to the preceding one: "... *(because) love is the sublimation of desire.*"

Love allows jouissance *to yield to desire by virtue of a relation with sublimation.* Lacan draws a precise boundary here. The metamorphosis at work in this aphorism thus needs clarification. *Desire is modified so that* jouissance *can yield to it.* But how does desire do this?

Clinical practice shows us that *desire is one thing and love another.* There are, obviously, sufficient seeds of conflict in this dichotomy that founds the speaking being. This is one of the constitutive disadjustments for which the subject has no other solution than to live with, trying generally to resolve it. *That love and desire are different from one another is not a phenomenon of the neurotic*; this is so for all speaking beings. It is a condition inherent to us, since to not ek-sist, the differentiation, the sublimation of one to the other, would not be feasible. And furthermore, sublimation can only take place in the order that founds the subject, that is, the signifier.

To summarize: according to these two Lacanian aphorisms, *jouissance* always yields to desire when desire changes into the condition called love, which occurs when there is sublimation. The viable transformation of desire into love is due to culture; this is absolutely congruent with various crucial developments of the teaching, which concerns us.

In principle and, apparently at least, the necessary finality of love is not physical union. Though this statement can be nuanced, it can be pointed out that *love is not directed at the body*. It seems to be able not to involve it. That's why sublimation appears as a relevant fact. From a Freudian point of view, it should be said that sublimation indicates a distancing of the immediate sexual object for the accomplishment of cultural aims. Due to this function, the passage from the search for satisfaction—both of which are so frustrating—to productive activities of a generic, anthropological order of "works" is made. However, this understanding of the concept is merely simplistic. The term *Sublimierung* denotes much more than the "displacement of sexual drives to socially valued ends." The merit for recovering this concept goes above all to Lacan—especially as of *Seminar VII, The Ethics of Psychoanalysis*—as followers of Freud (known generically as the "post-Freudians") had scorned it.

For the other psychoanalysis, sublimation is a process aimed at proper social adaptation. To fulfill a function properly, to concentrate adequately on a task, to make money, and other such things came to be the product—and examples of—effective sublimation. Nevertheless, the nucleus of sublimation has little to do with this condition of spurious behavioral happiness adapted to socially correct or, better yet, socially praised activity. Lacan's definition of the concept is an entire program in itself. *Sublima-*

tion consists, as he said, in "elevating the object to the dignity of the Thing."[1]

The definition provides the essential fact: *das Ding*, the grabbing and devouring Thing, which we mentioned in Chapter 2. Sublimation does not occur due to a necessity of social adaptation; it does not happen due to a tendency to live like a model citizen, carrying out methodical work in the best possible manner. *It implies more than the happy control or inhibition of drives and a jubilant turning towards production and creativity. It implies that one allows oneself to be caught by the Thing, not due to an act of will exactly but rather through an almost imperceptible advance in which the Thing continues to involve the subject using* jouissance *as the lure through which such a design promises to recover it.*

Sublimation absorbs the subject to a degree that can hardly be understood in terms of adaptation or routine. This can be observed by taking into account that the speaking being usually comes to forget or put off certain elementary needs on behalf of the sublimation marking him or her. This, as we shall see, should be emphasized in order to overcome one of the classical puzzles, which comes up in examining the theme of *creation*.

One of the customary formulations of this problem, around an issue usually referred to as "creative genius," is the following: taking cases that are known to be a combination of madness and artistic productivity, the question is asked, are these subjects artists because they are mad or despite their madness? Did they produce works of art in function of their "pathology"—in some cases very notorious—or did they manage to create thanks to being able to set their madness aside from their art?

---

1. Jacques Lacan, *The Ethics of Psychoanalysis*, trans. Dennis Porter (New York; Norton, 1992), p. 12.

Doubtless, there is no lack of famous artists to whom these questions may be applied. Now, sometimes creation is possible for artists because they apply all their psychic suffering to their art, and at other times the condition for productivity is based on the temporary suspension of the madness. Since it is impossible to formulate a general law in this regard, an all-encompassing answer is attempted: sometimes it happens this way and at other times that way. Finally, from this it is deduced that one must be broadminded in this matter and consider both routes, especially as the artistic terrain puts into play the supreme and intangible freedom inherent in arts. As can be seen from a plurality of cases, one passes to a doubtful and comfortable eclecticism that has nothing to say about the issue. The lack of an answer to this issue, nevertheless, comes from the fact that in this order of things the questions have been poorly formulated.

If sublimation is understood to be something other than effective social adaptation, as claimed by the other psychoanalysis through its tautological and incredible reference to "successful defenses," the possibility of developing efficiently a function or profession with adequate remuneration—along with the traditional method and habit of respectable work—is different from what Lacan was able to distill from Freud's notion of Sublimierung. Grasping the distinction is essential to understanding in what sense love can be a sublimation of desire, an incomprehensible proposition if we think in terms of a process of psychosocial adjustment. If there were one, how could someone literally be devoured by passionate love though his or her sexual drive finds itself inhibited and the union of bodies is left aside?

Lacan insisted, at various times in his teaching, on the relevance of the classical figure called *courtly love* (as in the case of the young homosexual woman for the *cocotte*). This modality of love consists in loving by foregoing at all times—as an act of "will"—physically approaching the loved one. It is a crucial phenomenon that is more than a mere historical curiosity about an oddly and well-assembled discourse, in spite of any contradictions imputable to it. In any case, the foregoing of physical union in courtly love must be examined more closely since the body is, in fact, at stake in some way. From the sublimation of desire, which is love, the body is filtered though veiled. *Although the body is decisive in the order of desire, since it is the condition of causality and peremptoriness, its presence in love is manifested in a more indirect, disdainful manner, including as an object to be avoided steadfastly or to be replaced by fetishized substitutions— as occurs in the discourse on courtly love.* The body here should be understood in the widest sense, if there is some degree of indefinition. Defining the terms more closely, the dimension of *a* should be taken into account, which always connotes the body under the label "partial object." The *a* is a fragment of the body, fallen away and unstuck, but body nonetheless and, as such, cause of desire.

Incorporating love as a fourth term—articulated with *jouissance*, anxiety, and desire—Lacan puts into act this system of components by threshing out once more astute clinical observations on the series of issues related to masculine and feminine sexuality: *the differentiation of sexualities,* for one. This is a very significant point, since misunderstandings about them abound, especially regarding the luring and much debated theme of feminine sexuality. We have already brought up in this seminar some of the crucial reexaminations of the cliché about "the castrating" or phallic woman. In the framework of the transitory four terms, *Lacan sets forth some interesting determinations about mankind in relation to sexuality and its articulation to castration.*

The man, in proposing himself as Eron, as desirer, "a-izes" the woman. This means that he transforms the woman into a since, in the end, to be a desiring being is to propose himself as lacking a, *opening in this way "the door to the* jouissance *of his being."* Now, what occurs when the man "*a*-izes" the woman? First, this situation supposes one is located on the second level of the framework of the division of the subject by the signifier, which is the level relating the object *a* and the Other to lack and anxiety. And here we find a key: "*a-izing*" *the woman provokes her anxiety.* This does not imply an irreversible course but refers to those moments in which the man puts the woman systematically in the place of the fragment of himself that has fallen away, come away, and that, obviously, he intends to reclaim. If this is about making the object *a* present—remember, anxiety is not without . . . an object—surely the object *a* acts as a substitute for provoking anxiety: *a*-izing can only bring about or set off the anxiety of the Other. However, since I claim to be *Eromenós* (loving), I decline that position, granting that love sublimation allows *jouissance* to yield to desire. *But if the man desires to "a-ize" the woman, the question that arises is, what does she want?*

Lacan answers the questions about feminine desire homologically to what has been pointed out about the masculine phantasy known as feminine masochism. He says in this regard that the woman has, correlatively, another phantasy: the myth of Don Juan.

Seminar X wisely points out that the myth of Don Juan is a phantasy, a feminine "dream." Lacan is also leveling a kind of criticism at the other psychoanalysis, which insists on believing that Don Juan refers to repressed masculine homosexuality, since it tells the story of a man who possesses "all" the women, but that at a "deeper level" (what astute analysts, to never stop perceiving something at a "deeper level"!) Don Juan is a homosexual who does not assume his homosexuality. Of course, Lacan obviates this "interpretation." He limits himself to specifying that it is a woman's phantasy. Therefore, in addition to canceling speculation about a supposed homosexuality of the mythic character, he clears the way for another type of development. He makes it clear that Don Juan is the one who can protect against the possibility of the loss of phallic value, since he sustains it on a constant basis, and no woman can take it from him. It is this that "feminizes" Don Juan from the woman's point of view. The character indicates the condition of an always present phallus (φ). So now, what does a woman want?

This question inevitably reminds us of Freud's famous question about the desire of the woman, which includes the reference to the unknown Dark Continent of feminine sexuality. Lacan answers Freud's concern this way: *the woman wants to experience* jouissance *through the man; she wants his* jouissance; *she wants to get off on his* jouissance. She wants his being and that is how she arouses his anxiety. Why? Because she can only get it by castrating him, since the only desire that can be realized implies castration. This is what the concept of *penis-neid*—penis envy—accounts for *and we should point out that this is not a conceptualization of femininity which shows penis envy deriving from anatomical lack.* By this twist, Lacan changes the idea that the woman starts from this lack, which would convert her into a deprived being. *It's worth recalling, as Lacan does, that he did not assert that the Real is full; he maintained that the Real lacks nothing even though "holes abound like ants" in the Real, or even if the Real is made empty.* Therefore, the body of the woman, insofar as Real, lacks nothing. Whoever asserts this any other way is neuroticizing the theory; indeed, from his or her own neurosis, the person conceives of the woman as lacking something, which he or she then relates to an infantile sexual theory, and then this kind of conception can even be decorated with a symbolic perspective indicating that some kind of elaboration has taken place, which adds insult to injury. This point is really crucial, as can be seen when these kinds of theories are related to what is said in some of the points in *Leonardo da Vinci and a Memory of His Childhood*, where Freud makes some lucid points related to cognition that have little or nothing to do with evolutionary psychology.[2] But we shall take that up in the next chapter.

We were saying that the woman lacks nothing in the Real. In support of this, we shall describe more carefully the way Lacan accentuates Freud's presentation of this issue. In summary, one can say that Freud considers that the woman starts from the castration complex when she is a child inasmuch as she does not "really" have the phallus. That is to say, from the point of view of her infantile sexual theory, regarding the universal premise of the phallus, she discovers she is lacking it. Everyone should have it and she lacks it; therefore, something has happened. That is why the first relation the girl articulates is to demand the mother give her what she lacks. Obviously, this demand cannot be met, so the demand is then made of the father, who also does not have it. This is how the passage from castration to Oedipus takes place in an inverse trajectory to that of the man's, who at first crosses the oedipal relation, which is overcome—insofar as possible and with the limitations of the case—through the castration complex. In short, this relation in the case of the man and woman follows opposite paths: with the girl, first there is castration and then Oedipus; and with the boy, first there is Oedipus and then castration. Focusing on this notion from the field of the Other, Lacan points out—and this is very interesting as he establishes a direct tie to psychoanalytical practice—that *the woman has an easier time with regard to the*

---

2. Sigmund Freud, *Leonardo da Vinci and a Memory of His Childhood*, vol. 11 of *The Standard Edition*, pp. 59–138.

position of analyst. This is not about biological sex but about positioning oneself in a certain manner with regard to the desire of the Other. Lacan points out that the woman finds herself less articulated to desire than the man. *Thus, she is more open to* jouissance. *And this is due to the difference in the path she has followed towards the phallus and castration.*

Consequently, the man does not take up the phallic value in relation to an initial search for it on the side of the mother but in principle finds himself with the phallic image (φ), incarnated in his penis. Now we shall examine how the phallic image can be negativized (-φ). The constant reference by the man to the establishment of castration as requisite for the link to the object determines that men find themselves in a more dependent position in relation to the issue of desire, which limits their being open to *jouissance*. It is not by chance that at the first level of the framework the letters are written without a slash through them. This indicates that there is not the same position inherent to the subject of desire. *The barring—which shows a specific "experience of the slash" (division)—is directly related to the negative sign "−" that marks the phallic image as it accounts for castration.* Both speak of a lack and of "being worked on." Insofar as every subject is the subject of desire, it can only be so because it has fallen from the position of sustaining the phallic image. In our graph of anxiety, this is viewed in the following manner:

$$\mathcal{S} \longleftarrow \text{anxiety} \longleftarrow (-\varphi)$$

Given the course the man follows, one can ask: *From where does the phallus come to the woman?* The answer is: *from the Other, as an addition.* This means that the woman finds herself in a second-degree relation to the phallus, since she is not confronted with the peremptoriness of the fall of the phallic image, of its negativization—castration—in order to accede to the order of desire. *The phallus comes to her through the desire brought from the Other.* This is how we understand that the woman dominates *jouissance* to a greater extent at the same time that she is attentive to the phallic contribution from the Other; that is how she can be open to her desire. This disposition, this greater sensitivity to the desire of the Other, can be translated into listening, and this is how the relation of the woman with the place of the analyst is easier. *However, we must be prudent here and not oversimplify by deducing from this sensibility that a woman is more inclined to be a better analyst than a man.* This ease can be transformed into a source of unquenchable raving. Observing certain developments of women analysts who are involved in the other psychoanalysis confirms this. These analysts tend to base their analyses on countertransference, that is, on what they "feel" when faced with their analysands. We need not recall here the innumerable mistakes this has given rise to. That is *why Lacan said once that women could be the best analysts when they are not the worst ones.* We point out the greater ease for women, which does continue to provide incentive to them. However, the risk of falling into the abyss is always in play since the constitutive limitation of desire, as in men analysts, is not as great a risk for them. This limitation, as we were saying, produces a greater restrictive effect but also functions as a barrier of containment against open-ended empathy.

At this point, we think it necessary to introduce some passages from Ovid's *The Metamorphoses* that Lacan goes into in *Seminar X*, as they present some decisive issues for psychoanalysis. What interests him most is the account in the fourth passage of Book III in which Juno blinds Tiresias. This passage and the surrounding ones are a crucial part of the text for us; indeed, immediately after this account, Ovid refers to the most widely known version of the Narcissus story. The Narcissus myth gives rise to one of the founding myths of psychoanalysis in Freud's explicit proposal.[3] In an earlier work, we had the opportunity to point out the relevance of the Tiresias episode from Ovid's *Metamorphoses* as this character also plays a defining role in the story of Oedipus, another founding myth.[4]

As the famous Sophoclean tragedy recounts, Tiresias was the blind seer who led the investigation into the plague assailing Thebes and knew who was responsible for the disgrace. Before Tiresias knew what happened with Oedipus, he had suffered the mandates of the gods, as explained in Ovid's work.

Tiresias was the wisest of all men even before being blinded by a wrathful Juno. His wisdom included knowing about feminine *jouissance*, to which he had access immediately after a strange occurrence. Let us see how his experience accounts for what Lacan set forth: *the dominance of desire in the man and* jouissance *in the woman*. Here is Ovid's account:

> Now while these things were happening on the earth by the decrees of fate, when the cradle of Bacchus, twice born, was safe, it chanced that Jove (as the story goes), while warmed with wine, put care aside and bandied good-humored jests with Juno in an idle hour. "I maintain," said he, "that your pleasure in love is greater than that which we enjoy." She held the opposite view. And so they decided to ask the judgement of the wise Tiresias. He knew both sides of love. For once, with a blow of his staff he had outraged two huge serpents mating in the green forest; and, wonderful to relate,

---

3. It is explicit because Lacan reads the account of the assassination of the Father—introduced in *Totem and Taboo*—as a mythical production that, since Freud, founds psychoanalysis. Even more, Lacan carries out an operation homologous to Freud's; he retro-founds it in the work of the creator of psychoanalysis as the latter did in Greek mythology.

4. Roberto Harari, "Eco de Narciso," *Del corpus freudo-lacaniano* (Buenos Aires: Trieb, 1981), pp. 103–111.

from man he was changed into a woman, and in that form spent seven years. In the eighth year he saw the same serpents again and said: "Since in striking you there is such magic power as to change the nature of the giver of the blow, now will I strike you once again." So saying, he struck the serpents and his former state was restored and he became as he had been born. He therefore, being asked to arbitrate the playful dispute of the gods, took sides with Jove. Saturnia, they say, grieved more deeply than she should and than the issue warranted, and condemned the arbitrator to perpetual blindness. But the Almighty Father (for no god may undo what another god has done) in return for his loss of sight gave Tiresias the power to know the future, lightening the penalty by the honour.[5]

Lacan focuses—as an apologue—on this episode to point out that "*those that experience* jouissance *are women.*" In *Seminar XX, On Feminine Sexuality, the Limits of Love and Knowledge. Encore,* this characterization is ratified by the introduction of the notion of *supplementary* jouissance: *a strictly feminine* jouissance—*not easily attainable—located beyond the phallic.*

In *Seminar X*, another very valuable reference is provided: it refers, once more, to castration inscribed as $(-\varphi)$, and its articulation with the object *a*. One can observe here to what extent concepts are not sharply separated from one another. At times (and other authors such as M. Marini[6] agree here) the places and correlates illustrated by *a* and by $(-\varphi)$ are not clearly distinguished. In spite of this sporadic indefinition, there is one passage in the seminar where a schema is drawn that distinguishes them. *In it, both functions reside in two different vases with the same design:*

---

5. Ovid, *Metamorphoses* (Loeb Classical Library 1994), pp. 147–149.
6. Marcelle Marini, *Lacan* (Paris: Pierre Belfond, 1986), pp. 197–198.

Lacan is using this illustration to show what happens when we name anxiety. First, anxiety is not without an object. And this implies—as was noted in Chapter 3—that *a* covers the lack bounded or marked off by (-φ), pouring the content from one vase to the other. In the ensuing semiplenitude, the phenomenon of anxiety cannot fail to appear. He calls the vase on the left primordial or original castration, a new name in terms of Freud. Under these circumstances, *what the subject desires when the a is poured—the object that should not, but does, nevertheless, appear—is to restitute castration*; hence, the subject sustains both the emptiness of the vase and the edge around the opening (-φ). It should be noted that when the vase encounters the poured *a*, it is half empty and half full. *The issue is not only the pouring, but also the transfiguration that is anxiety-provoking.* To account for this, Lacan makes his example more complex by modifying the edge topologically. In this sense, he proposes that we imagine that the edge of the vase (-φ), which, as we know, is round, be transfigured by uniting "two opposite points on its surfaces by turning over the edges." What do you get? *As in the Moebius strip, the internal side becomes the external one without crossing the edge.* He thus shows in graphic form how the *a* comes from elsewhere, from the desire of the Other. *This continuity, he assures us, is what characterizes anxiety.* What is the purpose of twisting the edge in this strange manner? It is highly useful in understanding that anxiety is not—as one might naively think—exclusively an internal phenomenon since the twist shows the difficulty in distinguishing inside from outside. So where is anxiety "located"? Is it inside or outside? We agree that it is located in the ego but it is also related, as to its very constitution, to the object *a*, to which no imaginary interiority can be feasibly attributed. *Structurally speaking, anxiety—Real—suspends the functioning of the imaginary mapping that intuitively recognizes the difference between an inside and an outside.* In this context, Lacan once more locates anxiety—beyond the apologue—as an edge phenomenon, citing Imre Hermann as the pioneer in the elucidation of such phenomena.

Through the small vases, Lacan considers the difference that should be made between lack and possible fullness, or semi-fullness, rigorously speaking. In Chapter 3 we made a very simple drawing of the issue between (-φ) and *a*, using what we called the "electric light bulb" schema.

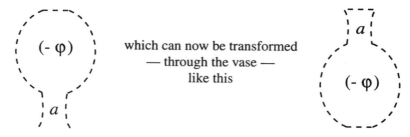

which can now be transformed
— through the vase —
like this

Considering what we have said about the vase, the idea is to account for greater difficulties in the relation between this lack and what blocks it "badly." This adverb needs to be changed slightly, since the blocking cannot occur without an unpleasant effect: anxiety. In addition, we repeat, Lacan reasserts that, when one is faced with anxiety, desire seeks to return to "primary castration." Obviously, this concept can appear surprising and strange at first: How can someone seek castration? If we understand that the person seeking castration is not doing so because he or she is a masochist or a transsexual—that he or she is looking to inscribe it in the body—and that the person does so through a passing to the act with the ablation of his or her genitals, it is feasible to point out that the *search fulfills a condition of normalization. It is about preserving lack.*

Lacan focuses on the necessity of preserving lack—unlike what a good many official psychoanalysts maintain with their efforts to make analysands "accept lack" in the sense of accepting "realistic" limitations—using the example of *circumcision,* echoes of which are often heard in psychoanalysis. *This practice corresponds to a strict marking of lack and sifting of* a. One of the lamentable readings of this ritual—and entire books have been devoted to this—interprets it as an aggressive action, which is castrating in the literal sense of the word as ablation of the flesh. From this, these essayists have decided that circumcision is traumatic, bad, and pathogenic for the helpless subject undergoing it. In summary, it is an inadmissible aggression and execrable from beginning to end. Ideas on the issue usually outline various reasons to make this practice into an anathema that in itself is viewed as highly damaging.

Regarding the main reading of this issue within the psychoanalytical movement, Lacan points out that this act is not only a sort of precept to obey—and in this sense has a normalizing influence that links one generation to the next in a calming manner—but it also connotes a crucial dimension involving the relation that the subject has with the field of the Other through a small fragment of flesh—*a*—that opens the issue to a situation beyond what is normative; circumcision is not merely the seal of a pact, given that it is exercised on the real that is the body, from which the foreskin falls away. Therefore, Lacan refutes interpretations that "analyze" the aggressivity latent in circumcision.

Very often analysands, in function of "psychoanalytically inspired" mass media messages try to liberate themselves in every conceivable manner from the unconscious pact linking them to their culture—to the historicity of the Other—which invites them to circumcise their children. They imagine that they should not do it because some expert said not to, in the name of psycho-analysis. In these cases, an analyst may think after all, why not stop doing this? In this way a disagreeable moment can be avoided by the son of an analysand; congratulations! Everything would be perfect if one did not observe in these cases that what was not consummated as a pact threatens the relation continuously, dis-rupting the assuming of the place of the father and/or the mother as much as of the son. The son, as we see in clinical practice, re-mains conflictual in cases such as these, "bolted into" the place of the remainder or avoided leftover.

Lacan works on the issue of circumcision in an exemplary manner, using a quote from the Bible. One passage from the Book of Jeremiah 9:24–25 has attracted and greatly perplexed transla-tors. The crucial part of the Hebrew text, according to the explana-tion in *Seminar X*, should be translated as: "I shall punish all those who are circumcised in their foreskins." This is a paradoxical phrase that translators, even the best ones, have tried to change. The translation in French is, "I shall act with rigor against all those who are circumcised in the manner of the uncircumcised," which has impeccable logic although it in no way reflects the original text.[7] The enigmatic phrase "I shall punish all those who are circumcised in their foreskins" contains, doubtless, something strange. What does it mean to characterize the presence of the foreskin as crucial? In addition, is not a man who is circumcised

---

7. Translator's note: compare the Authorized Version: "I will punish all them which are circumcised with the uncircumcised."

so described because his foreskin has been cut off? What is perhaps the most authoritative version in Spanish, from the *Biblia de Jerusalén* says, "There are days coming—oracle of Yahweh—in which I must visit all those who are circumcised in their flesh alone. . . ."[8] In this manner, it seems that the condition of circumcision can either go beyond the merely carnal or be limited to it. The text goes on: "Egypt, and Judah, and Edom, and the children of Ammon, and Moab, and all that are in the utmost corners, that dwell in the wilderness. For all these nations are uncircumcised, and all the house of Israel are uncircumcised in heart."[9] As can be seen, in this Spanish version the strangeness of the original text has also been lost, although the suggestive and allegorical formula "uncircumcised in the heart" has been maintained. *The Bible's teaching here is about the essential separation of a certain part—a fundamental part—of the body that is beyond the foreskin. Therefore, it is alluding to a function that forms a symbolic relation in the body itself, from which one part is alienated.* What Lacan notes is that *even in the figure that is presumably directed towards the spiritual, the reference to the body is maintained.*

Now the issue of being uncircumcised "in heart" should be taken literally. In order to point out this notion, Lacan uses Shakespeare's *Merchant of Venice*. The protagonist, Shylock, demands a pound of flesh from Antonio in payment for breach of contract. From his own flesh, extracted from the area closest to the heart. "The pound of flesh" is an obvious allusion to the object *a* and one of the definitions Lacan gave of it, which in this case is incarnated in the organ, through an ages-old cultural tradition—in the play—which we call the seat of love and for Semites

---

8. Translator's note: compare the New Revised Standard Edition: "I will attend to all those who are circumcised only in the foreskin."

9. Authorized Version, Jeremiah 9:26.

is the source of intelligence. In Shakespeare's passage—which also shows a certain anti-Semitic ideology through the stereotypical portrayal of a Jew—Shylock is offered substantial material payment in compensation for the breach. He obstinately holds out for the pound of flesh because, as Lacan points out, "it is always with our flesh that we must pay off the debt." This difficult matter is solved when Portia enters, dressed as a Doctor of Law, and after a long dialogue, sets out this dilemma:

> This bond doth give thee here no jot of blood;
> The words expressly are "*a pound of flesh*";
> But, in the cutting it, if thou dost shed
> One drop of Christian blood, thy lands and goods
> Are, by the laws of Venice, confiscate
> Unto the state of Venice.[10]

In fact, Portia had read the contract or bond in a more literal manner than Shylock, which impeded the mutilation of Antonio. The least that can be said of this passage is that it revolves around an entire dialectic about gifts and debts, showing how the *a* enters into a kind of interchange, in this case, restrained by the letter, which impedes the perforation. Shakespeare, with exemplary sharpness, uses the metaphor *strictu sensu* and not for its referential or figurative value. *Shylock wants the heart as an organ of the body. From this point of view, the* a *is inscribed no longer in the sublimatory dimension of love but rather in the search for the body*, as the evident presentification of what Lacan daringly calls the "*gut as cause*," an expression that seems the kind Quevedo would use given the creative shock created between two widely distant semantic fields. Indeed, something so seemingly metaphysical as *the cause* appears linked to the intestinal. And, in this sense, we should recall how Lacan praisingly called Melanie Klein

---

10. *The Merchant of Venice* 4.1.75.

"*la tripera*,"[11] due to her decided emphasis on phantasy life over the ego. This point leads us to another similar one in the seminar.

Lacan's intention in this part of *L'Angoisse* is to draw a distinction between *objectivity* and *objectality*. The object *a*, that pound of flesh linked to the heart, has an obvious relation to the order of desire, in its reference to the body. In the framework of the division of the subject by the signifier, we write the link in the following manner:

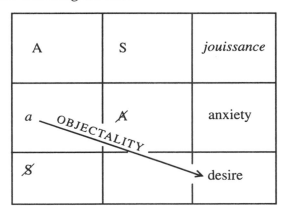

Lacan calls this a relation of objectality, which, as the "correlate of a *pathos* of the cut" must be distinguished from objectivity, which constitutes the self-proclaimed intention, at the very least, of the search within Western scientific analytical thinking. Lacan produces another aphorism in this regard: "*Something is omitted in the consideration of knowledge.*" What is omitted? To answer the question, he draws another audacious arc: what is omitted is "the desire, which gives life to the function of knowledge." But does this imply psychological essentialism? That is what he is seeking to evade, by writing in the structure. Thus, *each time the cause is*

---

11. Translator's note: "she who handles tripe or guts."

invoked, it is because it constitutes the blind spot in the function of this knowledge. As we said earlier, *the cause always accounts for a blank, an absence, a lost link.* One example we find in *Seminar XI* mentions the impact of the moon on the tides. This is doubtless an "objective" fact, for which a precise law can be established. However, if the changes in the tides are an *effect* of the moon, what is the cause by which the moon has an impact on the tides? Here we run into an element that has already been mentioned: an opening, a blank, and an absence, something that is omitted. Confiding in the Enlightenment ideal that credits science with progress, one could naively assert that the void will be filled in the future; but the space opened by the cause—and here we find Lacan's daring course—is related to the object *a*, that is, the object cause of desire in objectality, which unites what is irreducible in the effect of the structure, which is neither historical, nor "progress." Thus, the *a* will also see itself linked to objectivity, which articulates in a logically formal manner *"that part of our flesh"*:

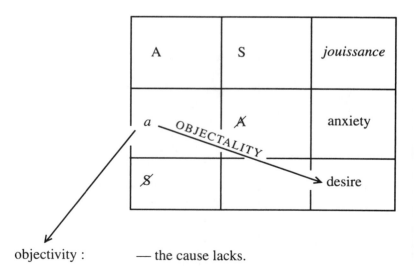

objectivity :   — the cause lacks.

In relation to presumed and scientific knowledge that is founded, the condition of objectivity should at least be placed between quotation marks, demonstrating that the cause is absent from it insofar as the authentic substratum of its function has been lost. *With this, these laws can be established and events can be foreseen in function of them; nevertheless, the dimension of cause finds itself obscured to the greatest possible extent.* There the omission of knowledge rules in "objectivity" itself:

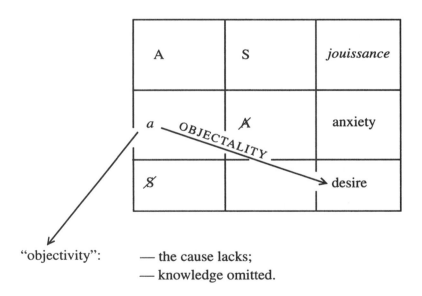

"objectivity":   — the cause lacks;
                  — knowledge omitted.

This is one of those moments where the way the framework of the division of the subject by the signifier has an impact on the order conventionally known as "intellectual" may be more clearly appreciated, since up until now it seemed that we were dealing with functions inherent in what psychology calls *affects*. However, it is clear that Lacan's proposal evades the usual point of view, which claims feelings distort or put obstacles in the way of thinking. Here a condition of structure is being accounted for: *the a marks an irreversible dimension from which the theme of possible knowledge is derived.* It marks something that in principle is regarded by Lacan as Real, as something that always returns to the same place. He articulates to the Real, as "a structural necessity," that the relation of the "subject to the signifier necessitates the structuring of desire in the phantasy." Why have I included this reminder here? To teach that the phantasy itself comprises knowledge, that is to say that there is already knowledge in the phantasy. But what kind? Before elucidating this issue, let us take note of what the framework states. In this way, the field now also covers, through the lozenge, the desiring subject, writing the phantasy as what sustains knowledge.

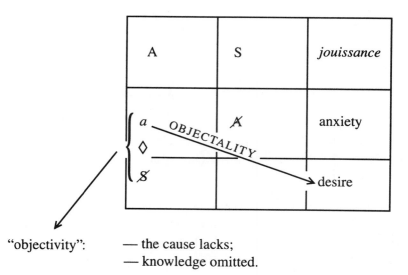

"objectivity":   — the cause lacks;
                  — knowledge omitted.

Freud's postulation allows us to conceive, as we have demonstrated, that it is not because it is scientific that it is possible to distinguish a theory from another that is an infantile sexual one. It belongs to the same order. If its structure is unveiled, they cannot be distinguished from one another. And what is the former? None other than the phantasy.

Here we propose another turn of the screw on the issue. When the cause lacks, what is this due to?

To answer the question *we must point out a particularity of the functioning of the phantasy. It reveals a syncope, temporally characterizable, of the object a—cause of desire—which at a particular phase is erased and disappears.* It is not noticed because it fades away. *The a, hidden, syncopated, accounts for the function of the cause.* What cause are we talking about here? "The cause lacks" signifies that the *a* is lacking insofar as it has undergone aphanisis. *The disappearance of the object cause of desire in the dialectic of the phantasy is what makes "objectivity" always approximate, and causes certainty to be provided only by anxiety.*

Another Lacanian articulation is linked to this: "The subject, by speaking, is implied in his or her own body through the fact of speaking. The root of knowledge is this compromise of his or her body." In the last instance, it is to this that knowledge refers. Now we can add a drawing in which the body is installed—according to this fact—within the perimeter of speech based on an elementary logic of classes. Thus, via the phantasy, the subject possesses whatever knowledge is, which is feasible insofar as the body is "wrapped" in speech; this, in turn, is what the fantasy bears witness to: those things that it knows.

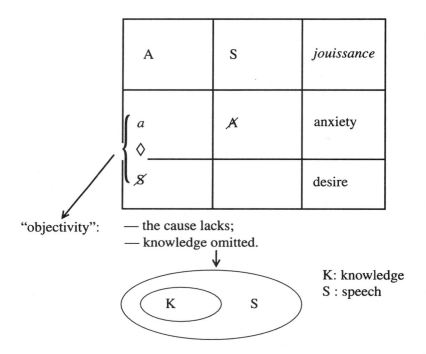

Now the question is, which body are we talking about when we say that it is "covered" or compromised by speech and that knowledge accounts for this body? To answer this question implies refocusing the issue of the body in relation to the object *a*, at the level of the processing it undergoes in the function of the phantasy. So, given that *the fantasy includes this body fragment*, which is the incarnation of the object *a* itself—whether it be called a pound of flesh, foreskin, or something similar—its articulation in the framework is the following:

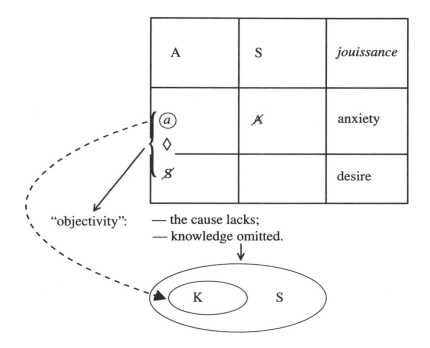

What Lacan encounters in elucidating the issue arising from the body in relation to the object cause of desire is what, in *Seminar X*, he calls *floors in the constitution of the object* a, which we will analyze later. For now, suffice it to say that starting from the original list of objects described by Freud—the oral object of the breast, the anal one of feces, and the (negativized) phallic one—two other markedly hallucinatory ones are added. The first is what Lacan refers to here as *the visual or spatial level*, which he would later call *the gaze* in *The Four Fundamental Concepts of Psychoanalysis*. He articulates another to this one, which he "extracts" from Kant's *categorical imperative*. It has to do with *the level that accounts for—according to Freud's initial proposal—the*

action of the superego as insisting in an unnamable, unchallenge-
able way on the carrying out of a mandate that is impossible to ful-
fill, a level that, as object a, is incarnated in the voice.

It is especially significant to end this chapter in referring to
the superego, since, if we add this to what has been said about
the feminine condition, a problem can surface in linking this
concept to the woman concerning her greater availability for
jouissance. Also, we should remember how Freud's argument
tends toward detecting *less superego impact on the woman.* The
superego in women does not appear like a formation that is
opposed to the ego (which is how it is generally located in the
man). It would even be possible to position these elements in
the following way: *superego, feminine.* That way we would account for the actual implication of the terms. This condition
refers to the *jouissance* domination we have just mentioned,
since the superego is what gives the order to experience *jouissance*
in accordance with the categorical imperative. *It commands,*
"*Experience* jouissance *all the time!*" It is precisely in this sense
that the order is impossible to fulfill. Whether its standards are
more or less strict has no bearing on the fact that the moral
precepts the superego dictates can be very restrictive and punishing. Its inscriptions involve values of consensus, the normative abruptness that is tautologically imaginary and not the
ultimate upholding of some legality or other, which is simply,
"I order you to experience *jouissance* ceaselessly," and at a
maximum level, of course.

In terms of structure, the superego insists in only one way,
as an imperative order, to experience *jouissance.* Since this is so,
it does not indicate an incitement to pleasure; however, it is not about
a compulsion for suffering either, as some have suggested on several occasions. The order insists on maintaining the tension of
the psychic apparatus without pointing to an end to the tension;

this would be an aim in keeping with the pleasure principle. To conclude, let us return to the issue of the woman.

In *Seminar XX*, Lacan clearly refers to the woman in his notation as divided. In this division, one part is directed to *the signifier of the lack in the Other* S(Å) and the other towards the *symbolic phallus* (Φ):

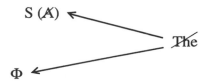

An aside on Lacan's notation to designate the woman. He writes "T̶h̶e woman," barring the writing of the definite article, which can be read as the already famous aphorism, *"The woman does not exist."* And that is how it is: *there is no sole essence, no universalization of femininity that is repeated in all women.* Returning to this T̶h̶e we can point out that one of the vectors, the one going from the woman to the symbolic phallus, is crossed by another relation, coming from the left, masculine side "of failure of the sexual relation":

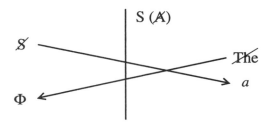

To summarize: *the non-ek-sistence of the woman as essence is related to the fact of the double definition of the woman, that is, in relation to the signifier of the lack in the Other and to the sym-*

bolic phallus. This partition can be found in clinical cases in various ways. One of the most frequent is the complaint by women analysands about the difficulty of reconciling two orders, as the ones of home and work can be, while "the man only has to take care of one thing." Though this jump from theory to analytical listening can seem abrupt, what the analyst hears is that *the woman claims and complains that she is divided*. Thus, the woman often faces the impossibility of "letting down her guard" or being able to have access to some kind of "stable" homeostasis, which reduces tension. Now, from the place of the man, a relation between the desiring subject and the object *a* is made, sought in the field of T̶h̶e a-*ized* woman. *The line starting at $ in fact designates the inevitable a-izing of the woman by the man, inscribed through the phantasy, the notation of which it writes*. The line that unites the barred subject with the *a* can only shield the man more in regard to *jouissance*, constraining the opening that in T̶h̶e woman appears as constitutive.

7

Knowledge Drive? The Graph of the Floors of a

In the last chapter, we quoted an elementary schema, related to the framework of the division of the subject by the signifier, which requires greater theoretical justification. We can now present a simplified version of that diagram in the form of two concentric circles. The outside circle refers to speech while the inside one illustrates the impact of speech on the body:

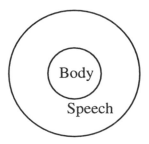

The schema indicates that the body is included, inscribed as such, in the function of speech. This general fact has extremely significant consequences on psychoanalytical theory and practice. In the first place, *the schema determines that the biological body is not the terrain of psychoanalytical practice.* Although anatomy is not foreign to us, as we shall explain in this chapter, biology is not the field where psychoanalysis operates. The body psychoanalysis deals with is *the body inscribed in speech.* This is not the body phenomenologists dissect in detail through the grid of lived experience. Several major texts, including the often-quoted *Phenomenology of Perception* by Maurice Merleau-Ponty, consider the body as a unit, a globality or general structure in that the whole presence of the body is involved in perception. And although this seems to overcome mind–body dualism, it makes the body into a "corporealized soul." One of the principal differences between psychoanalysis and phenomenology centers on this issue. Whereas psychoanalysis starts from a body in which, by definition, the function of the partial is lacking and cannot be totaled using any concept whatever, the latter presupposes with regard to the corporeal an initial unity that cannot be split. One major thesis of psychoanalysis—and obviously not acceptable to the "totalizing" claims of the phenomenologists—centers around *the object a, insofar as it deals with that part of the body that has become unstuck or separated—through the "involvement" of the signifying dialectic—and "as of that moment, inert"; that is, having been made into a statue.*

The object cause of desire is the piece that is determined as such at the moment it "falls away," separated from the body. This occurs because the body in question is implied in and by speech. It is not, hence, a part that we can conceive as having been granted some kind of autonomy that in turn produces it. *The a does not originate in self-generation; rather, it becomes unstuck and is the leftover of an operation of division that is carried out in function of the signifying order.* Consequently, it is a phenomenon proper to the speaking being. It is neither a fact related to biology nor does it answer to some metaphysical hypothesis. *The object a is thus produced by the action of speech in the body.*

Let us remember that in *Seminar X*, when dealing with the theme of the production of the object *a* in terms of speech, Lacan makes what seems to be a drastic conceptual leap. He points out that how we can know as subjects depends on the form in which the body, inserted in speech, is projected and set up in what we apprehend cognitively as reality. In this manner, he postulates that in function of the object *a*, speaking beings can "objectivize" this or that knowledge. Again, we refer to the distinction between *objectality*—related to the *a*—and "*objectivity*" as the requisite assumption of science. The condition all knowledge that is trying to elevate itself to a scientific category aspires to is written or ciphered in reference to *a formal and abstract object* through which some conception of the phenomena of reality are being sought, serially limited by the object. The two orders appear to be parallel and unrelated:

objectality.....................*a*
"objectivity"..................formal object, abstract

However, Lacan breaks with the supposed autonomy of "objective" knowledge, by observing that for an investigation of "objectivity" to be feasible, any pertinent epistemological review cannot do without considering objectality. In this way, as we have pointed out, *Lacan bestows on objectivity the gut as cause.* The "pristine" object of scientific knowledge proceeds from the visceral. The much-needed "objectivity" is not foreign, according to this consideration, to certain characteristics that refer to the corporeal separated ("internally") by the effect of speech. It does not become "unstuck," then, from any sphere of abstractions but from *functions linked to the body, which is of interest to psychoanalysis, and in which psychoanalysis is interested: what is implied by inert partiality.* In the last instance—a discovery with clear Freudian roots—*what makes some type of "objectivity" feasible is viscerally rooted in the link between sex and death.* This fundamental psychoanalytical axiom has a direct impact on the thinking about the bases of scientific knowledge. Although it sounds scandalous to some philosophies of science, psychoanalysis demonstrates that there is no possibility of thinking about "objectivity" that is not rooted—and this includes sublimation, of course—in the founding order: sex and death. With this background in mind, certain paragraphs of "Leonardo da Vinci and a Memory of His Childhood" should be reread. As we have said, Freud shows in his essay that what is cognitive does not depend on an evolution written into the organism but derives from manifestations involving sex and, as we would say, various destinies of the object *a*. In the text, we find the following fragment: "Psychoanalytic investigation provides us with a full explanation by teaching us that many, perhaps most children, or at least the most gifted ones, pass through a period, beginning when they are about three, which may be called the period of *infantile sexual researches.*"[1]

Before continuing with this quote, we should like to observe that Lacan, a formidable reader of Freud, did criticize certain points of Freudian theory that required adjustments. One of these is related to the passages in "Leonardo da Vinci and a Memory of His Childhood" following the one we have quoted, in which Freud makes formulations about what he calls *Wissentrieb*, knowledge drive. Other texts by Freud mention *Wissbegierde*, an appetite for knowledge, according to which the subject feels the need to apprehend certain legalities, certain causal relations

---

1. Freud, *Leonardo da Vinci and a Memory of His Childhood*, p. 78. Italics in the original.

of reality, driven by a specific drive that pushes him or her to knowledge. Lacan criticizes this consideration and says it does not exist. He says that what the subject suffers from is a passion for ignorance, contrary to *Wissentrieb*. In delving into this matter, Lacan points out that there are three passions: love, hate, and ignorance. *Freud's* Wissentrieb *is thus neutralized by Lacan through his notion of the passion for ignorance.* It implies that above all else *the speaking subject experiences* jouissance *and furthermore* "*wants to know nothing more about it,*" as he expresses it in *Encore.*[2] This has determinative consequences for psychoanalysis: indeed, the subject does not go into analysis because he or she, impelled by a *Wissentrieb*, wants to know more about him- or herself, but because he or she is suffering from a symptom and knows that the same something—which escapes him or her—wants to say. Though this seems amazing, *no subject has much interest in knowing what is happening to him or her, in being articulated to his or her textual, unknown knowledge.* The subject only apparently has this interest and, generally, this does not go beyond what the various currents of psychology usually propose as "self-knowledge" or the like. What is noticeable, in fact, is that the generalities proffered by the mass media and other vehicles about "knowledge of the self" function mainly to block the possibility of knowing what one wants to know nothing about; that is why they are so well received. The effect of all this psychological "knowledge"—which is referential—can only be, since it is generalized and prescriptive, an increase in collective not knowing. Confronting this is *the fundamental value that psychoanalysis sustains: the respect for singularity.* Keeping this in mind,

---

2. Jacques Lacan, *On Feminine Sexuality, the Limits of Love and Knowledge. Encore. The Seminar of Jacques Lacan. Book XX*, ed. J.-A. Miller, trans. B. Fink (New York: Norton, 1998), p. 106.

we can now turn to the next passage from Freud's essay: "So far as we know, the curiosity [here is the *Wissbegierde* literally] of children of this age does not awaken spontaneously, but is aroused by the impression made by some important event—by the actual birth of a little brother or sister, or by a fear of it based on external experiences—in which the child perceives a threat to his selfish interests."

We should stop here to say a few things. First, we can point out that from the outset Freud undoes any possibility of genetic maturation as sprouting from something formed internally; on the other hand, the "impression" of an "important event" for the child breaks in from the outside, in a moving manner, as an encounter with the Real that takes on a traumatic character. Second, it should be stressed that when Freud writes, "the actual birth of a little brother or sister, or by a fear of it based on external experiences," the space that is frequently opened for empirical questions is eliminated; questions such as, "What if the child does not have a little brother?" or "What if he is an only child?" These questions usually come up spontaneously. However, *this is not about situational phenomena but rather naming the structure*; what happens goes beyond lived experience per se to arrive at the fruitful vagueness of "external experiences," as Freud puts it, which are the basic support of the infantile sexual theories.

In Lacanian terms, we can say that something comes from the place of the Other, which involves the division constitutive of the subject; for example, matters related to castration. Remember the apologue: the boy discovers that the girl he sees naked has no penis. From this, he infers that he too might find himself in this condition. He does not have to deal with any concrete threat of castration. In the same way, there is no need that a younger brother be born; it is enough that others have one for the boy to assume the imminent and at least possible appearance of one for himself. These are both situations that open onto uncertainty, and that generate "narrow"[3] questions about the desire of the Other. These situations do not refer to empirical facts, since it is structure that is determinative. Thus the advice, in the style of "psychoanalytical childrearing," customarily dispensed to spare children from anxiety should be abandoned: whatever is said or done, the effects of structure and its accompanying shift cannot be eluded.

The paragraph we quoted ends in a striking manner, since it includes a concept to which Freud would later give special attention. He writes: "the child perceives a threat to his selfish interests." Here the reference to narcissism, the love of one's own image, starts to be crucial in the essay on Leonardo. Lacan has taught us that to write this situation in the manner below, where, as we know, the "m" is the ego and "i(a)" is the mirror image.

In the case we are referring to, narcissism is threatened by the possibility of a break in the relation sustaining it, which links "m" with the condition of ideal ego, which we propose writing as:

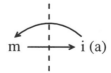

___

3. Translator's note: this is a play on words in Spanish between *angosto* (narrow) and *angustia* (anxiety).

Furthermore, the circumstances under which this "threat" (that the child becomes aware of) can have a significant impact do not refer directly to the nuclear family. A younger brother may well have been born to another child whom the first child hardly knows, but the personal reference, the threat of a break in the narcissistic connection, is taken from this situation, from the Other. Freud continues: "Researches are directed to the question of where babies comes from, exactly as if the child were looking for ways and means to avert so undesired an event. In this way, we have been astonished to learn that children who refuse to believe the bits of information that are given to them— for example, that they energetically reject the fable of the stork with its wealth of mythological meaning—, that they date their intellectual independence from this act of disbelief, and that they often feel in serious opposition to adults and in fact never afterwards forgive them."

The first thing we can see here is that the investigation undertaken by the child is very far from being a disinterested search for knowledge for knowledge's sake. Its objective is practical: "to avert so undesired an event." The stork story raises another interesting point. It is clear that the fable in question is an explanation offered to the child in place of a real one. It may even be that the child accepts this story when he hears it, but its inscription will be compared to later proof, thus giving rise to a retroactive effect from which arises, unexpectedly, the autonomy to which Freud refers.

Autonomy appears as an effect of the unexpected. This is simply the well-known phenomenon of causal retroaction that Lacan mentions frequently, whereby an S_2 causes the foundation of a new effect in S_1, which precedes it in the chain. A simple matheme is enough here to write the ciphered effect of autonomy of the "spirit."

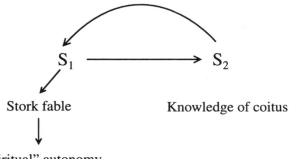

$$S_1 \longrightarrow S_2$$

Stork fable   Knowledge of coitus

"Spiritual" autonomy

The reaction of the child to the stork story and others like it can be observed when he or she compares it to other data. Indeed, why should a child necessarily believe what adults say? Therefore, although the parents have tried to "not traumatize the child" with precocious information that they suppose is beyond his or her fragile ability to understand, the effect of this frequently has surprising aspects to it. *Lies produce unwanted effects, which is a positive feature, although from a direction the parents least expect: the lies do generate autonomy as well as incredulity. With regard to the Other, the location begins to be one of an informed subject, a subject who for the first time encounters a deceptive Other.*

The text continues: "They investigate along their own lines, divine the baby's presence inside its mother's body and following the impulses of the lead of their own sexuality, form theories of babies originating from eating, of their being born through the bowels, and of the obscure part played by the father. By that time, they already have a notion of the sexual act, which appears to them to be something hostile and violent." So, if on the one hand it is certain that every neurotic attempt aimed at whitewashing the possibility of trauma leads inevitably to a failure, on the other hand, the child's approach to confronting the truth does not take place thanks to knowledge of the species. It is not that it is not suitable to deceive children because they possess a kernel of "true" knowledge, which is waiting for the right moment to reveal itself. On the contrary, *children's investigations lead to curious theories, as strange as they are common, which even repel true information*, such as, for example, that children are conceived through the mouth and are born through the anus. *This is a typical infantile sexual theory, which puts objectality in the foreground* as it approaches conception as something to be ingested—an oral object—and then finally expelled as if it were an anal object.

Freud uses his theories of infantile sexual theories in his essay about Leonardo to deal with what Lacan writes as *the passage from objectality to objectivity*. From art to science, Leonardo showed at crucial turning points in his discoveries and postulations traces of a phenomenon that made him fall into repeated failures. These were strange for someone like him, who seemed dominated by an intelligent yearning for all-encompassing and apparently exclusive knowledge. As much in his artistic work as in his scientific research and technical drawings, he was "a man who never finished." This is a decisive fact, found especially in the great number of paintings he left unfinished, which should be heard with all the connotations the verb *acabar*[4] has in our colloquial language, the Spanish of the Rio de la Plata area, which in this context can be used translinguistically.

The last point from this passage we shall examine may seem arbitrary at first though it is perfectly suited to our ends. Freud writes of the child: "But since their own sexual constitution has not yet reached the point of being able to produce babies, their

---

4. Translator's note: to finish; to finish (somebody, someone) off; to be finished.

investigation of where babies come from must inevitably come to nothing and be abandoned as insoluble."[5]

Let us stop a moment at this very direct reference in the passage. Here Freud is arguing that *a child does not have a body whose own flesh can conceive of what is involved in sexual relations.* The child is incapable of grasping what sexual relations consist of; he or she cannot inscribe them because it is knowledge alien to the body. The sexual act is unknown to the child until the possibility, the Real of making this concrete in his or her own body takes effect; only then can the child "know" something. And then the problem posed by Leonardo could be overcome: to not finish, disillusioned by the sterility and fruitlessness of his investigation, carried out, consequently, through a life of "chasteness." Now, is this not similar to what is being said in saying that what happens in an analysis cannot be understood if one has not gone through it oneself? By not ever going into the analytical situation, the theory remains as a knowledge that is more or less accessible, a conceptualization, or, if you like, some kind of abstract and speculative philosophy. This consideration is not meant to denigrate those who have not been analyzed; it shows that it is feasible to study Freud or Lacan in the same way that Kant or Hegel is read. One can master eruditely both authors though from there to being an analyst something irreplaceable is needed: literally, *to put one's body* . . . on the couch, in this case. To not go through this—which is not aleatory but determinative—is to not have the possibility of listening to an analysand; or, indeed to listen, but only by engaging in risks of the highest cost. Yes, *because the subject who analyzes without having been analyzed will only "see" analysands in the image of and similar to itself; this is exactly what the child does with its sexual*

---

5. Freud, *Leonardo da Vinci and a Memory of His Childhood*, p. 79.

theories. It conceives of coitus as anal violence or as urinating on oneself, indeed, "theorizing" from those functions that can attack its body. In summary, *one can know only through the "bordered" limits of the real of one's own body*. It is not too much to say that the body in question is simply the one subsumed to the function of speech, and the speech cuts off the *a*'s of the body.

Now we shall introduce the topic of *the floors—or the forms—in the constitution of the* a. To do so, we shall make use of this drawing, which Lacan used in one of the last meetings of the seminar.

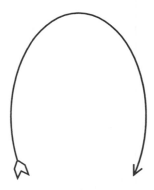

This figure comes from a tradition in Lacanian teaching. By inverting the direction of the arrow, we find the first drawing which becomes the *graph of desire*, constructed in the seminars entitled *Les Formations de l'inconscient* (of 1957–1958) and *Le Désir et son interprétation*, then consolidated in his paper "The Subversion of the Subject," and given its final form in *D'un Autre à l'autre*. It is necessary to distinguish the distances and even the breaks in play in the various formulations. Let us thus draw the main line of this graph with the two lines that intersect the main line, at homologous floors, in the opposite direction:

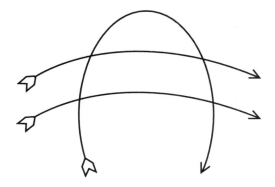

It is worth clarifying here once more, to dissipate any confusion. *A graph is completely different from a graphic drawing. In
place of the visual representation, which is a graphic drawing rooted
in the imaginary, the graph accounts for relations that are independent of its figurative presentation.* A graph points to writing the
structure, and it can do so through various graphic presentations;
despite this, it will continue to be the same graph.[6] It is important to point this out, because for more than a decade the translation into Spanish of Lacan's *Ecrits* has indicated the presence
of "graphic drawings" in "The Subversion of the Subject" rather
than what are in fact rigorous graphs. This text was presented
at the Colloquium of Royaumont in 1960, a year when the main
topic of debate (with the participation of philosophers) was dia-
lectics, although it was scheduled to be published precisely at
the end of 1962. That was the year Lacan began dictating *Seminar X*, reintroducing the old graph, and accounting for the main
terms of its intersecting nodes. Hence, the construction of this
new graph—not announced as such—testifies to the choice co-

---

6. This is the definition on which we constructed our *graph of anxiety*
in Chapter 2.

herent with one of the key points of Lacan's expository strategy, in accordance with the extremely important point he intended to teach. But prior to turning to this graph, we should recall—additionally, and as Lacan does—two defining items of each of these new nodes. First of all, it should never be overlooked at any time that *the a consists of a corporeal automutilation from which the subject is separated, "in a manner which is to a certain extent internal to the sphere of its own existence," with the aim of thus being able to constitute itself.* The paradigmatic example to evoke this production of the *a* is an *ambiceptor object*; the best example of this, as we have mentioned, is the placenta. Whose is the placenta? We posed this question in Chapter 4. *It is not possible to assert that it is the property of the mother, or of the child. In its quality as ambiceptor, it occupies an intermediary space between both mother and child.* Such is the location of the *a*, including the fact that *the remainder or leftover it implies for each side of the cut is dissimilar.*

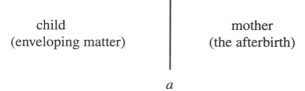

<table>
child | | mother
(enveloping matter) | | (the afterbirth)
 | *a* |
</table>

The reference to the placenta to account for the ambiceptor dimension of the object *a* is not without consequences on the intellection of the other *a*'s. If another *cut to the body* were mentioned instead of the placenta, for example, as the breast may be, it seems obvious that it can foreshadow an object *a* as belonging to the body of the mother. Nevertheless, to mention the placenta as the paradigm to be dealt with implies the marking off of something that does not immediately refer to the body of the mother insofar as it is *a partiality set up inside her body*, but whose ownership is debatable insofar as the enveloping matter is homogeneous to the newborn. To conceive of this partiality is unavoidable in *not* pointing to the presumed "achievement" comprised by the access of the child to the apprehension of the body of the mother as a totality; thus, the cut proper to the oral is made between the breast and the maternal organism; it is as if the breast were stuck to the latter. Indeed, *until weaning, the baby hangs from the breast as part of itself.* On the other hand, the cut is not an effect of the aggression against the breast. Finally, all this marks the huge distances from Kleinian conceptualizations, which we must examine briefly once again.

Melanie Klein and her followers assert that the first object relation to be established is with the breast. This is a partial contact at the beginning that is later healthily completed through establishing total relations. What is the basis for this assertion? Well, whether explicitly or not, it derives from the facts of evolutionary psychology. For example, Kleinians consider that the baby, when it manages to sit up, possesses a global perception of its surroundings, from which moment it can capture the totality of its object. A more advanced perception would moreover lead to the construction of total objects. Furthermore, the totalization of objects can also be rooted in the value bestowed on affect; beyond the first good and bad objects (idealized and persecutive) there is a greater tendency towards making objects conform with good and bad aspects at the same time (the depressive position). This totalization of the object is rejected very emphatically in the teaching of Lacan.

In this regard, *Lacan insists on the inexistence of total drive.* Likewise, he gives no credit to the possibility that total objects may exist. *The a is necessarily partial.* In any case, if we accept— as indispensable conditions—the presence of an object that is asserted as being total, this would be the object of love: the one coming from the jubilation brought about by the devolution of one's own image in the mirror, the i(a), projected later as i'(a). It is clear: "there is" in this object—in Gestalt terms—good form, seduction, attractiveness, fascination, and, in the last instance, deception. To summarize: *in the ideal ego, and in the object of love, unification is found.* This is an image that we should relate in a nonaleatory manner to a *sphere*, since it best describes this situation.

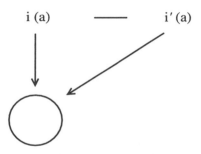

This unification accounts, for example, for the necessity to "round out" that is proper to the imaginary, to establish a close to the circuits, a perfect symmetry, a system of absolute correspondences. Where does this passion for "rounding out" come from, if not the love of good form, the fascinating capture?[7]

On the other hand, it is not feasible to totalize the object *a*, an object that is moreover not an object of love but a partial one.

---

7. However, the desire for castration also attacks the plenitude of the sphere, which can be observed, in our Rio de la Plata Spanish, in the use of an insult derived from this form to denigrate someone who is being called silly, or ill-informed. Indeed, *boludo* (which refers to a person) from *bola* (a ball, as in a sphere or an object used in sports) as much as *pelotudo* (which refers to a person) from *pelota* (mostly a ball used in sports) is an insult about the lack of an opening.

(In any case, let us remember that the object of love can be the "covering" of a hidden *a*.)

Now that we have reviewed these two characteristics, we can return to the construction of the new *graph*, which, as we said, Lacan did not designate as such. On the first line, then, he wrote "*floors*," *which are determined in function of the various forms of the object* a, *but in which the object* a *always remains the object* a. Along the trajectory of the arrow, ascending and progressive, are to be found the classic Freudian notions of oral, anal, and phallic objects:

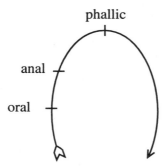

Based on the Freudian points, along the rest of the path described by the arc *Lacan proposes the presence of two new objects* a, which we have already mentioned. This is, strictly speaking, a part of his own doctrine. Now, the two new objects are postulated in a position that places them parallel to two of Freud's classic ones in an implicit, virtual trajectory that marks—not naively—the reference to a return direction, a regressive direction. In this way, *there is no progression without regression, and vice versa with regard to what is related to the analytical reconstitution of repressed desire.* The arc, furthermore, implies that nothing similar to good form will be drawn according to this graph. If a close occurs, it will not be in the manner of a perfectly drawn circle. In the end, there might be a "close" that questions the imaginary plane, as the one the topological cut known as the *interior eight* proposes to us, which is specifically the support of the *repetition* (with difference) insofar as it marks the register with a double loop.

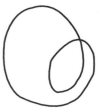

The topological support is made necessary to avoid the temptation of "rounding off" the "regressive face" of this structure and to avoid closing it reproductively. Anyway, the graph we are concerned with remains open, like the one of desire. In addition, Lacan puts forth, in correspondence to the anal object Freud had postulated, the object *a* that he will call—in the last third of the seminar—the *scopic* object.

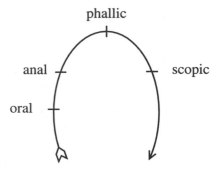

The *scopic object* is exhaustively examined in *Seminar XI*, with particular emphasis on the *gaze*. Nevertheless, the appearance in *Seminar X* of this object *arises at first in relation to vision.*

Lacan goes through an extensive explanation through zoology and ethology to account for some striking phenomena about what happens to the eye in animals. He goes into biology and physiology to point out how the eye—the pair of eyes—is made up. Before going into this point, we should examine the other object *a* introduced in *Seminar X*. At that moment of construction of the graph, *Lacan designates the voice as the superego.*

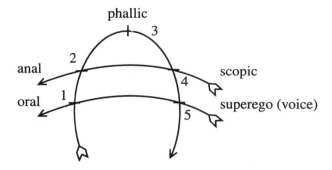

The graph of the floors of *a*

The inclusion of the superego underlines that the voice remains exemplified by the Freudian instance, which can be heard usually in psychoses in the form of verbal hallucinations: insults, violent swearing, belittling, threats, and seduction.

Furthermore, we added the lines showing the floors of the arc, uniting them to what was presented in *Seminar X* in order to *show the great similarity between the graph of the floors of* a *and the graph of desire.* Simply put, *one is the mirror image of the other.* Doubtless, our drawing is based on how *Lacan relates the anal to the scopic and orality to the superego.* About this last point, the work of Melanie Klein on the oral-superego line should be retained. Doubtless, the Kleinian clinical grasp has been keen, though founded on erroneous and contradictory theoretical presuppositions. The conceptual incorrectness was not an obstacle to perceiving in an especially pertinent manner what Klein called early *superego, primitive archaic superego,* or *maternal superego.* All these categories accounted for an instance that has terrifying contours, which has little or nothing to do with the impelling agency of a socializing order as a hypothetical stipulator of agreement with norms or standards of behavior acceptable to a culture. The superego detected by Melanie Klein did not advocate incorporating sociocultural normativity but it is ruled by the devouring tension marked, for example, by the vampirism of the Desire of the Mother.

As for the anal-scopic axis, Lacan pointed out that the second term is examined in detail in some classic psychoanalytical developments. In this regard, he recommends an article by Otto Fenichel. Lacan recovers the value of certain points in the text though the text itself and others related to it show themselves to be "insufficient." This fact goes to show to what extent Lacan recognized he was dealing with an analyst, though he disagreed deeply with the general conception put forth by Fenichel. It is pertinent to recall this, since on the analytical terrain the most common insult for a colleague with whom one has great or little disagreement is, "You are not an analyst." With characteristic and implacable intellectual rigor, Lacan preferred to point out that there were those who made mistakes, at times egregious ones, but this did not stop them from being analysts. For this reason, the fact that Lacan used fragments of an author like Otto Fenichel, who is often greatly criticized—justly—can come as a surprise.

Many references to the desire awoken by the scopic a—in short, scopophilia—can be found in a wide variety of cultural traditions. In Spanish we have a very interesting one that involves classical Spanish culture of the Golden Age. In an earlier text we analyzed the relation between the scopic and the anal, pointing out the connection even in a vulgar word we commonly use, *ojete*[8] which designates "anus."[9] It undoubtedly comes from the field of the scopic to designate what is strictly anal. The interesting thing is that this correlation is not a new or isolated fact. Indeed, Francisco de Quevedo y Villegas, in a short text entitled *Gracias y desgracias del ojo del culo*, had already related the anal opening to the eye.

Though there is an indubitable connection between the scopic and the anal, what is crucial, in any case, is to differentiate between the objects corresponding thereto. Cleverly, Lacan puts off until the end of this presentation clarifications about the anal object and its impact—and this is a traditional theme in psychoanalysis—on the obsessional neurotic in particular. He first deals with the scopic.

As object a, the scopic is what best hides castration due to one of its basic qualities: the space of vision is homogeneous. In what appears in my field of vision it is impossible to draw a precise cut. Where does a crack appear, the fissure necessary for castration to be given a boundary, the *béance*, the opening through which an excision can be made? *The cuts in the scopic object a can only be made through an inexorable degree of arbitrariness, which impedes accounting for castration.* Although the subject is the one who has the access through which what produces a perception can be cut off, this partition cannot be made in function of castration, which by definition arises from the Other and not from the will proper to any "subject of representation." This situation can be demonstrated easily if we use the comparative

---

8. Translator's note: literally, "big eye."
9. Roberto Harari, "Un ojo muy particular," *Discurrir el psicoanálisis*, pp. 173–174.

route of the phenomenologic supports comprised, respectively, of images and words.[10] With regard to verbal language, a word can be split due to certain rules that dictate where they can be divided. A term such as "amboceptor"[11] can be divided according to certain rules that articulate monemes and phonemes. If we remove this or that letter from the word, writing it, for example, as "amboeptor," the meaning is limited by the transgression of a semantic norm: the idea is lost. A simple change of letter determines an outright change in the effect of the meaning: in the word *pala* (shovel) a "b" can be substituted for the "p" making it *bala* (bullet). The cut authorized by the language makes it so the term creates a new meaning, which is not achieved if a combination is used with a letter that the language in question does not contain, for example, "xala."[12] Here, there is no possibility of producing a communicable meaning except in some private idiolect, the price of which can be psychosis. *In schizophrenia, indeed, one can often observe the proliferation of neologisms that transgress the linguistic code.* But the rules of division do not apply to the scopic. There is nothing from the Other indicating where a cut is to be made. The constrictive order operating in verbal language and from which the subject cannot escape except with serious risks are not observable in the

---

10. For a long time we have emphasized, in accordance with the teaching of Lacan, that the Imaginary is not something satanic from which to flee in a terrified manner. We find a reason for this in the image, as in the examples of blind Oedipus and the two paintings of saints by Zurbarán. As the seminar says, "it is about image, since what is irreducible about *a* is of the order of the image . . . in the form i(a), my image, my presence in the Other has no leftover. I cannot see what I lose there."

11. Translator's note: *amboceptor* is a Spanish word that we have previously translated as "ambiceptor" (see page 190). It has been left in its current form because of the analysis that the author performs on it.

12. Translator's note: *xala* has no meaning in Spanish.

scopic except in birth and beauty marks, for example. *The zero point, which Lacan says is where the "mystery" floor of castration hides—and its anxiety—is displayed across the entire field of vision. Desire is supported by an annulment or cancellation limited to its central point—the scopic a—which determines effects of fascination, contemplation, and fragile "suspension of the unsticking of desire," insofar as desire depends on castration. That is why the phantasy is on the scopic level, insofar as its function is to try to elide desire.*

Now *each floor of the object a has a particular type of relation with the Other.* The fact that the paired objects share the same floor implies they have something in common, but also the location on different nodes of the graph indicate that their differences should be pointed out. Where is the differentiality, for example, between the oral object a and the superego? Were there not one, there would be no reason to single out an object different from the one postulated by Freud. *It is precisely the differential relation of each object with regard to the Other—of which they are a leftover—that Lacan attempts to write with what we call the graph of the floors of* a. If it has been agreed that the function of making cuts is decisive in defining objects a, and that, furthermore, the function is distinctive in the specificity of the scopic object, it is the right moment to go back to anatomy—as we suggested at the beginning of this chapter—from an etymological standpoint. Freud has a famous remark about this: "Anatomy is destiny." Lacan criticized it on various occasions but nevertheless provides a feasible meaning for it in this seminar. At first reading, this sentence seems to indicate that everything in life is ruled by the biological design of the body. Our destiny would thus be subsumed to the structure of the body: anatomy is a written destiny from which escape is impossible; or, attempting to escape it takes place at the risk of, and due to, "aberrations."

Now, if we agree that the body in the psychoanalytical sense is the one inscribed in speech, Freud's aphorism appears completely unjustified. However, Lacan proposes a reading of it whereby it becomes, as we said, approachable.

Anatomy is destiny, and it can be so if we look at the etymology of the word "anatomy." It refers us to the Greek root *tomein*, which means "to cut." On the same line are words such as "dichotomy" (to cut into two), or "atom" (what cannot be cut). From this point of view, if the object *a* is something produced by the effect of a cut, Lacan lucidly asserts that to approve the aphorism is not without pertinence. *Everything, really, that can be known about the body is related to the function of a cut.* Anatomy—even when it is used as a synonym for dissection—was born in the cutting of cadavers that inaugurated the field of observation of organs and systems. To do so, the various types of obstacles, especially religious ones, had to be overcome so that the dead bodies could be viewed as nonsacred. As it became possible to make cuts to look inside bodies, anatomical knowledge began to accumulate. Hence, anatomy is history; it is a signifier and it is not brute, empirical corporeality. The shift Lacan exerts on the sentence Freud said he could recognize in Napoleon is remarkable; the sentence involves much more than its manifest content. *That is why a cut in the body itself gains all its scope from destiny, that is to say, from the articulation of the subject with the function called desire.*

Returning to the graph, it is pertinent for us to now examine the peak—drawn—of the arrow: this is exactly the position of "third" or three assigned to the phallic object, the only one not paired up with another *a*. As we were saying, a year later, in *The Four Fundamental Concepts of Psychoanalysis*, Lacan limits the "alphabet" of objects to only four: the breast, feces, the gaze, and the voice, which in turn are articulated to the oral, anal, scopic, and invocatory drives, respectively. What happened to the object *a* known as phallic—lacking, voided—in *L'Angoisse*? Here we need to ask why there is this reduction in the number of objects. *The fifth object in question has a quality that places it in a difficult situation insofar as it can be asserted that, metaphorically, it is present in the four others.* Lacan provides a subversive account in this regard, which constitutes a fundamental underpinning of what should be called the Lacanian clinic.

What happened in the psychoanalytical movement generally after Freud contended that the end of analysis occurs when one is faced with the last limit marked by the bare rock of castration? Before answering this question, we should recall here, in Lacanian terms, though the phallic as an image is designated by the Greek letter (φ), castration is merely the (φ) preceded by a minus sign:

$$(\varphi) \qquad\qquad (-\varphi)$$

phallic image   castration

Putting a minus sign in front of the phallus indicates that castration cannot be split or divided from the phallus. The strict correspondence between the phallus and castration had already been introduced by Freud himself in a 1923 text, "The Infantile Genital Organization." *Lacan uses this relation at one of the most important points in* Seminar X *to begin teaching that there is an end to analysis, as signaled by Freud, but that this end can, and must, be overcome.* The bare rock of castration is for Freud a *non plus ultra:* one cannot go further in an analysis. This end is not one that is conceived only in chronological terms. Why? Because, regarding time, the sessions can go on indefinitely; but in analytical terms nothing would happen during them. In some way, in the continuation after running into the rock of castration, *the main difficulty to overcome is how to cut off the interminable analysis.* Once more Freud: his first problem was how to get analysands to stay in analysis; the second was to achieve their leaving it. Once he had developed the analytical device, this was not the least of the inconveniences that he had to face in finishing adjusting it. Now, *Lacan asserted that one could go beyond what is obtainable in analysis. This is a program that is indubitably very pretentious, but based on a very sure grasp of the avatars of the post-Freudian analytical movement, along with, it is clear, his experience in the direction of the treatments in his charge.*

When analysts were confronted with the limit pointed out by Freud, what they did was to go back even further in the archaic phases to the ones they considered to be at a place "before" castration. For example, Melanie Klein emphasized this in her theory, focusing on the oral object. Through her attention to orality, it seemed to her that she had obtained answers to what happened at the most "profound" or "primitive" strata of the subject. In a conception shaded by its entanglement with an evolutionary substratum, it was asserted that, the more one went back to the supposed "stages," the more one could accede to the unfathomable depths, which, it was said, possessed a crucial, determinative scope. Here is where most of the post-Freudian derailment—which obviously is not limited to Kleinism—occurred, and to which Lacan tried to put a stop. A good reading shows that when reference was made to orality or anality, there was a ceaseless, albeit implicit, metaphorization of the phallus. The issue is not about the autonomy, for example, of the oral but the slippage or shifting of the phallic, which comes to cover the predicate of other "leftovers." In this way, one can find the form in which an object *a* functions by substituting the writing of the phallus as castration. This can be written in the following formula:

$$\frac{a}{(-\varphi)}$$

This is one of the ways to conceive the reason for the disappearance of the lacking phallic object a in *Seminar XI*, after its having been located at the peak of the arrow in the graph of the floors of a proposed in *L'Angoisse*. The object a substitutes, in this manner, the place of castration. The only thing is—and here we must recall the apologue of the little containers, presented in the preceding chapter—the cover is never total or full. If it were, castration, which is in turn the pillar of desire, would be liquidated; therefore, by only being a semiplenitude, *it continuously impels the launching of desire anew, as the point of anxiety and the point of desire do not coincide. But in this nonveiling of desire by anxiety, what place should then be assigned to Freud's "bare rock" anxiety, which Lacan proposes to surmount*, or, stated better, which he asserted to have already surmounted "on many occasions." The conceptualization of the "beyond" took many forms in Lacan's work. Here, let us just deal with the directly implied reference. We say that *the neurotic does not move back when confronted with castration except by making his or her own castration what lacks in the Other, A. Giving his or her castration a positive sign, it is made into "the guarantee of this function of the Other,"* which *"slips away or drains away in the undefined reference of significations." This last point is what accounts for an interminable analysis: that is why the aim of bringing it to an end is inherent to the analytical method and not an adventitious or sumptuary element of this method. In fact, if at the end of a Freudian analysis, the analysand—whether man or woman—insists on reclaiming the phallus, it is because he or she has not given up the omnipotent phallus, the function of which is to be found in whitewashing an irrefutable fact of the structure; that is, the "something missing" of the relation between the object and desire has not been differentiated at each floor "from that which the constitutive lack of satisfaction is about." This is an utterance, in our judgment, that is not completely clear, and that, doubtless, caused Lacan to make more pertinent formulations later on.*

Now we shall turn to the *a* introduced in *L'Angoisse* as the superego, which would soon come to be simply the voice. The name for this is is simple, although as object it is complex to grasp. For now it refers—as every object *a*—to the putting into act of a void, which is implicit in the (-φ). However, Lacan introduces the theme through *the plenitude of the object* a *called the voice*.

In this regard, let us note in one of the floors of the graph in "The Subversion of the Subject" the following display of elements:

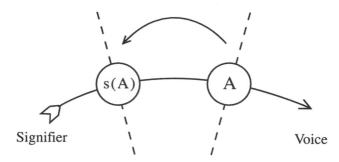

On this floor the vector of the signifier goes to the Other, A. On returning from A—retroactively—the node originates that calls *the signified the Other: s(A)*. In this symbolic operation there is something that cannot be subjected to the effect of retroaction: the voice, which "falls"—as this graph shows—as something that exceeds the Other. In this way, this operation does not result in an exact product, but rather, something is discarded as a remainder, as object *a*, in the last instance.

In principle, *the location of the object a in the graph indicates that the voice is an effect of the signifier. This advances its elaboration, though it is also problematic since all the a's—as products of a cut—are generated by the signifier.* It is assumed here that there is something that does proceed from a different order. That the breast be cut off—not physically but through the action of the signifier—can be imagined as the starting point for conceiving of an oral object. The same is true of the anal object. With greater difficulties, as we saw, one can imagine the process in the case of the phallic and scopic objects. But regarding the voice, how should the cut be conceived? It would seem that it always circulates in the same way. What difference would there be between the voice and the fact of speaking? Are they not perhaps the same thing? No, they are not. *The voice is not the same as speaking; inversely, one can argue that the voice is precisely what speaking lacks. Stated differently, in speaking, the voice lacks. Hence, on the contrary, the voice is present—let the paradox have value—in muteness and a-phony.* However, we point out that Lacan presents the voice as plenitude. Where, then, can it be grasped?

The example given in *L'Angoisse*—through plenitude—is biblical, insofar as it can be "manipulated" and "exemplary." It refers to the Jewish ritual *shofar*, the horn of a ram, used as a wind instrument to celebrate *Rosh-Hashana*, the new year and *Yom Kippur*, the day of atonement. Lacan points out that on these occasions, when the deep sound of the horn is made, one can perceive what is being transmitted by this act capable of creating "an auricular affect." It is curious that Lacan, who was not Jewish, should refer to something that seems to be merely the emission of pure sound, with no signifier. *The notes sounded by the* shofar *have no signifying quality, since they are not articulated under a signifying regency.* But the sound, he remarks, is one that—beyond the atmosphere of solemnity, faith, and even repentance, or the precise ritual in which it is used—causes a "profoundly moving" state. What is special about the playing of the notes of this instrument? And here the cultural inscription is given: it refers to the Bible and the places in it which mention the *shofar*.

The *shofar* appears in the Scriptures at a moving moment: Moses meets Jehovah before the Ten Commandments are given to him. It is a crucial moment when a pact is renewed. The *shofar* is sounded every time a pact is sealed between humans and God; it indicates respect for a circumstance that returns. The passage reads: "And it came to pass on the third day in the morning, that there were thunders and lightnings, and a thick cloud upon the mount and the voice of the trumpet exceeding loud; so that all the people that was in the camp trembled."[13]

The trumpet here is the *shofar*, in the Hebrew version. The effect of these facts on the people should be noted. Was it merely the thunder and lightning or the clouds on Mount Sinai that caused the fear in people? Or was it the sound of the *shofar*? The text from Exodus then says: "And Moses brought forth the people out of the camp to meet with God: and they stood at the nether part of the mount. And Mount Sinai was altogether on a smoke, because the Lord descended upon it in fire. And the smoke thereof ascended as the smoke of a furnace, and the whole mount quaked greatly." In this chapter, the translators of the *Biblia de Jerusalén* have a footnote that greatly clarifies what comes next: "Lit. 'with (or in) one voice'." This word, when used in the plural, always means thunder (cf. v. 16). Also, in the singular, it can mean "the thunder," but here it may express the intelligible voice of God, which "responds" to Moses. The adoption of this meaning is a particular characteristic, proper to the

---

13. Translator's note: Authorized Version, Exodus 19:16.

God of the Hebrews, different from the god of the philosophers, since far from being an abstract entity, this god appears, has a dialogue with, and has an impact on, his creatures in a singularly forceful way.[14] At the end of the passage we have quoted, it is said that the sound of the *shofar* became louder and louder. We must underline that with regard to both the thunder and the voice, it is important that the *shofar* sound continually during the moment of the pact on Mount Sinai, as a background, marking the presence of God, a God who descends to impose—and this too is an interesting fact—a signifying constellation: the Ten Commandments.

Lacan, in addition to the biblical reference, takes other specific examples from Theodore Reik, who wrote various essays on what is mistakenly known as "applied psychoanalysis." One of them is on ritual and deals with the issue of the *shofar*. Reik's approach allows Lacan to discuss the presence of a "full" *a*, as can be seen in other biblical passages. For example, in 2 Samuel 6:15, one can read of what happened with the arrival of the ark of God in the city of David after other events: "So David and all the house of Israel brought up the ark of the Lord with shouting, and with the sound of the trumpet." This is another moment of renewal of the pact, of the Alliance; this is what constitutes an encouragement of the remembrance of God—with both genitives.

Lacan also points out—and this is a detail worth noting due to what happened to him—that the *shofar* is also played in moments when the alliance is suspended for one member of the community. *In the ceremony of major excommunication, when someone is expelled from Judaism—as was the case of Baruch de*

---

14. To what extent this particularity may have to do with the condition of being Jewish requires study.

Spinoza—the shofar *is sounded to announce the separation of a member of the community from it, and also to renew the membership of those who remain.*

The theme of excommunication is not a whimsical one for Lacan. It is the starting point of *Seminar XI*, the first chapter of which he would entitle "Excommunication," referring to his own expulsion from the International Psychoanalytic Association, which was in the making while Lacan was holding *Seminar X*. The *shofar* is also sounded when someone, reputed to be a traitor, is expelled from the horde or the group. The renewing of a pact therefore includes not only what is festive but can also be used to excommunicate dissidents in an irreversible manner.

8

Voice, Gaze, Phallus. Faire "l'amourir"[1]

In the desperate search for a "before" by the various currents of post-Freudians, perhaps there is a course other than the attempt to take psychoanalysis onto the ever-tempting terrain of metaphysics. Contrary to what might be supposed, conceptions such as these—far from being lost in gratuitous and/or ludicrous abstract speculations—have determined clinical rules that have very serious consequences. From the outset, a strong dose of evolutionary psychology has filtered through these considerations, since they share the metaphysical *episteme*: the intrinsic maturation of the subject. We have had opened to us the possibility of another, non-Manichean reading proposed by Lacan: this one demonstrates that when a movement up and along an incline occurs, it provokes by the same token a movement down and along a decline, and the reciprocal is also true. When a movement forward is made in one instance, something goes

---

1. Translator's note: a Lacanianism derived from a combination of *faire l'amour* (to make love) and *faire mourir* (to make die). See page 224.

backward in another. *This echoes one of the dictates of castration: what is gained on the one hand is lost on the other.* But, since generally what is lost is not known, one believes only that one has gained. Given this nonabsolute return, there emerges concomitantly an intellection different from Karl Abraham's obstacle comprised of linear stages or phases of psychosexual development. *The floors of the graph of the a's are not phases to be gone through.* They are only called floors in function of a cut by different objects *a*. Lacan wisely observes that something of the *a* is kept on all the floors, though the *a*'s must be differentiated: *one object* a *is not the same as another, since, as we shall see, each one relates the subject* (S) *differentially with the Other* (A), *as a remainder of the latter due to the constitution of the former (in accordance with the framework of the division of the subject by the signifier).*

Now, it is suggestive that, in deliria and hallucinations, the scopic and the auditory (two environments involving the *a*'s sustained by the senses with no direct contact with the body)— are decisive and preferential areas. Furthermore, both these objects *a* initially "arise" in a more veiled manner; it is more problematic to grasp the relations they have to the body, their "carnate" relations, than Freud's *a*'s. Lacan says this clearly about the scopic object *a*; to our understanding, the same can be said of the voice. Thus, there are only specific cases in which one can note the superego operating to a certain extent in an isolated manner in the psychic realm, that is, with apparent autonomy. For example, this occurs in delirium found in situations of severe deterioration; auditory hallucinations where insults by "them" prevail; or the predominant, manifest self-loathing, as occurs in melancholia. In these situations, the superego appears as if it were independent, proffering irreversible sentences without appeal or cessation. Here, in our understanding, *the condition of remote reception operates to support a greater possibility of "disincarnated" symbolizing or veiling.* This argument seems acceptable to explain why Lacan added objects to the classic ones of Freud. That is to say, *this argument can help grasp what caused an impact so this advance was achieved.*

We shall now turn to an examination of matters related to these "strictly" Lacanian *a*'s. We shall start—on the down side— with the voice-superego, pointing out its link with a singular *cut effect. Lacan made an interesting observation about verbal hallucinations that are found in certain types of psychoses, in discussing the impact interruption has on these voices.* One characteristic that becomes obvious in Freud's text, "Psycho-Analytic Notes on an Autobiographical Account of a Case of Paranoia," and even in Schreber's own *Memoirs of My Nervous Illness*, is the insistent presence of interrupted messages, received as "they say to me" by the subject who suffers from *dementia paranoides.* Lacan had taken this into account in his *Seminar I, Freud's Papers on Technique*, when he explained why certain circumstances of daily life appeared in dream formations. One simplistic idea about this considers that what psychoanalysis calls the *day residues* are selected from among the unimportant events of daily life by a kind of wise intelligence, which selects them because they provide a better mask for the hidden meaning of dreams. It should be noted that people who maintain this are proposing the existence of a sort of homunculus, working within the subject, who astutely controls certain levers unbeknownst to the one providing shelter. In the case of dreams, this entity selects the most appropriate of the day's residues to disguise the latent content of the dream. To this widely disseminated grasp of the issue calling for a mystic inside wisdom can be opposed *the hypothesis in Seminar I that proposes that daily residues are constituted by virtue of an interrupted message.*

When an event from the day passes into the category of the day residues, it is because they have produced an unfinished message; some situation or other in which something could have been, or was about to be, said, was not said, due to some circumstance or other. *The condition of interruption, linked to the message, causes a coincidence with the structure of desire, which by definition has a dimension of lack or inconclusion. This is why, through structural homology, it becomes inevitable that desire—and this can be observed through a close reading of Freud's work—is transferred to these insignificant events that are converted into what we know as the day residues.*

The condition of interrupted message also links desire to what is involved in the decisive dimension of clinical practice: interpretation. If desire and interpretation share the same structure, to the point of being able to signal that the former is the latter, analysts should think that a valid interpretation finds its "culmination" in an open state: *an intervention that ends in suspension marks, which is not assertive; that is, far from the apodictic, from the closure caused by a concluding or pedagogical sentence.* Though, on the one hand, the interpretation must be polyvocal, on the other, the opening effect obtained through an unfinished message, where not-all is said, produces in the scope of clinical practice a result ripe for a change in the subjective position in play.

The reference to interrupted messages—overwhelming in their pathological extremes in deliria structured by auditory hallucinations—makes it possible to understand, in addition to what we have just said, *how the superego does not have precise and clear mandates, being, in this sense, an especially diffuse instance with regard to what is involved in the clarity of its signifying articulation.*

Going back to the *scopic*—which will give us an opportunity to develop it more fully—we should recall here what was said in our previous chapter, that is, that *the scopic is the floor of the phantasy itself.* Stated differently, the phantasy is a very specific formation in which the scopic plays a decisive role. Here we must clarify a term, since the word used by Freud was *Phantasie*, which is the German that responds lexically, though not conceptually, to "fantasy." In Lacanian teaching, a *phantasy* is differentiated from the activity of daily imagination, the *fantasy*. Kleinians have also sought to differentiate between the fantasies responding to what classical psychology calls imagination and "unconscious phantasies." In the latter case, both the Kleinians and Lacan encountered a special instance, closely related to the sexual entrapment of the subject. *Indeed, the phantasy is closely linked to a masturbatory condition, as of the constitution of its very origin; often, it is a precondition for the subject's having an orgasm.* Although a behaviorist conception can lead one to think that the subject participates—when the time comes—in "normal" heterosexual coitus, psychoanalytical listening usually discovers that the phantasy is the sine qua non condition for the analysands to be satisfied. This means that the appeal to the phantasy as a recourse "makes up for" what is lacking in the sexual encounter; thus, insofar as the process of producing phantasies is active or activated, the subject can have an orgasm. Now, if sometimes the deployment of the phantasy occurs concomitantly with a "normal" sexual encounter, in others it appears as a kind of capturing of the subject in which his or her sexuality is manifested independently of the presence of any partner; it is clear we are referring here to the practice of masturbation. In all these cases, the subject is usually present as an actor but at the same time is the spectator. *Hence, phantasies activate a subject that looks as a spectator at what is developing before it, and also looks at where it is.* This is how the scopic appears as the inexorable floor of the phantasy. Some fragment of the subject is, in the phantasy, something that gazes at it from the stage, which is not necessarily an eye.

In one of my cases, to cite an example, a woman analysand could only have an orgasm by "blotting out" the coitus she was engaged in with her partner and simultaneously phantasizing situations in which she appeared humiliated. As long as the phantasy was degrading, putting her in servile positions, and she was given violent commands and even physically punished, she could achieve orgasm. The phantasy, in this case, as in most cases, was not manifested straight out. Furthermore, the resolving of the process of phantasy-making could only begin by starting with the analysand's first surname, and how it produced an effect of meaning linked to the condition of being humiliated; in particular, she had to walk on her knees over grains of corn. It was the inscription of this master-signifier that could account for how she had articulated herself to the primary condition of *jouissance* as humiliation in her sexuality, as a way of making present in the mode of a demand her failed version of the father.

Beyond this precise example, it is possible to observe how the fantasy sustains the subject, allowing the construction of a great part of the subject's life in function of this formation. In this case, in addition to having recourse to the process of phantasy to achieve orgasm, the same phantasy became reality since in fact she "managed" to be humiliated and even beaten by her husband, due to monotonous and enduring disagreements stemming from daily life. *Far from remaining isolated on the terrain of the internal imaginary, the phantasy determines material effects in the life of the subject.*

The scopic floor, in reference to the phantasy, allows Lacan to shed additional light on "The Wolf Man," a classic case of psychoanalysis, which is crucial regarding the ground it covers and the thinking it sparked. In "From the History of an Infantile Neurosis," Freud provides an account of a discovery related to what he called *primary, universal, originary phantasies or protophantasies* (from the German *Ur*); that is, *those that are recognizable in every subject, independently of his or her singular lived experience.* In this famous case, the protophantasy in question—the dominating one—is the one known as the *primal scene*, that is, the fact, presumably witnessed and overheard, of the traumatic parental coitus. In analysis, at least, the primal scene tends to appear as an auditory issue before a scopic one. However, in "The Wolf Man," the importance of the visual becomes determinative. This case history has given rise to a flood of interpretations. Many people have examined it exhaustively, among them, Lacan. *He observed, in particular, Freud's persistence—inopportune in his judgment—in attempting to detect the effect of the fact that the patient had witnessed the coitus of his parents.* But we were saying that the phantasy that appears at a particular moment in analysis, and that becomes consubstantial to it, has the scopic as a defining element. Why is this so? In this sense, the seminar underlines, and adds to, what the well-known wolf dream offers to be grasped: five wolves were gazing at the fascinated subject from the branches of a tree, through an open window. *From this suddenly opened window, Lacan takes the "fenestrative" function of the phantasy, at work, for example, in defenestration (cf. Chapter 3); also, he shows that the dream shows the phallus, while veiling it behind the "catatonia of the image," which is none other than the astounded dreamer, fascinated by what he sees.* Lacan concludes that "what is gazing at the Wolf Man and which, in a way, is nowhere to be seen, is like an image," transposed, "from the state of detention of his own body, transformed into the tree . . . filled with wolves." This image puts the subject "on the axis of *jouissance*, an arborified *jouissance*, which stares entirely at him."

Now, as the window in this dream is an exemplar and is elevated to the category of a concept, the same occurs with *the scopic, insofar as it is linked, according to Lacan, to the totality of the protophantasies, and not only with the primal scene we mentioned.* We are now going to consider these protophantasies. There are five of them, although usually only three are discussed; indeed, there are many writings that only mention three. Our schema includes the three customary ones, leaving a blank at the beginning for one that is omitted:

$$\textit{protophantasies} \left\{ \begin{array}{l} \text{a.} \\ \text{b. seduction} \\ \text{c. castration} \\ \text{d. primal scene} \end{array} \right.$$

In a classic, "*Fantasme originaire, fantasmes des origines, origine du fantasme,*" J. Laplanche and J.-B. Pontalis have rigorously elucidated what is at play in protophantasies: they are a response to the question of the origin of something.[2] In particular, they account for a type of origin in which the order of sex enters into action. The unknown element in the blank space in point "a" is not accidental; it indicates that one of the protophantasies that is usually not considered occupies an initial position in more than one sense. But let us analyze one of the more common ones, for example, the protophantasy of seduction.

The infantile sexual theory of seduction would answer the question of how a subject can come to be a sexuated one, providing a precise answer: I was inoculated with sexuality from the outside. The insistence with which Freud's hysterical patients imputed

---

2. Jean Laplanche and Jean-Baptist Pontalis, "Fantasy and the Origins of Sexuality," in *Formations of Fantasy*, ed. Victor Burgin et al. (London: Methuen, 1986), pp. 5–34.

at one time or another seduction scenes to members of their families or to persons they knew as the origin of their sufferings is well known. It is here that at a specific moment a break is produced and Freudian theory is displaced; this ranges from accepting that these seductions were facts of "reality" experienced by his patients, to viewing them as protophantasies with a "nucleus of truth": *sexuality is constituted from the field of the Other.*

As for the protophantasy of castration, it can be pointed out that it answers the question about the origin of the condition of each sex. How is it possible that there be two sexes? Why are there men and women? In psychoanalysis, this question can be translated as: Why is there a phallus and castration? It is precisely castration that accounts for the difference between the sexes. *It is here that the distinction is made between the phallic and the castrated.* At a logical, later time, another question derives from this one: *If they are different, what do they do between themselves?* The primal scene is an attempt to answer this question. The three protophantasies are logically coupled and, in this series of problems, the scopic is involved as the structuring agent of the answers to the various questions. To summarize: from the origin of sexuality, through the origin of the division of the sexes, until arriving at the origin of children, since those who are coupling in the protophantasy of the primal scene originate new life.

This is the classic triptych of seduction, castration, primal scene, which is what Laplanche and Pontalis limit themselves to. Now Freud adds two more to these in a footnote in "Three Essays on the Theory of Sexuality." Due to the insistence of his patients, Freud noted, around 1920, that two protophantasies that had not been contemplated at first appear in an unequivocal and insistent manner. One was the return to the womb, which we shall now write in the first blank, and we shall include also the second one that was omitted by them in the remaining space, which is blank at the moment.

$$
protophantasies \left\{
\begin{array}{l}
\text{a. return to the womb} \\
\text{b. seduction} \\
\text{c. castration} \\
\text{d. primal scene} \\
\text{e.}
\end{array}
\right.
$$

As we have had the opportunity of pointing out, there is no nostalgia for some lost protection in this protophantasy. It answers the question about the origin with a sinister twist that accounts for the condition of reintegration to which the Desire of the Mother tends. *It does, therefore, not refer to a warm fetal ambiance but rather to the anxiety-provoking threat coming from the desire of an Other who devours.* Its sinister-like dimension is completely opposed to the yearning for a rosy time prior to birth.

Lastly, we find in the fifth place a protophantasy that responds in a more convoluted manner to the questions about origins. It is called the *family novel*.

$$
protophantasies \left\{
\begin{array}{l}
\text{a. return to the womb} \\
\text{b. seduction} \\
\text{c. castration} \\
\text{d. primal scene} \\
\text{e. family novel}
\end{array}
\right.
$$

This protophantasy derives from a narcissistic modality in answering the subject's question about origin. It does not refer to origins in general but to the appearance of oneself. We have already provided an account of this situation, in which a subject postulates itself as the child of a couple who are not the ones who raised the subject by phantasizing circumstances in which he or she was the victim of a substitution at birth. In the phantasy, "legitimate" parents are referred to as having marvelous traits and as being blessed with noble attributes, light-years away from ordinary parents. The subject manages to convince him- or herself that its real parents are not the ones who were present while he or she was growing up. Now, when the family novel is spoken about, "of the neurotic" is usually added to it from the title of Freud's text. Nevertheless, it is necessary to clarify that what we are saying here goes also for psychosis. In inaugurating the Clinical Section of the University of Vincennes in 1977, Lacan, when asked if the same categories such as barred subject, object *a*, and so on, were valid in psychosis as in neurosis, answered, "Yes." He affirmed it seriously. Not only is the family novel a proto-phantasy shared by neuroses and psychoses but it also involves the phantasies themselves.

In recent years, an insistence on teaching that the dimension of phantasy has no bearing on psychosis has gained certain ground. To accept this, in our judgment, would be to demolish any attempt to conceive of psychosis as structure. *The conceptual error is the following: in psychoses, the dialectic of the neurotic, that is, the prevalence of demand, does not occur.* As we know, what the neurotic does is to replace the *a* of the formula of the phantasy by the D of demand:

$$(\mathcal{S} \lozenge \ a)$$
$$\downarrow$$
$$(\mathcal{S} \lozenge \ D)$$

Indeed, this is not what happens in psychoses; this movement of substitution, which *speaks of metaphoricity*, does not happen. Nevertheless, one does not deduce from this that there is no phantasy. Before the liquidation of a structure, it is pertinent to choose to perceive the differences specific to it. *The psychotic also desires.* Listening to a delirium makes it possible to point this out. For example, is there not, by any chance, a phantasy in Schreber? If even Freud designates it by these terms, *let us agree that the problem consists in being able to account for how the "destiny" of the phantasy is modified in the psychotic structure, before crudely rejecting the phantasy outright.*

So there are five protophantasies, and five floors in the constitution of the distinct objects *a*. Also, *the object cause of desire participates necessarily in the basic grammar shaped by the protophantasies. The a is elaborated, processed, and located in them, thus gaining special relevance for the structure of the subject. In this way, the necessary feasibility of articulating each element in the first series to one in the second arises, or is presented to us,* as Juranville[3] says; these recur sufficiently so that the issue can be posed in this manner. But first we must return to the complex floor where the scopic is located in order to make new statements about the following phallic floor on the return line that runs through each of them

Let us recall the weight of the gaze in the case history of "The Wolf Man," observing in what manner he viewed the primal scene. With his admirable capacity for reading, Lacan underlines in this scene the condition of being watched in a somewhat equivocal manner. Nothing in the scene should be taken as anecdotal; the fact that the Wolf Man glimpsed the coitus of his parents is in no way to be scorned; rather, the situation produces effects of teaching in Lacan's analysis of it. *Glimpsing marks a fact of structure.* This is, obviously, about half-seeing, and not

---

3. Alain Juranville, *Lacan et la philosophie* (Paris: PUF, 1984), pp. 191–194.

directly and fully seeing. There is something subtracted in this primal scene, hidden from the gaze. In this way, the plenitude of seeing is cancelled out by the phallus, which does not appear in its entirety. Also, we should recall the Wolf Man's immediate reaction to the scene. Defecation constituted his answer to the never-ending murky scene that arose before him, which he could not see as a whole. *Lacan does elevate these facts to the level of exemplar.* This means—returning to the central theme of *Seminar X*—returning once again to the link between anxiety and sexuality, or the reason why the phallic condition is decisive. *The relation arises because, when the phallus is expected in one place, it does not appear.* It can only be glimpsed, since it is subordinated ceaselessly to a condition of sliding, of subtraction. Starting from this statement, Lacan points out that this is what happens in the dimension of the phallic. *Insofar as the phallus does not show up at the meeting with the subject who gazes upon it, when all is said and done, it does not cease producing an effect of dissatisfaction.* It can always have been something different from what could be seen; also, what is traumatic is very often found in this property of slippage.

Lacan makes new, very wise clinical observations in this regard in *Seminar X*. Everyone knows cases, he points out, where a woman has her husband in analysis. What this woman fervently desires in this situation is to be analyzed by the same analyst as her husband. There is no other alternative for her desire, he says, since in these cases what she is seeking is a repositivization of the phallus. And he writes what happens in this case in a striking manner. This woman is attempting the following:

$$- (-\varphi)$$

The repositivization is sought by no other means than the negation of the negation of the phallic image, that is, of castration.

Through the desiring peak that she believes her husband has reached in his analysis, she tries to do something with the little phallic image (φ) that she has been lucky to get, Lacan stresses. Undoubtedly, he is referring here to the anatomical support, constituted by the clitoris, for the phallic image in the woman, which implies "taking the phallus for what it isn't." All she obtains thus is a power close to what she imagines about the *jouissance* of the other, committing thereby an aberration "regarding her own *jouissance*." As we have already said, another one of the ways the woman can be confronted by the problems inherent to the phallic condition she disdains is to sustain it by constantly exciting the men around her. Since the phallus is missing from its place, the hysteric appeals over and over again to seduction in fleeing the confrontation with the detumescence of the penis, which means the phallic image succumbs. To avoid this, she finds no better solution than to maintain tumescence. Now one of the decisive points in taking this situation into account is that, from the side of the one exercising the seduction, there may not be a commitment located in her body to sustain the phallic image. The phallic image comes from the Other, it is located in the Other. *It is precisely in the Other—and not over her—where she obstinately seeks to sustain this theory of the phallus—to keep it from falling—as an instrument of power.* Hysterical seduction contains crucial references about this phallic issue: we should not be astonished that, to obtain the insignia of this ever-present tumescence, the woman renounces her own *jouissance*. This sort of feminine "hypergenitality," which is explicit, frank, and declared, inducing the man to remain in a state of constant excitation, can correspond to a situation of frigidity. This concomittance should not be surprising, *since this supposed hypertrophy of the genital is not seeking jouissance itself but rather disdaining it, insofar as it maintains tumescence and sustains desire, suffocat-*

ing the possible source of anguish. Also, and concomitantly to this, if the function of orgasm is to get, *without a doubt,* maximum satisfaction, why can it not be seen that *due to the feature of certainty they share, orgasm is equivalent to anxiety*?

For sure, the theme is developed in such a way to a point of insistence in the teaching of Lacan: What happens in what is called the "normal" union between man and woman? To go back to the issue, we turn this time to *set theory,* to what are known as *Euler circles.* Man and woman seem, in the sexual act, to be reunited, to be covered by a manner that their desires lead them to reach:

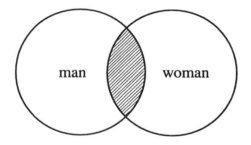

In principle, one observes here an area of intersection. However, *what appears to be the region of contact is precisely what causes an obstacle to there being a full relation, a union in the strict sense.* This failed area, interposed between the man and the woman, summons castration without a doubt, since what is shown here is the evanescence of the phallic (lacking) condition: *"for each of us, it is what alienates us from the other when it is reached."* If there is *jouissance,* it is only partial, completely away from the absolute involvement of bodies; as tight as the embrace may be, it cannot embrace all the imaginary. Thus the phallus, promising union, only impedes it. Man and woman seek it "on the level of genital mediation," which is where the phallus is not to be found. That every sexual union is condemned to fail ends up providing little encouragement for hedonist utopias; also, this is a basic milestone on the path that later allows Lacan to state—in a formalized way—his classic negative aphorism: "*There is no sexual relation.*" Man and woman do not "fit" fully; there is not an even proportion between the two, since "*the other is either the other or the phallus, in the sense of exclusion.*" Nevertheless, this does not hinder their believing that a complete union is feasible, despite the fact that it cannot be written.

The fantasy of love, as seen in classical reference to the myth of the androgyne presented in Plato's *The Symposium*, leads to the search for the "other half," "the other half of the orange," for an assurance of plenitude. However, once the distinction between love and sex has been made, this question arises: What is being asked of the partner in the sexual act, this limiting encounter that is an obstacle? Lacan's answer is direct: *what is being asked is the satisfaction of a demand that has some relation to death, with the "little death," a fact Lacan dubs as* "faire l'amourir."[4] As to what sex involves, to *faire l'amourir* is something very different from innocent lovemaking, since the latter does not explain the resting, postorgasmic state. *The condensation that creates this neologism unites magisterially the two coordinates that have always been present since the very beginning of the psychoanalytic undertaking: sex and death.* Why not put forth a more tolerable connection, such as, for example, friendship and religion, or even sex and life? Is perhaps what is intransferably psychoanalytical an arbitrary, gratuitous conjunction? As we shall see, the coming reflections make it possible to show that a crucial and inextricable relation pertains between the two vectors of sex and

---

4. Translator's note: see note 1, p. 209.

death, and not between other and/or pairs. The decisive point to grasp is that what is at stake here—beyond *the homologation of sexual* jouissance *and the little death*, a confirmation that is in no way whimsical—is legitimately sustained from its basis in the real of biology.

One fundamental rule of biology that involves the reproduction of sexuated species is that, for them to exist, the individuals must procreate and then die. The life of Homo sapiens, one species among those that follow this rule, also moves in this direction. This is what sexuated reproduction necessarily entails, unlike what is implied in the division—splitting in half—of more rudimentary organisms. For example, a protozoon split into two gives rise to new beings. No participation by another microorganism is necessary for this to occur. There is no sex in the process, nor is there death, for that matter, since reproduction can occur indefinitely through these splits in an internal process. *It is the sexual difference of more complex species that involves death.* Each type of species must accomplish the cycle of being born, feeding itself, growing, reproducing itself, and dying. An individual of the human species achieves something separate from him- or herself with the indispensable participation of someone different, of another sex. The child will prolong the project of the species, but the life of the singular individual who engendered it can only be extinguished at some point. *Sex and death are thus coalescent phenomena.* There is nothing artificial in this correlation; it is a condition we are part of from the biological structure that is indicated in this search for the "little death," through which new life may arise, prolonging the species.

Regarding the common points that the connection between sex and death in Freud—and of course Lacan—might have with a philosophy such as Arthur Schopenhauer's, several distinctions should be made. The German philosopher was the author of notable intuitions but his conception of the woman—to use one example of many possible ones—did not in any way coincide with Freud's vision, *according to which the search for the phallic insignia, after following a libidinal course marked by the lack of an object, culminates in the feminine "bet" on the child (as an object a to be separated from, Lacan adds)*. In Freud's doctrine, it is not necessary to rely on a "knowledge of the species" as in Schopenhauer's will. The philosopher writes in *The World as Will and Representation*: "Sexual instinct is, generally not, in itself and outside any exterior manifestation, anything other than the 'will to life.' But this has a generic character: the relation between two individuals (subjective love) is only a 'stratagem' by which nature achieves its aims. And it is in the product of the union, the child, where the will to life of the species is finally objectified."[5] Thus, marking the fallacy of postulating an Other of the Other, the misogynist philosopher did not differentiate between the sexes, making them mere puppets of what is, in the end, a theistic design.

We can now move to a new understanding of a decisive point made in *Seminar X*, which we have already touched upon at other times during our work here: the uncanny. Let us remember in this regard that *the uncanny is produced when what is destined to remain hidden arises and nevertheless manifests itself*. Freud takes up, to give a definition of this, a formula of Schelling. Lacan takes his reading of this one step further. What is this situation about? he asks himself. And here we have the answer: *the uncanny does not fall away when, from the place of the desirer, the other is located in the place of the desirable; it occurs when the desirable suddenly manifests itself as desiring, since the desirer is what*

5. Arthur Schopenhauer, *The World as Will and Representation*, cited in P. L. Assoun, *Freud, la filosofía y los filósofos* (Barcelona: Paidós, 1982), p. 206.

was veiled. In clinical practice one can clearly observe this in the sexual problems manifested by some male analysands faced with women who, suddenly and completely unexpectedly, show themselves to be "overdesiring." Lacan writes this in an even stronger manner. He advises that one note the classic effect of the uncanny produced when an inanimate being—an object of contemplation and thus of desire—starts to move. Let us imagine, for example, that a statue suddenly starts to move before us. Who would not see in this the threatening sign of the uncanny? What would this movement imply if not that it is the desirer that desires us, since the hiddenness has been dis-covered? Beyond however fantastic this example might seem—various manifestations of which are to be found in the most diverse cultural traditions—we should point out that it strikingly illustrates how this unveiling inversion—instituted by the eye—of what is desired into desirer can only be uncanny, since the desire of the Other turns back, ungovernable, towards the subject, which arouses anxiety. *What does the Other desire? Well, it wants me, as I do not know what I am for it. A dimension of devouring is manifested and lurks behind anxiety.* Between the lines, we should read here the condition where the primordial Other is seeking to reintegrate what it has produced. The subject thus finds itself helpless in the face of a desire that is the desire of the Other with regard to the subject itself in its quality of wholeness. This desire aims to reintegrate the subject, apprehend it, subject it to its domination by reingurgitating it. *In this situation of the uncanny, the trait inherent to the protophantasy of return to the mother's womb—not in the least idyllic—must be recognized.* At least, this is one of the originary phantasies in which the subject is, in a literal way, *devoured by anxiety.* In such a way this protophantasy makes a sudden appearance at moments when the desirable gives way to the desirer, assuming uncanny contours; *thus, when the*

subject falls into a situation of hopelessness, the constructed phan-
tasy operates as the giver of an answer—tranquility-producing—
to the question for the desire of the Other.

Another point that needs clarification in relation to the graph of the floors of the object *a* is, once again, the *cause*. This notion, far from being resolved through metaphysical speculations, has decisive clinical consequences, in particular with regard to the obsessive and the resulting domination of the anal floor.

When we talk about cause, David Hume observed, we are merely referring to a relation between an antecedent and a consequent. That was his idealistic criticism of the notion of cause. The Scots philosopher concluded that the cause was none other than a mental category, locatable only in the psyche. One thing happens and then another; both are related but the motive is not known, Hume explained, since there is intrinsically no explicit reason for why something causes one thing to have an effect and not another. Lacan, as we have shown, points out that this absence in the register of the cause must be attributed to the object *a*, thereby distancing himself from Hume's criticism. *The innumerable works that philosophers and epistemologists of the most diverse tendencies and epochs have dedicated to the problem of causation are due, in the last instance, to circling around and around the object* a. *This perdurability indicates, thus, that the series of problems posed by the category in question is not fallacious, insofar as the* a *participates irreducibly in the structure.* Of course, the *a* is not in view; it is not "full" view but, rather, it is marked as void of an object. It is this emptiness that determines what is unknowable of the cause. In this way, psychoanalysis finds itself with another preoccupation shared by philosophy and science, on the same footing as the much (and necessarily) reworked *objectivity*, as we saw in Chapter 6.

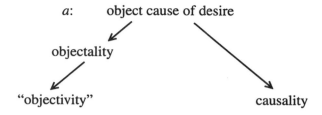

In an intellectual maneuver of the concept, Lacan jumps from one discourse to another. Linking fields that do not appear to have any relation to one another, he suddenly asks himself the purest kind of "*conceptista*"[6] question: What happens to the obsessive neurotic in relation to the cause? Although obsessions and the dimension of cause seem to be heteroclitic concepts, a certain internal relation operates here, he asserts.

First of all, it is necessary to observe what happens to the obsessive and his symptom, and when he can manage to stipulate that he needs to know its cause. Obviously, there are many people who have obsessions, but the fact that they do does not imply that they admit they do. In this sense, they remain outside the analytical perimeter. The obsessional neurotic begins to be so at the very instant he recognizes he is at the mercy of his obsessions; only with this can psychoanalysis do anything, *since there is no symptom as such unless the person suffering from it recognizes it. Also, it should be added that many times the first step in analysis is to constitute the symptom.* Now, when the subject recognizes his or her obsession as a symptom, that is where the answer about the cause comes up. In the same way that philosophers do, the subject puts forth that the ill being, the obsession he or she has,

---

6. Translator's note: a literary style of seventeenth-century Spain, characterized principally by bringing closely together semantic fields that are apparently vastly distant from one another.

originates in a causal enigma. It is something, it seems, that nobody imposed on the subject but that he or she cannot get rid of. *What is the cause of what is happening? And why, if it is disobeyed, does he or she experience anxiety? This is the principal place, consequently, for accounting for the relations between anxiety, which is obvious, and desire, which is obscure.* What then functions as a cause in the obsessive? Taking the cause–effect pair into account, we can say that *if the object is the cause, the desire is the effect.* Of course, "an effect has nothing to do with the effectuated," since the effect lacks or is lack. *The symptom, hence, is not an effect, but a result.* Desire is what we as analysts try to circle, or circumscribe—which in itself is very arduous. For its part, *the symptom is the mark by which the analysand goes into analysis, and that fulfills the function of the result of the* béance *caused by desire as the lack of effect of the causal* a. All of which can be represented thus:

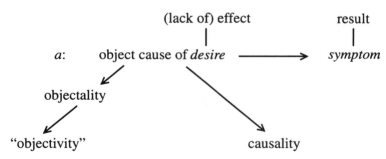

From the *a* to the symptom, there is no cause–effect relation but rather a mediation in which the *béance* of desire itself is at work. This indicates that we should ask ourselves what happens, in each analysis, to *the object* a *veiled in and by the symptom, since it is not reduced, as a result, to the mere play of signifiers.*

Approaching its articulatory function from the field of obsessive neurosis, the anal object ends up—once more—being a model of the primordial character of every *a*: this is what Lacan called, towards the end of *Seminar X*, "that which can be ceded." The *a* is conceived, then, as the object that is constituted by falling away. As a consequence of this, *another of the synergetic readings of anxiety can be introduced, a reading that understands anxiety as irrupting when the object* a *is on the verge of falling away.* Furthermore, the point prior to the imminent hand-over or yielding to the object *a*—which implies a degree of self-mutilation in so doing with regard to the voracious desire of the Other—is implied by the function of anxiety as signal. In the case of the obsessive, it is very clear that the demand in play—the demand of this floor—is educational: it is related to control over the sphincter, formulated—in an exemplary manner—by the mother.

It is worth underlining that *Seminar X* contains developments that might relocate some series of problems, which, though they are not dealt with by the seminar, are carried by, are instigated by, its itinerary. For example, the theme of the protophantasies is not explicitly dealt with by Lacan in 1962/63; however, the precise allusion to the five floors of the *a* does refer implicitly to originary phantasies; we shall now take up this articulation as mentioned.

In this regard, the prefix "proto-" connotes, surely, a condition related to what is regressive and archaic. If we recall what was said at the beginning of our meeting here and remove the connotation of risk from the word, one could think that *protophantasies are desirable formations that serve as the basis for the construction of more elaborate phantasies through combinatorial procedures.* It is from these universals—as an effect of structure—that the singular, unrepeatable, and fundamentally used phantasies, revealed by the subject in analysis, are derived. The five would operate as ultimate units, similar to mythemes, phonemes, and others. Based on these antecedents, *we propose call-*

ing *protophantaises "phantemes": minimal and irreducible phantasy units*.[7]

To show how and to what the five phantemes are articulated, we shall put them in a *new framework*, in which each is taken into consideration according to certain differential characteristics. This framework, as we shall see, has several entrances.

Having specified the floors for the constitution of the object *a* and the five phantasies pointed out by Freud, we have two headings and can correlate the items under them in the following way:

Phantemes	*a*
return to the womb	oral
seduction	anal
castration	phallic
primal scene	scopic
family novel	superego

Now we have to locate each of these phantemes and the object *a* corresponding to each one in relation to the remaining heading: the first can be called *the relation of the subject (S) with the A (Other)*,[8] a point which is also marked in *Seminar X* by five different modalities. Then, we shall *include the various threats that these phantemes claim to give rise to, in a column we shall call* "dangers." Lastly, we shall articulate various *phantasies* that account for the way in which the subject manages to be through

---

7. Harari, *La repetición del fracasso*, pp. 139–143.

8. This is a point that implies the display of the developments related to the framework of the division of the subject by the signifier, as worked out in Chapter 5.

them. As we are dealing with psychoanalysis, we should recall that this subject can only be in lack. *To be something, it is clear, is related to the movement of the drive, which is that which makes itself. Stated differently, the search is directed toward getting points of* jouissance *anchored through the Other, where the knotting makes sexuality be.*

The framework that will emerge as the final result of our proposal might seem assertive or even dogmatic, but its links are merely the legitimate fact of having gotten the various *a*'s to correspond to their respective phantemes, and extracting the logical consequences thereof. The guiding principle of this attempt comes from the postulation that *the phantasy provides the system of formation and processing of the* a's. These do not fall out of some platonic sky but rather, in the same way that they find support in the body crossed by speech, they are gestated and oriented within the phantasy structure.

9

From the Phantemic Framework to a New Version of the Matricial Framework

The columns of the framework we began in the previous chapter continue with a heading that we are calling *the relation of S with A*, in accordance with the five variations taken from the framework of the division of the subject by the signifier (Chapter 5).

Before going into this, we should recall that each of the object *a*'s is gestated in a different originary phantasy structure, that is, a phanteme. Now, instead of naming these as we have up until now, that is, in a manner leaning very often on the function of the drive or the psychic instance, we are now going to unify the terminology, designating them according to their customary "incarnation": *the oral a is thus the breast; the anal, feces; the phallic—in its condition of missing object—the phallus; the scopic, the gaze; and the superego, the voice.* As for the relation S has with the Other, the A, by virtue of the articulation of the five phantemes with their respective objects, it is necessary to start from a preliminary punctuation: in the five singular categories we are considering, *the reference to the desire of the Other is always present, such that each a floor always retains the com-*

mon trait of the object a. One should not forget here that *anxiety is, first of all, the sensation of the desire of the Other*, and it signals the imminence with which this desire is managing to fulfill its objective, that is, to reabsorb the subject or one of its *a*'s from the place of the Other, so that this latter can be reencountered due to the cession in play. This circumstance is valid to show that the *framework* we propose calling *phantemic*—by respecting the myth constituting its origin—is useful to clarify the guideline of the path: anxiety, obviously. Here Lacan makes a variation to his well-known proposition, "the desire *of* the Other." At one point in the seminar he speaks of ". . . *in* the Other" to point out the different categories. Why does he make this modification? In our judgment, he is driven by the theme he is exploring, which *privileges the radically Other*; the "of," on the other hand, due to the very ambiguity of its genitive, summons the possible juncture of desires—"I take mine from the Other"—which does not in the least illustrate the condition of anxiety.

Consequently, he begins by linking the breast to *the necessity in the Other*, to which we articulate the phanteme of the return to the womb:

Phantemes	a	Relation of the S to A
return to the womb	breast	necessity in the A
seduction	feces	
castration	phallus	
primal scene	gaze	
family novel	voice	

To understand what Lacan means when he mentions a necessity in the Other, it should be taken into account that the oral constellation supposes a logical moment and not a developmental one. The logical aspect at play is defined by the middle floor of the framework, which unites castration with the phallus object *a*; furthermore, the necessity in the Other takes into account the distinction Lacan makes between necessity and desire. Necessity refers to what is related to the animal, instinctual order, whereas desire is exclusive to speaking beings. Though a necessity is assigned to this floor of the framework, it should be understood as a primordial, newly mythical moment, though not, thereby, fallacious or inefficient. Lacan uses this conceptualization as a *theoretical fiction in which the Other is recognized in its constitutive relation to what is precisely a pre-subject—or subject of* jouissance—*as an instance where only the order of necessity is present.* Insofar as it is present or absent, it marks a distinct modality of the relation to the subject in its larval state (as it is not yet lived as the signifier for the Other). Between satisfaction and its resurgence as necessity in a continuous recycling, this dimension has an intrinsic characteristic of *rhythm, since it is about the breast that does not cease to lack.* According to Lacan, this floor or stage is placed in the *presignifying mythical moment,* already mentioned, *where the lack in the Other can barely be made out* at its most primitive level: that of necessity. On the floor below is written another concept, the clarification of which is crucial: *the demand in the Other*:

Phantemes	*a*	Relation of the S to A
return to the womb	breast	necessity in the A
seduction	feces	demand in the A
castration	phallus	
primal scene	gaze	
family novel	voice	

The demand in the Other can best be seen in the condition of anality. Strictly speaking, something very similar to the sphincter demand is implied *in the phanteme of seduction, which indicates that if the subject is capable of doing this or that, the Other will provide something as a reward.* A dialectical exchange is at play here that illustrates symbolic exchange, since *something that is significant for the Other announces its presence.* Lacan points out that it is here that one can observe the issue of the *gift* and *oblativity* in the way that Freud, at this same level, showed the status of the *gift.* We should stop here to specify, for example, what is apparently given in the relation between a man and a woman. Is something given here, or, more drastically, can we assert that neither the man nor the woman gives anything and that *the gift is a metaphor?*

The demand in the Other arises with the requirement to account for what happens on this floor we are examining. The demand the child puts forth with feces is, "Give me something that is yours." The fragment the subject concedes is, at the outset, a piece of itself. But once the feces come away from the body, they no longer belong to the subject. The Other has gotten them; Lacan remarks that once they have been expelled, the condition changes to such an extent that the subject must come to the conclusion that they are not parts of himself to be valued. Here a dialectic with two times comes into play. *First, the subject exalts agalmatically[1] what is about to appear and be given up or fall away from it, and be given up as a present, a gift, as a pledge of symbolic exchange. Next, this initial gift becomes what " it is"; no more than waste.* It is something the subject must not want anything to do with, since it is "not its own," nor should it belong to the subject even though it continues to be so. In the same way, we can say that, though the object *a* feces has a similar importance in

---

1. Translator's note: the *agalma*, as previously explained, is that which shines in the Other.

the constitution of the subject, it does so because *feces come to symbolize the presence-absence itself of the phallus, which is also played out in two times.* Said another way: the object *a* feces has the impact it does because *it* is "*symbolic of castration.*" In the case of the phallic object, the issue centers around the tumescence and detumescence (or aphanisis of the phallus). On the floor of the anal object *a*, the subject goes from appreciating the feces—before they are expelled—to being required to throw them away after they are expelled. The demand in the Other gives rise to this oscillation, to an ambivalence observable in a prevalent manner in the obsessive neurotic in the form of doubt, in the indecision leading to the *procrastination,* discovered by Lacan, consisting of the *indefinite delay of putting desire into act* along the lines of "leaving for tomorrow what you can do today." Everything centers around this anal object that is so definitive. In this regard, it is interesting to note a text by Dominique Laporte entitled, with no intention of euphemism, *Histoire de la merde* [*The History of Shit*; Trans.]. Here we find, rather surprisingly, the relation that forever has united the speaking being with this particular type of waste. What should be pointed out is that feces are not always granted the characteristics common to waste. Rather, on many occasions that are not necessarily dependent on a perverse structure, the opposite occurs. Laporte wrote the introduction of the French version of a book for which Freud wrote a prologue in the German version, *Scatologic Rites of All Nations,* by John Gregory Bourke. In terms of Laporte's own book, it is interesting to quote certain phrases that refer to the ambiguous place given the anal object, which, being waste, is also what is called *manure,* that is, something that is put at the service of creating life. Laporte writes this: "Shit, a principle of life, fecundates as spirit. It is known, through his diary, that Michelet, precisely when lacking inspiration, would go and *in-*

spire in the latrines the suffocating odor of his creation which the *animating* (in the literal as well as figurative sense) breath brought to his spirit."[2] Ingeniously, the author also is playing here with the idea of "animating breath." The famous historian made use of nothing less than the nauseating fumes of the latrines for inspiration. An intake of something that is smelled and refers to the anal *a. This reference to the air as vital breath, understandable here as a metaphor for intestinal gases*, is not casual.

Furthermore, when Lacan goes into the notion of birth trauma in the seminar, he points out that this event is traumatic not so much due to the violent separation of the neonatal infant from the mother but rather from the fact that the *infans* is almost suffocated by being abruptly brought into the medium of air, which is different from the one that until that moment enveloped him. This is Lacan's reading of what Freud pointed out at the beginning of *Inhibitions, Symptoms and Anxiety* as the initial moment of the sensation of anxiety, which constitutes its irreversible foundation in corporeity. In the physiological description of the phenomenon, what is preponderant is the *lack of air*. The reference to inspiration—in which, as we have seen, the anal object plays such an important role—leads to the idea of *anima*, a Latin word approximately equivalent to the Greek *pneuma*, which means both "soul" and "breath," and from which arises the notion of vital breath. The word "inspiration" itself refers to the idea that if one breathes in air, one's very soul is being inspired. In this regard, Laporte makes a long analysis of texts by Georges Bataille and Roland Barthes to deepen this association. This contemporary book by Laporte and the classic one by Bourke are indispensable in

---

2. Dominique Laporte, *Histoire de la merde* (Paris: C. Bourgois, 1978), p. 39. Italics in the original.

examining the implications of this *stool* object, the theoretical approach to which is so problematical. This precise designation by Lacan refers more to the *fecal clod* than the feces itself. It is clear that by using a term such as this one, one avoids uttering indecent words when dealing with this issue. In this regard, a considerable number of what are known as "dirty words" unequivocally refer to feces, the anus, defecation, and constipation. If someone is fond of using them, that is, is *copralalic*, he or she is said to have a "dirty mouth," an obvious slip from the anal to the oral floor.

The obsessive is one, in the way he is capable of making a certain twist, a certain inflection in the analysis, who elects to assume the place of the anal object *a*, offering himself according to the destiny of feces itself, as dejecture, as an object to be expelled. *But also, given his original condemnation to not reach any end whatever, he attempts to get the Other to authorize him—to make demands on him.*

Returning to the *phantemic framework* that we are elaborating, we add a third form of the subject's relating to the Other, which is linked to the castration-phallus axis; it is characterized as *jouissance in the Other:*

Phantemes	*a*	Relation of the S to A
return to the womb	breast	necessity in the A
seduction	feces	demand in the A
castration	phallus	*jouissance* in the A
primal scene	gaze	
family novel	voice	

Indeed, all of this new linkage is solidly congruent. What experiences *jouissance*? We should remember here that *jouissance* is located, focused, limited to the object face of the phallus. Beginning at this point in the seminar, we can say that since *jouissance* is phallic, it never ceases to summon what can be located as *jouissance* in the Other, as if it were establishing a hypothetical reversibility of the relations. *This jouissance in the Other, which Lacan later discusses as "jouissance of the Other" in* Seminars XIX *and* XX, *for example, is proposed for the first time systematically in* L'Angoisse. Hence, is it correct to speak in terms of the *phallic drive*? This is difficult, given how much Lacan insists upon the fact that *the phallus never ceases slipping, as the signifier of desire.* Thus, the phallus is a virtual presence that is not present, precisely by being present. And that is where the *jouissance* of the phallus is located. Jouissance *in the Other correlates to the castration-phallus articulation—castration is borne from the object side of the phallus—as of the moment in which the hypothetical phallic drive tries to establish itself.* This is difficult to conceive in a homogeneous, coherent manner, unlike the other drives (oral, anal, scopic, or invocatory), given the convergence in the phallus of the drive with desire, and the signifier with the phallic object. This *jouissance*, although difficult to grasp because it rests on something that is continuously subtracting itself because it is sustaining its place in another place, is a necessary step in providing a place for another modality of the subject's relation to the Other. This is a theme that Lacan would enlarge upon greatly during *Seminar XI*, and that implies *the gaze*. In *L'Angoisse* he calls this floor *potency in the Other:*

Phantemes	*a*	Relation of the S to A
return to the womb	breast	necessity in the A
seduction	feces	demand in the A
castration	phallus	*jouissance* in the A
primal scene	gaze	potency in the A
family novel	voice	

Now, it is rather restrictive to call this relation potency. To be more precise, one wider approach is to use the term indicated: here we should then make a characterization in terms of *omnipotence*. This is the condition of the gaze that leads Lacan to postulate it from the beginning as *something that is outside, and even more, is everywhere*. But it has no location; indeed, if the subject looks from only one place, that is but a lure; the subject is first looked at from all points or everywhere. This omnipotence—linked to an *all-seeingness*—is, rightly, what is first of all attributed to God. This is a major characteristic because *due to the all-seeingness, the Other institutes the world and commands it*. It can see everything because it is, in the first place, That Which sees all as a Universal Eye. Lacan's reasoning here is very keen; he points out that gods belong to the Real, thereby connoting their irreducibility to the signifier, to history. In this way, *there is no progress* linked to advances in the sciences or supposedly objective knowledge that could turn the question of the existence of God into one of decadence or incredulity. This is not about ascribing to the God of this or that religion; what is at stake in any belief is this postulation of omnipotence, from the point of view of an idea of an all-seeing eye that can be in all places at the same time, watching over all points in the universe, in accordance with "*contemplative possession*." The notion of panopticon—as used by Jeremy Bentham—comes from this presumption of all-seeingness proper to the Supreme Being. This is where Lacan says that *the true dimension of atheism belongs to those who have managed to eliminate the phantasy of omnipotence. This phantasy, furthermore, is the form the ego ideal adopts to cover anxiety at this level.* Against this stand all manner of believers with their different theistic constructions, including the category of those who say they do not believe in the existence of the gods.

It is worth observing that in *L'Espace et le regard* by Jean Paris,[3] which unravels what could be called the *philosophical history of vision*, the author comes to very similar conclusions to those of Lacan. At the beginning of the book, Paris discusses the gaze in a painting, in a portrait, insofar as the gazer and the one who is gazed upon are in a reciprocal, dual relation to each other. Paris then notes aspects of the work of painters such as Brueghel, which seem to appear as painting of nonseers; the difference here is that Brueghel broke with the dual relation, with reciprocity. Later, Paris considers a series of works where one can see figures with half-opened eyes, and finally he discusses a series of paintings of particular interest to him due to an issue that he calls the *seers*.

---

3. Jean Paris, *L'Espace et le regard* (Paris: Seuil, 1965), translated into Spanish as *El espacio y la mirada* (Madrid: Taurus, 1967). Paris does not quote Lacan, nor does Lacan quote him, though they both knew some of the same people, including Merleau-Ponty and, as we shall see, Roger Caillois. Paris and Lacan also had the same publisher, Seuil. What we do know is that Paris was a Joyce expert. His book, *James Joyce par lui-même* (Paris: Seuil, 1957) is well known.

[Note added for the English edition of this book]: Two later circumstances have finally permitted me to situate Jean Paris: the first is owed to the generosity of the eminent French philosopher, essayist, and poet, Jean-Pierre Faye, who sent me several volumes of the discontinued review *Change*. Lacan and Paris both sat on the editorial board of the magazine, adding their talents to an enterprise that, in its moment (publication began at the end of the riots of 1968), constituted a gamble of the vanguard in the field of literature. The second reference concerns the book of Élisabeth Roudinesco, *Jacques Lacan— Esquisse d'une vie, histoire d'un système de pensée* (Paris: Fayard, 1993), the Spanish version of which I had the pleasure to present, together with its author, the following year in Buenos Aires. In it, Roudinesco pauses over a tasty anecdote, narrated by Paris, which involves him as much as Lacan: "He— Lacan—turned up one night at one in the morning at the house of Faye because he wanted to use a portmanteau word that I had devised." With these two references I hope to have clarified the relationship between the two for the English readers of my book.

Who does Jean Paris call a "seer?" Coinciding almost exactly with Lacanian teaching, he writes: "Before any other attribute, God sees. The Sun is his Eye, the lamp of the sky, like the human eye is the lamp of the body. . . . All medieval art, until the heart of the Renaissance, retains this celestial character of the Seer which sustains the spirit as a variety of the Light."[4] Later developments in the text are also very striking due to the attractive quality of the writing, which comes close to poetry. For example: "Divine, human, bestial; dominion is undoubtedly of visual origin, and instantly we see how two classes of beings are drawn: one who exercises it and those who suffer it. What the former sees must obviously be forbidden to the others: from here springs the necessity for the gods to remain hidden." In summary, he who sees without being seen shall be a god. In the next line, with almost the same words as Lacan, the author writes, "The gaze is, then, the principle of power. To see is already to conquer, to assert a magic position of the object. . . . To reflect, to see clearly, to be lucid, to foresee a problem, to perceive a solution, to unveil, to shed light, to update a point of view, a way of seeing, a vision of the world, etc. From 'illumination' to 'natural lights,' from 'clear and distinct ideas' to the 'reflection' of the materialists, to the 'perspective' of the relativists. . . . One can thus conceive through what confusion the divine Gaze was able to spring from ours, by feeding on the privileges that are denied to us. His dominion is the infinite: his clarity, like that of the stars, reaches unfathomable distances everywhere."

Evidently, many developments could be followed starting from the beginning of Paris's book, but all the approaches, in our judgment, to the issue of the gaze are summed up in this

---

4. Paris, *El espacio y la mirada*, pp. 26–27.

brilliant, conclusion-like sentence: "God's omnipotent gaze is thus opposed to the weak gaze of man."[5]

Further on, to our surprise, Paris gives the reader a rigorous series of classical authors frequently quoted by Lacan: "The analogy of vision and knowledge sheds light on the mystic ambition of discovering the world through God's very eyes. For San Juan de la Cruz, Jakob Boehme, Angelus Silesius, to return to Him would be, beyond any visual frontier, to introduce themselves into his optics, to melt themselves in them. . . . We already know the words of Meister Eckhart, 'The eye through which I see God is the same eye through which He sees me'."[6]

Strikingly, the last sentence is a famous mystical saying that Lacan uses textually. Beyond any influence there might have been between Lacan and Paris, what is important is to point out that the two work from dissimilar theoretical tools but arrive at similar conclusions about the theme of the power in the Other as it relates to the gaze.

It is worth emphasizing once again the decisive nature of this floor of the framework, since it is the one in which *the object a is whitewashed to the greatest degree*, due to the syncope, the evanescence of its action. Furthermore, it should not be forgotten that *this floor is the one of the phantasy itself*, and *it is the phantasy that institutes reality*. Also, here we would like to reiterate *the strength of the ties between the gaze and the uncanny*.

As for the last floor, which articulates the family novel as phanteme with the object a called the voice, what Lacan calls— this time with all the weight on the punctuation—the *desire in the Other. This relation is more closely linked to the signifying chain, which, it is clear, has the object side in the voice*; that is, it is about

5. Paris, *El espacio y la mirada*, pp. 36–39.
6. Paris, *El espacio y la mirada*, p. 45.

being in earshot of the Other so it sends out its voice, hidden by speaking. Thus—like the gaze—the voice cannot be separated from the subjective aspect of the Other, postulated as the principal site to activate its desire:

Phantemes	*a*	Relation of the S to A
return to the womb	breast	necessity in the A
seduction	feces	demand in the A
castration	phallus	*jouissance* in the A
primal scene	gaze	potency the he A
family novel	voice	desire in the other

The clinical point to be taken into consideration on this level centers on the recurring problem of obsessive neurosis. What happens to the obsessive with his *impossible desire*? He or she does not manage to fulfill it, and *keeps emphasizing the failure to do so.* Furthermore, what he or she does continuously and by all means is to try to not fulfill something, as if obeying a desire which he or she seeks to have demanded of him or her by the Other. "I don't do it because I want to"—that is his or her alibi—"but because it is asked of me." That is *where the demand in the Other appears, which "covers" the desire in the Other.* Now, Lacan warns us in this regard to be very careful when this happens in an analysis, that is, when the obsessive starts to locate him- or herself comfortably in the place of being the serf of the Other, since if he or she falls into this condition *the subject will have identified itself with feces.* We should say that, while the obsessive appears as an obsequious slave, asking permission, getting the Other to show him or her what he or she should do each step of the way, thereby hiding his or her own desire, at the same time he or she is also putting him- or herself in the place of waste, in a condition where all that is left is to be thrown away.

This is a serious risk, which should be taken into consideration, since it is not unusual for the analysis to take such a turn in the direction of the cure. When this situation arises, the cure can be paralyzed if sterile behaviorist "analyses" of the aggressive or rebellious and/or submission fantasies are proffered by the analyst.

As we set forth in the previous chapter, the next column in the *phantemic framework* involves *dangers*. This is what Freud called "a situation of danger" in *Inhibition, Symptoms and Anxiety* and in the *Thirty-second Conference*. To our understanding, these situations can also be articulated to our framework, given the extent to which they illustrate Lacan's assertions about the fact that danger anxiety is a signal of *the imminence of the giving of what may be ceded: the* a—that is, what a does the desire of the Other want me to be for it? What does a want from me (why don't I know it)? Or, directly put, what wants (me)?

The first of the dangers that should be pointed out, which are linked to the phanteme of return to the womb—which engenders the oral object *a*—and with the relation of necessity in the Other, we have already included in our work. We call it, as Freud does, *helplessness (Hilflosigkeit)*. *This refers to the state of absolute "psychical and motor" defenselessness, which is empirically verifiable, of an* infans *at birth.*

Phantemes	a	Relation of the S to A	Dangers
return to the womb	breast	necessity in the A	helplessness
seduction	feces	demand in the A	
castration	phallus	*jouissance* in the A	
primal scene	gaze	potency in the A	
family novel	voice	desire in the other	

In our judgment, Freud's intellection gives rise to the way Lacan understands the child in *Seminar XX*: the entire child is an object *a*. It should be said that in the structural situation in which the *infans* is thrust into the world from the primordial Other, its specific cession is one of integral corporeity. Put otherwise, *it is a leftover that leaves no leftover*. On the next floor *a more precise moment is marked in which something is lost, configuring what Freud calls the loss (of love) of the object*. A valid example one can imagine of this is the following: let us suppose a subject in a situation in which the Other appears on the verge of being lost or about to stop loving it. *This changes the valence of the presence of the Other completely, since if what the Other demands is not fulfilled, the presence can become an absence*. We can recognize here the action of *seduction*, the *gift*, and *anal exchange*:

Phantemes	*a*	Relation of the S to A	Dangers
return to the womb seduction	breast feces	necessity in the A demand in the A	helplessness loss (of the love) of the object
castration primal scene family novel	phallus gaze voice	*jouissance* in the A potency in the A desire in the other	

As for the third danger, we should repeat what we earlier entered in the framework as a phanteme. This is *castration*, which here functions as *a threat to the subject*. What does this imply? That this threat carries the Law as symbolic, thus transcending the defensive limits of the phanteme related to it. *Castration, as the dangerous installer of the phallus, thus forces the ceding of a* jouissance *that is believed to be lost and that is, rigorously speaking, impossible*.

Moving directly to the last floor, we find in *Seminar X* itself an orientation for the encounter with the corresponding danger, since Lacan interchanges the voice with the *superego*. And fear of the superego is another of the dangers Freud postulated. *What returns in the voice, if not the obscene ferocity of an inertial danger of the "prehistoric" Other, which answers with the originary "royal-like" norms of the novel before which the singularity of desire is ceded?*

Phantemes	*a*	Relation of the S to A	Dangers
return to the womb	breast	necessity in the A	helplessness
seduction	feces	demand in the A	loss (of the love) of the object
castration	phallus	*jouissance* in the A	castration
primal scene	gaze	potency in the A	
family novel	voice	desire in the other	superego

As can be seen, a decisive floor—linked to the gaze—remains blank. One category is missing that is not named in the Freudian texts. To save this absence, we shall have recourse to a reference Lacan takes from ethology. We refer—to exemplify the danger in question—to "the praying mantis of voracious desire, with which no factor unites me . . . [which is an exemplary] case where the Other would be radically Other." This reference could be hermetic were the scientific and literary source from which it springs not taken into account, which is simply a text of Roger Caillois. He undertook various studies like the one we are considering, which he called *diagonal sciences*. In a book entitled *Méduse et Cie*, he inserted a brief text on the praying mantis, which Lacan worked on intelligently. Around 1960, Caillois writes the following in this book that brings together diagonally zoology with mythology, anthropology, literature, and psychology: "I had attempted almost twenty years ago to establish a relation between certain facts which appear not to have, and maybe do not have, relations between them: these concern the sexual habits of the female praying mantis who devours the male during intercourse; the extraordinary interest generally shown by mankind towards this insect which is to be found either divinely or diabolically in all the places the latter is found: from Provence, Greece, Rhodesia, southern Africa; the fear *(frayeur)*,[7] testified to by numerous myths and obsessions that a daemonic woman devour, kill or mutilate he who unites himself to her at the moment he favorably agrees to such a union."[8]

Further along, Caillois wonders if these quasi-ethological, or rather, comparative psychology-like comparisons are valid, and responds that they are. It is worth observing to what extent the specific points of this French essayist "are Lacanian." For example, he points out that the praying mantis is an insect, an order that is to be found—on the zoological scale—at the extreme opposite of the order of the speaking being. Nevertheless, he observes that both species possess language, though in insects this is an exceptional phenomenon, as is the case with bees, where, unlike the *sapiens*, it is not possible to transcend the limits imposed by "a code of fixed and unchangeable signals."[9] The "correspondence" is also found in the formation of complex societies. Except for the differences—crucial, we might add—the similarities are curious. All this is used by Caillois to *outline a suggestive "parallel" between the praying mantis and the devouring woman of so many mythical accounts or "fabulations."* In the legends, the women fascinate their prey with their gazes. The female praying mantis also paralyzes the male with her ocelli, which find themselves excluded from the vibration of the eye-

---

7. See Chapter 5, this volume.
8. Roger Caillois, *Méduse et Cie* (Paris: Gallimard, 1960), p. 25.
9. Caillois, *Méduse et Cie*, p. 27.

lids, from the aphanisis. After enumerating initial facts, Caillois points out that the gaze in itself becomes devouring and "swallowing up" (from the French *engloutir*). This could be rendered as "to eat with the eyes," a commonly used expression in the colloquial Spanish of the Rio de la Plata region. Similarly, it is worth remembering in this regard how certain women are graphically characterized as being "maneaters." *The petrifying and "outside" localization of the gaze metaphorized by the omnipotent praying mantis illustrates clearly what can be ceded on this floor, whose capture usually remains covered over by the world and reality.* This capture ensures against anxiety since the cession on this floor seems not to be completed. Its emergence, hence, signals what is radically Other. Because of all this, *we propose calling the danger corresponding to the scopic level the praying mantis.*

Phantemes	*a*	Relation of the S to A	Dangers
return to the womb	breast	necessity in the A	helplessness
seduction	feces	demand in the A	loss (of the love) of the object
castration	phallus	*jouissance* in the A	castration
primal scene	gaze	potency in the A	praying mantis
family novel	voice	desire in the other	superego

In the text quoted from Jean Paris, the relation uniting the gaze and devouring is not absent. The postulation of the (omni) potency in the Other correlates to an impotence in the subject, who is converted into a victim by virtue of being looked at from the ocellus.

Our framework requires a new column to finalize its relevance. Here we shall place the phantasies that Lacan demonstrates—in *La Logique du fantasme*—constitute axioms: indivisible utterances or sentences, all unquestionable insofar as primordial "truths," and from which consequences should be drawn coherently and consistently. Thus, the consequences of these phantasy axioms structure the life of subjects. In this regard, we recall the place of the *a* in the formula of the phantasy ($\$\lozenge a$). It should be observed that the *a*'s are not objects located in front of the divided subject but rather, first, *the subject is its object in the phantasy*. Therefore, this is about something of the order of being ("is"). Thus, the first fundamental axiom, related to its floor, is *the phantasy of being swallowed, ingurgitated again by the primordial Other in a helpless reabsorption by the maternal womb*:

Phantemes	*a*	Relation of the S to A	Dangers	Phantasy Axioms
return to the womb	breast	necessity in the A	helplessness	being swallowed
seduction	feces	demand in the A	loss (of the love) of the object	
castration	phallus	*jouissance* in the A	castration	
primal scene	gaze	potency in the A	praying mantis	
family novel	voice	desire in the A	superego	

As of now, we assert that this axiom does not refer to any empirical type of state; it does not in any way name an anthropophagia about to be consummated. What the axiom does assert is that the then presubject is related to the Other that seeks to devour it in function of its lack: necessity. *The anxiety in question is recognized then as an anxiety of being devoured.*

On the following floor is the phantasy axiom that is frequently found in everyday speech in a variety of ways. This is a decisive phantasy through which the subject locates itself in the place of the anal object *a*. To be colloquial and blunt, we define it as *the phantasy of being shit*:

Phantemes	*a*	Relation of the S to A	Dangers	Phantasy Axioms
return to the womb	breast	necessity in the A	helplessness	being swallowed
seduction	feces	demand in the A	loss (of the love) of the object	being shit
castration	phallus	*jouissance* in the A	castration	
primal scene	gaze	potency in the A	praying mantis	
family novel	voice	desire in the A	superego	

This is one of the habitual ways that a subject can achieve—through putting this phantasy into act—that the Other demand that it place itself in the place of stool in order to be ejected, humiliated, won over, thrown away as waste. *It is fundamental that this phantasy axiom be considered to capture a decisive function played out in destiny neuroses.* In repetitive-failure compulsion, for example, in which a demonic design seems to be fulfilling itself—Real—from which the subject cannot get away, this axiom is preponderant. The subject over and over finds itself involuntarily implied in situations where it comes to occupy the place of feces, which corresponds to the loss (of the love) of the object.

The following item is the axiom related to what we have seen as a *phanteme* and as a *danger: castration.* This is the axiom of being mutilated—through the symbolic order, of course:

Phantemes	*a*	Relation of the S to A	Dangers	Phantasy Axioms
return to the womb	breast	necessity in the A	helplessness	being swallowed
seduction	feces	demand in the A	loss (of the love) of the object	being shit
castration	phallus	*jouissance* in the A	castration	being mutilated
primal scene	gaze	potency in the A	praying mantis	
family novel	voice	desire in the A	superego	

What does being mutilated consist of? It implies a being that is restricted, enclosed, which leads to the localization of a *jouissance* that can only be partial, given the aphanisis of the phallus (-φ). *Mutilation leads to the imaginarization[10] of plenitude, as* jouissance *in the Other. Thus, mutilated, the subject is the guarantor of the castration of the Other.*

As for the fourth level, linked to the *a* gaze, the axiom corresponds to the danger incarnated by the praying mantis—"contemplative possession" in function of "mirroring of potency"—*the axiom of being possessed.* What is phantasized is *the capture through the gaze of the Other:*

Phantemes	*a*	Relation of the S to A	Dangers	Phantasy Axioms
return to the womb	breast	necessity in the A	helplessness	being swallowed
seduction	feces	demand in the A	loss (of the love) of the object	being shit
castration	phallus	*jouissance* in the A	castration	being mutilated
primal scene	gaze	potency in the A	praying mantis	being possessed
family novel	voice	desire in the A	superego	

The subject thus phantasizes being possessed by an all-encompassing gaze. As for the element that completes the framework, it is linked—in accordance with the theme of origins and the family novel—to the arrival of the subject in the world. The axiom in question is none other than *being given birth to in a somewhat dishonorable manner.* To use our slang, we would say it is about *being (badly) born.*

---

10. Translator's note: a neologism of the author, taken from the Lacanian category of the imaginary.

Phantemes	a	Relation of the S to A	Dangers	Phantasy Axioms
return to the womb	breast	necessity in the A	helplessness	being swallowed
seduction	feces	demand in the A	loss (of the love) of the object	being shit
castration	phallus	*jouissance* in the A	castration	being mutilated
primal scene	gaze	potency in the A	praying mantis	being possessed
family novel	voice	desire in the A	superego	being (badly) born

In our Rio de la Plata speech, to refer to someone as being "badly born" is an insult that discredits the person's honor in function of his or her origins, of his or her maternal forebears.

Our study of *Seminar X* shall conclude, as it does, with a final examination of the matricial framework developed in the first two chapters of our work. This is one more reason to show to what extent the development of *L'Angoisse* does not follow a linear or progressive path. In relation to the already completed framework, Lacan proposes examining it in relation to the second and fourth floors of the graph of the *a*'s with the aim of *calibrating the specifications that the variables of the framework adopt in function of these floors.* Furthermore, this issue arises again in positioning the condition of obsessive neurosis. We shall now examine this theme in light of the diagram where the inhibition, symptom, and anxiety elements of Freud's triptych, the guideline of the entire seminar, were diagonally located, as well as the remaining six operators. These elements were positioned, we recall, in the framework according to increasing intensity along a horizontal axis of *difficulty* and a vertical axis of *movement*. Working on the framework by es-

tablishing these initial terms, Lacan places new elements between the relations of contiguity and double entry. Stated another way, focusing on the problem of desire in the obsessive
neurotic, he defines how each one of the factors becomes increasingly singular in this area according to movement, difficulty, and the anal and scopic *a* floors. Now, insofar as the
scopic floor shows newer and more complete specifications—
in our judgment—we shall point them out first, though articulated to the anal ones. And it is the anal, precisely, from where
it encounters the appearance of inhibition, as the first item in
the framework. *From this "museum-like symptom," articulated
at the beginning of the seminar, he moves to characterizing it in
function of the desire in play.* This is desire that "can take on
the function of what we call a defense." In inhibition, what is
achieved is the introduction in a function of another desire
different from the one that, in a natural way, is found to be
implied in the satisfied function. The erotization of functions
can be understood in this manner. In this regard, one should
not forget Lacan's emphasis on Freud's classic example of the
issue, which has the value of an exemplar: inhibition works
on the (loco) motion.[11] But although Lacan points out with regard to this that another desire is superposed on the desire in
question, it should be taken into account that in this constellation *another term appears linked to these desires, through which
desire is implied in inhibition: this term is the act.* Here we can
locate three linked terms, *inhibition, desire, and act*, with which
we begin to draw this new version of the matricial framework.[12]

---

11. Translator's note: a pun. (Loco) motion is "crazy" motion.
12. It should be said that our drawing of the framework does not reproduce both those of the seminar to which it refers, since it incorporates
explicitly articulations that are not developed in the visual drawing of the two.

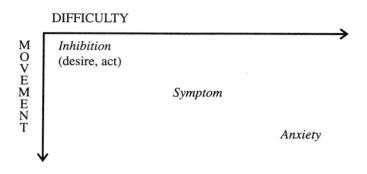

Regarding the act, Lacan makes another attempt to be precise. He says that this concept ". . . is an action . . . in that through it is manifested the same desire which was destined to inhibit it." As can be seen, he links the definition of the act with inhibition and desire. *An act, in this respect, is as much the result of originary desire as of the desire destined to inhibit it (as a defense).* As its name suggests, what is at stake in inhibition is a phenomenological retraction of the subject. The act, on the contrary, overcomes inhibition because it succeeds in articulating both a desire as well as what in principle was oriented toward defending the subject from the former, *culminating in an action.* But this action is not merely about motor activity—which is contingent—but rather an "insistence in the Real" that has the character of *"a manifestation of the signifier where . . . the detour that makes a gap of desire is inscribed."*

Now the obsessive, captured in the structure of the second floor of the phantemic framework (seduction-feces-demand in the Other, etc.), does not cease to point out also the fourth floor—linked to the *a* gaze—to attempt to fulfill his desire. Paradoxically, the desire of the obsessive neurotic around this can be characterized as *the desire to not see:*

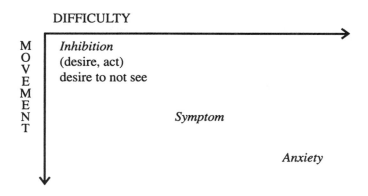

DIFFICULTY

M
O
V
E
M
E
N
T

Inhibition
(desire, act)
desire to not see

Symptom

Anxiety

This particular state of blindness sought by the obsessive has little to do with the tragic dimension of blindness—the *ojos "a-terrados"*[13] of Oedipus—since the *"human drama is not tragedy but comedy."* He seeks only the situation that we can illustrate by paraphrasing the old adage: there is no better blind man than the one who does not want to see. This is one of the modalities by which the obsessive subject—located in the place of inhibition—seeks to articulate a desire that, by definition, is impossible.[14] *Anxiety, on the other hand, is rejected in function of the seizure by the specular image, i(a).*

As we have pointed out, Lacan postulates what he calls *emotion* farther along the movement axis than inhibition. Here too, he locates a new term linked *to the misrecognition proper to another type of desire, the desire of not-knowing.*

---

13. Translator's note: a pun. "Terrorized eyes," literally, eyes that have been disinterred or are on the ground or earth.

14. Roberto Harari, "El obsesivo llega a la conclusión (Acerca del deseo imposible)," in *¿De qué trata la clínica lacaniana?* (Buenos Aires: Catálogos, 1994), pp. 115–127.

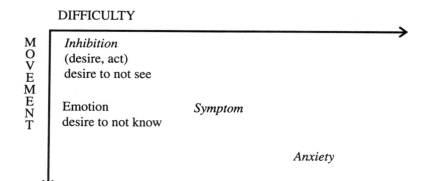

DIFFICULTY

M
O
V
E
M
E
N
T

Inhibition
(desire, act)
desire to not see

Emotion   *Symptom*
desire to not know

                                        Anxiety

This desire to not know brings about a problem through its operation, because that operation puts into play anxiety confronted by an unknown. Which unknown? The one that punctuates that the subject does not know, in this situation, what the Other wants of it. This occurs in such a way that, *in his attempt to "achieve" the consummation of desire by defending himself with another desire, the obsessive remains easy prey to the Desire of the Other.* That is how *desire* is positioned in the place that, in principle, Lacan reserved for *emotion*.

As for the maximum degree of movement, which in the first exposition of the framework was occupied by what was called *dismay,* now, in the scopic, is correspondingly placed the *ego ideal.* This variance is justified by the fact that the ideal "*is the most comfortable at introjecting the Other.*" Specifically, the ideal is formed from a trait of the Other; following Freud here, we say that it is a *unary trait.* Now, *this introjection moderates anxiety because it seems to respond through identification to the question of the subject about the Other, that is, its desire for the cession it seeks.* So we must enter the ideal in the schema as it is written in Lacanian notation, that is, as $I(A)$.

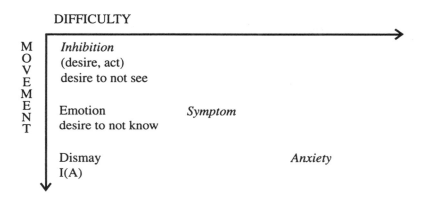

DIFFICULTY

In the position following inhibition, which refers to a greater degree of difficulty, Lacan locates another phenomenon linked to the obsessive's experience. Where the *impediment* had been placed, he now emphasizes a condition of *impotence*, which he asserts as the correlate to upholding the previous desire to not see. But this "being chased into the trap," is not, clearly, only a redoubling of inhibition; thus, *impotence, the not being able, is also a not being able to carry out fully the desire not to see and the desire to retain. The consequences are, in the latter case, compulsion, and in the former case, the "peeping" of the a.* Now, remembering that *the floor of the gaze is the floor of the potency in the Other*, this impotence necessarily refers to its antithesis, which Lacan locates in the central position in the matrix. Consequently, *the postulation of impotence in the impediment is made to correspond to the phantasy of omnipotence in the Other in the place of the symptom.* In fact this phantasy, as we saw, is simply the potency in the Other, the modality through which the subject is possessed and subjugated by the Other, which can be verified in the cession known as symptom. Thus the impotence–omnipotence pair will be placed in the following manner in the framework:

DIFFICULTY

M O V E M E N T	*Inhibition* (desire, act) desire to not see	Impediment impotence	
	Emotion desire to not know	*Symptom* omnipotence	
	Dismay I(A)		*Anxiety*

We could say that the *symptom*—in one reading—is simply *the attempt arising from desire to fulfill, in the phantasy, the omnipotence of the Other*. The subject submits to the all powerful Other, which often presents itself in the obsessive problematic as God— we should recall the Seer here—pressing the symptom towards an ideational religious construction. Indeed, *the symptom ends up being, like God, unpredictable, ungovernable, and inscrutable*.

In the place corresponding to acting out, Lacan surprisingly locates another concept that we have already considered in Chapter 4, the concept of mourning:

DIFFICULTY

M O V E M E N T	*Inhibition* (desire, act) desire to not see	Impediment impotence	
	Emotion desire to not know	*Symptom* omnipotence	
	Dismay I(A)	Acting-out mourning	*Anxiety*

One frequently observes a depressive condition in the obsessive neurotic, who lacks the self-reproaching characteristic of the melancholic. It is the melancholic that provides the clinical support for proposing what Lacan will write in the place of the *passing to the act* rather than in the place of *acting out*. Very close to anxiety and hiding it, he locates this last type of action that abandons the scene: *suicide. This mainly applies to the melancholic, since, in the case of the obsessive, suicide is a phantasy.*

DIFFICULTY

M O V E M E N T	*Inhibition* (desire, act) desire to not see	Impediment impotence	
	Emotion desire to not know	*Symptom* omnipotence	Passing to the act suicide
	Dismay I(A)	Acting-out mourning	*Anxiety*

Suicide shapes the paradigm, the apologue, of what characterizes passing to the act in the scopic. Then, in the place corresponding to anxiety—based on Freud's original triptych—the term and the experience of it will remain imperturbable. Obviously, this is anxiety "whilst always covered." There remains, nevertheless, a blank to be filled in, which had belonged to the condition that Lacan called "*embarras.*"[15]

We pointed out, in the passages where we introduced this term, that it referred especially to a difficult situation. This is a

---

15. Translator's note: see Chapter 1, page 19, and footnote 7 for an explanation of this term.

situation in which the subject suffers *the greatest difficulty in what is implied in a successful outcome to the obstacle presented*. Towards the end of *Seminar X*, Lacan will again take an unexpected turn, putting in place the *concept of anxiety*, which, in addition to alluding to a specific element, is the title of a work by Søren Kierkegaard. Reading this work can provide insight to grasping this term, one of the inspirational sources of the seminar:

DIFFICULTY

M O V E M E N T	*Inhibition* (desire, act) desire to not see	Impediment impotence	Unease concept of anxiety
	Emotion desire to not know	*Symptom* omnipotence	Passing to the act suicide
	Dismay I(A)	Acting-out mourning	*Anxiety*

A new version of the matricial framework of anxiety.

This concept, it is clear, "tends" to anxiety. Nevertheless, *the conceptual order, in which the anxiety-provoking phenomenon seems to be involved, in some way becomes domesticated by being caught on the symbolic terrain of the signifier that provides its limit.* If there is a signifier, there is slippage; hence, as we have already pointed out, there cannot not be deception. *Outright anxiety, on the contrary, has a crushing degree of certainty since it is the "only connection" to the Real, and, as such, constitutes the "only ultimate grasp (prise) as such of any and all reality."* The concept of anxiety thus implies an attenuated order of what anxiety itself is, since symbolically, the "true" connection we mentioned does not have a place. Lacan leans on Kierkegaard then, which distances him from Hegel.

In Appendix C of *Inhibitions, Symptoms and Anxiety*, one of the main points to be differentiated, according to a concern that Freud himself considered unresolved, is the relation between *mourning* and *anxiety*. Visibly and outwardly, the two issues seem unrelated. However, Lacan returns to them, wondering, *why does Freud point out that mourning and anxiety both refer to the loss of an object?* And since he says this, what difference is there between the losses in both cases?

In the case of *anxiety*, the situation is quickly clarified. *Anxiety takes place when the imminent cession of the object a-Thing threatens.* Thus the implication refers directly to the order of *desire* and its manifestations. On the other hand, regarding *mourning*, Lacan shows—and the framework illustrates this—that we are on the territory of the ideal. We are thereby facing something that is related decisively to the phenomenon of *love*, which, given that it is *a* determined narcissistically, upholds desire through i(a) before upholding it through the object *a* gaze. This latter remains hidden in spite of being "the true object of the relation." *The working through of mourning consists in consummating again "the loss brought about by the accident of the destiny of the loved object."* That is to say, the work of mourning seeks to link memories and hopes to the loved object in a very detailed manner. This process seeks *to restore the nexus with the hidden a for which another substitute can be found in the end.* The lost object—i(a)—was merely also a substitute for *a*. Also, *in acting out, the substitute comes onto the scene, pointing to a homology with the work that mourning carries out with the object.*

Once Lacan proposes this intellection for the case of mourning, he immediately positions melancholy, thereby echoing the classic text of Freud. In melancholy, suicide, with its exemplary dimension, accounts for another dialectic between *a*—still the fourth level—and i(a). *In the case of suicide, the specular image merely fulfills the function of being removed.* It must be attacked up to its last instances in order to arrive in this manner at the unknown and hidden object *a* by *crossing the frame, the window, of the phantasy.* The act resulting from this objective, in its most extreme form, is none other than *the defenestration of the subject identified absolutely with the* a. The subject, being *a*, falls, hurls itself down.

Another point included by Lacan in the final passages of *L'Angoisse* is related to the issue of mania. He says of the manic that *"what is at play is the nonfunction of the* a"; *not its being not known.* When this function, which makes a cut in the signifying chain by *"ballasting"* the subject does not exist, what happens clinically speaking is the *flight of ideas.* The subject finds itself carried along by an incessant and apparently lawless series of associations where a minimum trace provides a link with the following one, and on and on in an "infinite and game-like" metonymy. The consideration of mania, as that of melancholy, opens in this manner a territory distinct from the one of the mourning-Ideal-love register, although its fruitful characterization is still in its early stages. In any case, what Lacan does indicate about mania provides an example of the productive nature of the framework he sets out at the end of *Seminar X.* The matricial framework thus reveals itself to be an apt conceptual operator to produce different combinations—for example, based on each of the floors of *a*—starting from the originary combinatorial structure. Stated differently, beyond being a descriptive diagram, it is *a genuine piece of conceptual machinery* due to the articulation of its terms. Suffice to put it to work for it to show its results. This is undoubtedly true of all of this unequaled seminar of Lacan, the introduction to which ends here.

Index

relation to the Other, 44–45, 232, 235
relation with object, 65, 112
sublimation
and creation, 151–152
of desire, 149–150, 152
suddenness, 53–54, 62, 129
suffering, 11, 14, 21
degrees of, 18–19
as universal, 7, 53
suicide, 263, 265–266
superego, 174, 210
and need for failure, 98–102, 100
in phantemic framework, 249–250
voice of, 195–205
superego object *a,* 232, 235
symbolic exchange, 54
symbolic phallus, 175–176
Symposium, The (Plato), 93–95, 97, 224
symptoms, 74, 85
in analysis, 27, 92, 229–230
relation to inhibition and anxiety, 8–12, 15–16, 19–21

taxonomy, 30–34
therapeutic relationship, 29–30, 156–158
therapist. *See* Analyst
thetic consciousness, 65–66, 68
Thing, the, 71–74, 73–75, 77, 151
"Three Essays on the Theory of Sexuality" (Freud), 217
topology, 2, 6, 16, 70, 194

tracks, and signifiers, 41
transference, 96
acting out as, 84–85, 97
and therapist as object cause of desire, 90–91
transitional objects, 114

unary trait, 46–49, 260
uncanny, the, 61–64, 73, 129, 226–228, 246
"'Uncanny,' The" (Freud), 9, 62–63
unconscious, 51, 63, 66, 89
affect, 12–15, 22
as crucial discovery of psychoanalysis, 66
in framework of the division of the subject by the signifier, 136–137
subject of, 117–118
"Unconscious, The" (Freud), 12–15
Unheimliche, 9. *See also* Uncanny, the
unification, 47, 192–193
unknown, in danger-fear-flight schema, 128–129

voice, 200, 210, 211
relation to family novel protophantasy, 246–248
superego as, 101, 195–207, 235

Winnicott, D., 114
Wolf Man, case study of, 214–215, 220–221